# THE GOTHAM LIBRARY
## OF THE NEW YORK UNIVERSITY PRESS

The Gotham Library is a series of original works and critical studies published in paperback primarily for student use. The Gotham hardcover edition is primarily for use by libraries and the general reader. Devoted to significant works and major authors and to literary topics of enduring importance, Gotham Library texts offer the best in literature and criticism.

Comparative and Foreign Language Literature:
Robert J. Clements, Editor

Comparative and English Language Literature:
James W. Tuttleton, Editor

# The New Thoreau Handbook

*Walter Harding*
*Michael Meyer*

New York University Press · New York *and* London

**Library of Congress Cataloging in Publication Data**

Harding, Walter Roy, 1917-
  The new Thoreau handbook.

  (The Gotham library of the New York University Press)
  An earlier version published in 1959 under title:
A Thoreau handbook.
  1. Thoreau, Henry David, 1817-1862.  2. Thoreau,
Henry David, 1817-1862—Bibliography.  3. Authors,
American—19th century—Biography.  I. Meyer,
Michael, 1945-   joint author.  II. Title.
PS3053.H32  1980        818'.3'09        79-53078
ISBN 0-8147-3401-4
ISBN 0-8147-3402-2 pbk.

Manufactured in the United States of America
10  9  8  7  6  5  4  3  2

# Permissions

For permission to quote from and summarize their unpublished doctoral dissertations, we are indebted to Raymond Adams, Professor Emeritus of the University of North Carolina; Wendell Glick of the University of Minnesota, Duluth; William L. Howarth of Princeton University; and Anne Whaling of the University of Texas, Arlington. We are also indebted to The University of Chicago Press for permission to quote from J. Lyndon Shanley's *The Making of Walden*, copyright 1957; to Cornell University Press for permission to quote from Lawrence Buell's *Literary Transcendentalism*, copyright 1973, and James McIntosh's *Thoreau as Romantic Naturalist*, copyright 1974; to Duke University Press for permission to quote from Alexander Kern's "The Rise of Transcendentalism, 1815-1860" in *Transitions in American Literary History* edited by Harry Hayden Clark, copyright 1954; to Holt, Rinehart and Winston, Publishers for permission to quote from Charles R. Anderson's *The Magic Circle of Walden*, copyright 1968; to Alfred A. Knopf, Inc. for permission to quote from Walter Harding's *The Days of Henry Thoreau*, copyright 1962, 1964, 1965; to Princeton

University Press for permission to quote from Robert F. Sayre's *Thoreau and the American Indians,* copyright 1977; to Twayne Publishers, Inc. for permission to quote from Walter Harding's *The Variorum Walden,* copyright 1962; and to Yale University Press for permission to quote from Ethel Seybold's *Thoreau: The Quest and the Classics,* copyright 1951. Further, we are indebted to *The Graduate Journal* and to Joseph J. Moldenhauer for permission to quote from "Paradox in Walden," copyright 1964; to the Modern Language Association of America for permission to quote from Fred W. Lorch's "Thoreau and the Organic Principle in Poetry," copyright 1938; and to *Studies in Romanticism* for permission to quote from Nina Baym's "From Metaphysics to Metaphor," copyright 1966.

# Preface

Although Henry David Thoreau was once one of America's most neglected nineteenth-century authors, modern students have more than made up for the neglect. The scholarly work on Thoreau is prodigious—so prodigious, in fact, that only the extreme specialist can hope to assimilate more than a small part of it. The standard edition of Thoreau's collected works runs to twenty volumes, and the new one currently being edited will run to probably twenty-five. *Walden* has been issued in nearly two hundred different editions. There have been nearly one hundred book-length biographical and critical studies written about Thoreau and more than one hundred doctoral dissertations. Newspaper and other periodical articles concerning him number in the thousands. Obviously some guide is needed through this vast welter of publications.

In 1959 Walter Harding wrote an earlier version of this *Handbook*. In it he attempted to survey every known piece of Thoreau scholarship available. But in the intervening twenty years, Thoreau scholarship has multiplied so rapidly that it is no longer feasible to survey everything within the covers of one volume; therefore this *New Thoreau Handbook* is selective rather than comprehensive. Instead of listing every article on a special facet of Thoreau, we have cited only the most comprehensive; we refer to others only if they contain new and different material. Although we have read in full all the doctoral dissertations on Thoreau that are available through University Microfilms (plus such others as we have been able to lay hands on), we have cited only those with something new and significant to offer. With rare exceptions (exceptions made when we have had some special reason for believing them to be particularly significant), we have ignored the vast multitude of masters' theses, for so few of them upon investigation have proved to be useful. Although we have tried to examine as many foreign works as possible, we have not cited very many simply because they are not generally available in American libraries. In other words, this survey is limited to particularly significant works and to works generally available in a good university library.

We have divided the handbook into six major sections. Chapter One summarizes Thoreau's life and discusses and evaluates the major biographies. Chapter Two discusses each of Thoreau's works and recommends the best edition(s) of each. Chapter Three points out the sources of his ideas and attitudes. Chapter Four summarizes his ideas. Chapter Five discusses his artistry. Chapter Six surveys the changes in his reputation over the years. For quick reference, a brief chronology of Thoreau's life has been placed at the beginning. A short checklist of the leading bibliographies of Thoreau is given at the end of the book. The chapter divisions are necessarily arbitrary, and inevitably there is some repetition, but we have tried through cross-references and an extensive index to eliminate as much duplication as possible.

Each chapter is divided into two sections. The first and longer attempts to summarize and evaluate the significant scholarship on the subject. Bibliographical references there have been cut to a minimum in order not to distract the reader. The second section of each chapter concentrates entirely on the bibliography, showing the reader the sources of our information and where further details may be found.

A large portion of any handbook such as this is necessarily devoted to evaluation. Objectivity is of course the ideal in any such case, but unfortunately it is not always a human characteristic. ("There is no such thing as pure *objective* observation. Your observation, to be interesting, i.e., to be significant, must be subjective," said Thoreau [J, VI, 236]). We have tried to be fair and honest in our judgments. In general, Walter Harding is responsible for the writing of Chapters One, Two, and Six, and Michael Meyer for Chapters Three, Four, and Five.

Michael Meyer wishes to acknowledge that his work was supported in part during the summer of 1978 by funds from the Foundation of the University of North Carolina at Charlotte. Walter Harding wishes to acknowledge the helpful assistance of the staff of the Milne Library at the State University College at Geneseo, New York, and of the many members of the Thoreau Society who have regularly kept him informed of new Thoreauviana. And they both wish to express their appreciation to the National Endowment for the Humanities for their Summer Seminars for College Teachers program, which brought the two of them together at the Transcendentalism seminar in Concord, Massachusetts. From that acquaintance grew this volume.

# A Note on Bibliographical Abbreviations

All quotations from Thoreau's writings are from either the new Princeton Edition of his *Writings* or from the 1906 Houghton Mifflin edition—the former if they were in print at the time of writing this volume; the latter if the former were not available. All references to these editions have been indicated by a parenthetical note immediately after the quotation: "PE" and page number if referring to the Princeton Edition; "W," volume number and page number if referring to the first six volumes of the Houghton Mifflin edition; and "J," volume number and page number if referring to the last fourteen separately numbered *Journal* volumes of the Houghton Mifflin edition. Both the Manuscript Edition and the Walden Edition of the 1906 Houghton Mifflin printings have exactly the same pagination as do the 1949 separate Houghton Mifflin edition of the *Journal* and the 1962 Dover edition of the *Journal.*

For all bibliographical notations in the "Sources" section of each chapter, we have abbreviated "Thoreau" to "T"; "Henry Thoreau" to "HT"; and "Henry David Thoreau" to "HDT" to save space. We have also adopted the abbreviations of the Modern Language Association Annual Bibliography for references to periodicals. We have distinguished between the *Thoreau Society Booklets* and the *Thoreau Society Bulletin* by referring to the former with roman numerals (i.e., *TSB* IV) and the latter with arabic (i.e., *TSB* 42). For unpublished masters' theses and doctoral dissertations, we cite the university and date of the completion (i.e., Harvard Univ., Ph.D., 1937).

# A Thoreau Chronology

1817  Born in Concord, Massachusetts, July 12.

1818  Family moved to Chelmsford, Massachusetts.

1821  Family moved to Boston, Massachusetts.

1823  Family returned to Concord, Massachusetts.

1827  Earliest known essay, "The Seasons."

1833  Entered Harvard University.

1835  Taught school in Canton, Massachusetts, between college terms. Studied German with Orestes Brownson.

1836  Visited New York City with father peddling pencils.

1837  Graduated from Harvard. Began *Journal*. Taught for a few weeks in public schools in Concord.

1838  Opened private school. Delivered first lecture at Concord Lyceum. Made first trip to Maine.

1839  Made excursion on the Concord and Merrimack rivers with brother John. Edmund and Ellen Sewall visited Concord.

1840  Published his first essay, "Aulus Persius Flaccus," and his first poem, "Sympathy," in the *Dial*. Wrote *The Service*. Proposed marriage to Ellen Sewall.

1841   Went to live with Ralph Waldo Emerson for two years. Published numerous pieces in the *Dial*.

1842   Contributed many more pieces to the *Dial*. Brother John died, January 11.

1843   From this point on, lectured almost annually before the Concord Lyceum. Helped Emerson edit the *Dial* and contributed further articles and poems to it and to the *Boston Miscellany* and the *Democratic Review*. From May to December tutored William Emerson's children on Staten Island, New York.

1844   Contributed further pieces to the final volume of the *Dial*. Accidentally set fire to Concord woods. Built "Texas" house.

1845   Began work on his Walden cabin in March. Moved in on July 4. Published "Wendell Phillips Before the Concord Lyceum" in the *Liberator*.

1846   Was arrested and put in jail overnight in midsummer for nonpayment of taxes. Made trip to Maine woods.

1847   Left Walden Pond in September to spend a year in Emerson's house while the latter was lecturing abroad. Published essay on Carlyle in *Graham's Magazine*. Began submitting natural history specimens to Agassiz at Harvard.

1848   Delivered lecture on "The Rights and Duties of the Individual in Relation to Government" ("Civil Disobedience") before the Concord Lyceum, January 26 and February 16. Delivered first lecture outside Concord, in Salem, at invitation of Hawthorne, November 22. Published "Ktaadn and the Maine Woods" in the *Union Magazine*. Returned to live at his father's house.

1849   Published *A Week on the Concord and Merrimack Rivers*, May. Published "Resistance to Civil Government" ("Civil Disobedience") in *Aesthetic Papers*. Made first trip to Cape Cod. Sister Helen died, June 14.

1850   Made second trip to Cape Cod. Visited Fire Island, New York, searching for the body of Margaret Fuller Ossoli. Made excursion to Canada with Ellery Channing.

1853   Made second trip to Maine woods. Published "A Yankee in Canada" in *Putnam's Magazine*.

1854    Published *Walden,* August. Lectured on "Slavery in Massachusetts" in Framingham, published in *Liberator.*

1855    Received gift of Oriental books from Thomas Cholmondeley. Visited Cape Cod. Published portions of *Cape Cod* in *Putnam's Magazine.*

1856    Did surveying at "Eagleswood," Perth Amboy, New Jersey. Met Walt Whitman in Brooklyn.

1857    Visited Cape Cod and the Maine woods. Met Captain John Brown.

1858    Published "Chesuncook" in the *Atlantic Monthly.* Visited the White Mountains and Mount Monadnock, New Hampshire.

1859    Father died, February 3. Lectured on "A Plea for Captain John Brown" and "After the Death of John Brown."

1860    Camped out on Mount Monadnock with Ellery Channing. Published "A Plea for Captain John Brown" in *Echoes of Harpers Ferry;* "The Last Days of John Brown," in the *Liberator;* and delivered "The Succession of Forest Trees" as a lecture at the Middlesex Cattle Show, later published in *Transactions of the Middlesex Agricultural Society.*

1861    Visited Minnesota with Horace Mann, Jr., May 11 to July 10. Revised many of his manuscripts.

1862    Died, May 6. "Walking," "Autumnal Tints," "Wild Apples" appeared posthumously in the *Atlantic Monthly. Walden* and *A Week on the Concord and Merrimack Rivers* appeared in second editions.

# Contents

Preface                                              vii
A Note on Bibliographical Abbreviations               xi
A Thoreau Chronology                                 xiii
1. Thoreau's Life                                       1
2. Thoreau's Works                                     31
3. Thoreau's Sources                                   91
4. Thoreau's Ideas                                    121
5. Thoreau's Art                                      160
6. Thoreau's Reputation                               202
Bibliographies                                        225
Index                                                 227

# 1.

# Thoreau's Life

I

Henry David Thoreau was the only member of the famed "Concord group" of the mid-nineteenth century who was a native of the town of Concord, Massachusetts. Born on July 12, 1817, in his grandmother's farmhouse on Virginia Road, on the outskirts of the village, he was the product of a heterogeneous ancestry—Scotch, English, and French. His paternal grandfather, Jean, an immigrant from the Isle of Jersey just before the Revolution, had accumulated a considerable estate as a Boston merchant. But Thoreau's father, John, had quickly lost his share in a series of unfortunate shopkeeping experiments. Thoreau's maternal grandfather, Asa Dunbar, a Harvard graduate, had abandoned a career in the ministry for one in law in Keene, New Hampshire. Thoreau's mother, Cynthia, was an energetic woman with a gift for talking and a keen interest in the world of nature around her. In nearly every respect she contrasted with her quiet-spoken husband, a fact that in no respect seemed to flaw their harmony. An older sister, Helen, and a brother, John, were five and two years older, respectively. A second sister, Sophia, was born in 1819. Helen was so quiet and self-effacing that little record of her remains. A teacher by profession, she apparently helped pay Henry's way through college. Her death from tuberculosis in 1849 is not even noted in her brother's *Journal.* John was the sparkling, vibrant member of the household. In the opinion of many of his fellow townsmen he was the genius of the family. Although John never attended college, he joined with Henry in operating a private school for several years. His tragic death from lockjaw in 1842 had a traumatic effect on Henry, who developed a serious, indeed nearly fatal case of sympathetic lockjaw. Sophia, like Helen, was quiet and self-effacing. During Henry's final illness she devoted herself to his care and, after his death, to the defense and enhancement of his reputation. In Thoreau's later years the household was filled with a goodly company of maiden aunts, an eccentric bachelor uncle, and an assortment of spinster and widowed boarders.

Thoreau's father's financial misfortunes continued for some years after Henry's birth. The family moved from Concord to nearby Chelmsford, to Boston, and, in 1823, back to Concord again. Finally the father hit upon the manufacturing of pencils, a trade already successfully practiced in Concord, and managed to earn a small but steady income.

Comparatively little is known of Thoreau's youth. Apparently it was the typical childhood of any small-town, early-nineteenth-century American youth, except that the family's penchant for natural history and reading gave him an unusually strong background in those fields. His home was a center of religious discussion, and the various members vacillated back and forth between the Trinitarian and Unitarian churches in the town. Thoreau himself never joined any church, and when upon achieving legal maturity he received a tax bill from the Unitarian church, he made haste to sign off from its rolls. Yet when he died, Emerson, much to the dismay of some of his friends, insisted that he be buried from the Unitarian church.

Henry was enrolled in Concord Academy, one of the better college preparatory schools of its day, where, under the direction of Phineas Allen, he received a sound education directed primarily at the entrance requirements for Harvard College. Thoreau probably joined the Concord Lyceum in his early teens (it was founded in

1829), and he continued an interest in its activities throughout his life. His earliest extant essay, "The Seasons," written in 1827 at the age of ten, is not a particularly remarkable work, but it displays his already awakened interest in nature.

He entered Harvard College in 1833 at the then not unusually early age of sixteen. Our conception of his life at college has changed considerably in recent years, thanks to the efforts of scholars in uncovering various hitherto unknown documents. The old picture, based primarily on the memoirs of his classmate the Reverend John Weiss, depicted him as a shy, retiring, and somewhat eccentric student, almost completely ignored by his classmates, who later astonished them when he became the best-known member of the class. But now we have a clearer and quite different picture of a college lad who joined in friendly discussions with his classmates, wrote facetious letters to them, and attempted to come to the rescue of one of the pranksters impaled on the horns of faculty discipline. When he attended classes regularly, his grades were well above average, but a long illness in his junior year lowered his final standing. Even then, however, he stood high enough in his class to take part in a disquisition at the graduation ceremonies.

It was also in his junior year that Thoreau took advantage of a college ruling that permitted him to drop out for several months to teach and thus add to his income. He had the good fortune of going to Canton, Massachusetts, where he met Orestes Brownson, then the pastor of the local Universalist church. The two immediately struck up a friendship and embarked on a study of German together.

One of the most frequently repeated legends about Thoreau is that he refused to pay five dollars and so never received his college diploma. His diploma is extant today. But there is a basis for the legend. Harvard granted a master of arts degree to all, as Edward Emerson once commented, "who proved their physical worth by being alive three years after graduating, and their saving, earning or inheriting quality or condition by having Five Dollars to give the college" (Raymond Adams, "Thoreau's Diploma," p. 175). It was this semifraudulent degree, not his B.A., that Thoreau rejected.

On graduation from Harvard Thoreau applied for a position in the Concord schools and was accepted. But his teaching experience there lasted only a few weeks. A member of the school committee insisted that he must not "spare the rod" in disciplining his pupils. Thoreau, in reply, called six children at random from his class, feruled them, and handed in his resignation, telling the committee he could not accept its interference.

For some months thereafter Thoreau searched for a new teaching position, but the depression of 1837 was at its height and no jobs were available. As an alternative, the next summer Thoreau opened in his home a private school that immediately prospered. In a few months his brother joined him, and they moved the school into the then vacant Concord Academy where it continued until March, 1841, when, because of John's rapidly failing health, they were forced to close it. They had no difficulty in recruiting pupils. Children of the leading families of the town were among their students, and out-of-towners boarded with the Thoreau household. The teaching techniques used were those of twentieth-century progressive education. The ferule was abandoned. Many classes were held out-of-doors. Wherever possible the class situations were related to real life. John was apparently the favorite of the pupils, but Henry's abilities were also recognized.

It was in these years that Thoreau's one romance occurred. Ellen Sewall was the daughter of the Unitarian minister in Scituate, Massachusetts. Her aunt, Prudence Ward, had long boarded with the Thoreau family. In the summer of 1839 Ellen visited in the Thoreau household for several weeks, and both John and Henry fell in love with her. In July, 1840, John visited her in Scituate and proposed. In her surprise she first accepted him, only later to reject him when she realized that it was Henry she loved. In November, Henry proposed himself in a letter to Ellen, then visiting in Watertown, New York. Unfortunately, the battle between the conservative Unitarians and the Transcendentalists was at its height, and Ellen's father, shocked at the thought of having a "radical" in his family, directed her to write a letter of refusal. "I never felt so badly at sending a letter in my life," she later said. But in 1844 she married Joseph Osgood, a Unitarian minister in Cohasset, Massachusetts, and spent nearly fifty years of happily wedded life with him. Henry Seidel Canby probably evaluated the romance accurately when he said, "I doubt whether he [Thoreau] wanted to marry her; for after the idyllic opening of this relationship she became more and more for him an experiment in the philosophy of love" (Thoreau, pp. 121–22).

Her younger brother, Edmund, was for some time a pupil in the Thoreau school. Edmund, too, captured Thoreau's heart, and Thoreau wrote his poem " Gentle Boy" about him. The psychological implications of this incident are only now beginning to be explored.

It is not known exactly when Thoreau and Ralph Waldo Emerson became acquainted. The evidence is so contradictory that we can assert only that sometime within a year or two after Emerson settled in Concord in 1835, the two met and that their friendship ripened rapidly after Thoreau had returned to Concord from Harvard in 1837.

Thoreau developed a warm affection for Emerson's second wife, Lidian, an affection that has been exaggerated by Canby in particular. Most biographers agree that it was more a mother-son relationship than anything else.

In 1841 Emerson invited Thoreau to join his household as a handyman about the yard. Thoreau, unlike Emerson, could wield a hammer and a saw. In return for his services he was to receive free room and board. Paul Hourihan ("The Inner Dynamics of the Emerson-Thoreau Relationship") suggests that Thoreau served to confirm Emerson's faith in the truth and applicability of his own ideas. The Dial had been founded in 1840, and gradually Emerson shouldered its responsibility as Margaret Fuller, the nominal editor, became more and more discouraged with its progress. Thoreau was asked frequently to contribute. Despite the fact that Miss Fuller often blue-penciled his writings, he saw thirty-one of his contributions printed in its pages in the four years of its publication. Emerson gradually turned many of the editorial duties over to Thoreau and asked him to edit the entire April, 1843, issue.

In January, 1842, Thoreau's brother John died suddenly of lockjaw, and fifteen days later Emerson's son Waldo died as suddenly of scarlatina. The double tragedy undoubtedly served to weld even more firm the friendship of Emerson and Thoreau. It is obvious that in later years a rift developed. Each complained in his journal of a lack of understanding on the part of the other. Some of the misunderstanding may be blamed on Thoreau's sensitiveness to the frequent accusations that he was an imitator of Emerson and some on his desire to be completely independent. Some of it too may be blamed on Emerson's growing conservatism. But the break was never complete. Emerson delivered Thoreau's funeral sermon in 1862 and aided in the posthumous publication of a number of his works.

Later in 1842 Nathaniel Hawthorne brought his bride to the Old Manse to live. Thoreau soon paid a call and the two became friends. Whereas Hawthorne always felt a little ill at ease in Emerson's presence, he delighted in Thoreau's independence and individuality, although at times he found Thoreau a bit crusty. In later years Hawthorne did much to spread Thoreau's fame in England, and it has been suggested that Hawthorne based the Donatello of his *Marble Faun* on Thoreau.

Another influential friend was Bronson Alcott, who, attracted by Emerson, had moved to Concord in 1840. With the exception of occasional brief residences elsewhere, he remained in Concord the rest of his life. He was quickly drawn to Thoreau and was among the earliest to recognize his genius. Although Alcott could rarely be enticed out into the woods and Thoreau was more than a little amused at Alcott's impracticality, the two spent many hours in congenial conversation. Thoreau never succumbed to Alcott's invitations to join the ill-fated Fruitlands experiment.

In 1843 Emerson decided it was time for Thoreau to see more of the world and obtained a position for him as tutor for his brother William Emerson's sons on Staten Island. Thoreau accepted, thinking it would give him an entrée into the publishing world in New York City. But the experiment was a failure. William Emerson had little of his brother Waldo's kindly interest in Thoreau's career. Thoreau was homesick from the moment he left Concord in early May. A visit home at Thanksgiving time was too much for him, and he returned to Staten Island only long enough to pack up his belongings. Thoreau found one new friend in New York, Horace Greeley, editor of the influential *New York Tribune,* who was to be a benefactor for years to come. Greeley offered his services gratis as Thoreau's literary agent and for the remaining years of Thoreau's life spent many hours annually in placing Thoreau's essays in magazines and touting his two books in the pages of the *Tribune*.

Just before Thoreau left Concord for Staten Island, Ellery Channing, Margaret Fuller's brother-in-law and nephew of the great Unitarian divine, William Ellery Channing, moved to Concord. Apparently he was already acquainted with Thoreau, for he had asked him to supervise the preparation of his new Concord residence. But it was after Thoreau's return from Staten Island that their friendship ripened. Channing became Thoreau's closest companion for the rest of his life. They were an oddly assorted pair. Channing was as irresponsible to his obligations as Thoreau was meticulous. Channing was earthy and shocked Thoreau with his off-color stories. But the two had in common an unbounded love for the outdoors, and they spent most of their time together roaming the woods and fields and rivers of Concord.

It was in 1844 that an incident occurred that blackened Thoreau's reputation among his fellow townsmen for generations to come. In April he and Edward Hoar, son of the town's most prominent family, went fishing on the Sudbury River. They built a fire on the banks of Fairhaven Bay to cook their catch, but the fire got away from them and was soon roaring through the dry woods. Thoreau ran to town for help, but then, realizing the fire was out of control, instead of returning he climbed a nearby hill to watch. The townspeople were enraged, and it has been suggested that had not young Hoar been his companion, he might have been prosecuted. Even today he is known to some Concordians as "the man who burned the woods."

It was also in 1844 that, after moving from house to house for many years, Thoreau's father, with Henry's aid, built a house out beyond the Concord railroad station in the section known as Texas. The house was destroyed by fire and hurricane in the late 1930s.

For some years Thoreau had been mulling over the advantages of living a simple life in comparative solitude. Maintaining himself in town was taking more of his time than he wished. Ever since John's death he had wanted to memorialize an excursion they had taken together on the Concord and Merrimack rivers in 1839, but he never found the time. Once he was on the verge of buying the

Hollowell farm on the outskirts of Concord. Another time he considered building a cabin on Flint's Pond in nearby Lincoln, but the owner of the land was unwilling. Then, in October, 1844, Emerson purchased some woods on the north shore of Walden Pond, a mile and a half south of Concord, to prevent their destruction. Soon afterward Thoreau entered into an agreement with him that he might build a cabin there and in return clear and replant part of the land.

In March, 1845, Thoreau started construction of the cabin with a borrowed ax, and on Independence Day he moved in. There he succeeded in his endeavor to simplify his life, to reduce his expenses, and to write not only *A Week on the Concord and Merrimack Rivers* but also the major part of his masterpiece, *Walden.* He lived there two years, two months, and two days.

In late July, 1846, Thoreau spent a night in Concord jail for nonpayment of his poll tax. It was primarily a protest against a government that supported slavery. Sam Staples, the Concord constable and a longtime friend, misunderstanding Thoreau's intentions, offered to pay the tax for him. But when Thoreau refused, Staples arrested him. That night, under cover of darkness, someone (probably Thoreau's maiden aunt, Maria, shocked to see her nephew in the local jail) paid his tax, and the next morning he was released. It has been recorded that he was angry when released and implied that his wrath was directed at the fact of arrest, but contemporary witnesses assert that he was angry because the payment of his tax forestalled effective protest.

There is a legend that Emerson visited Thoreau in the jail and asked, "Why are you here?" and that Thoreau replied, "Why are you not here?" The story has been discounted because there is no record of Emerson's visit. But the tale has been handed down in the Emerson family as true, and the incident could just as well have taken place outside the jail after Thoreau's release.

The arrest inspired Thoreau to write his most famous essay, known variously as "Resistance to Civil Government," "On the Duty of Civil Disobedience," and more commonly as "Civil Disobedience." Thoreau first delivered it as a lecture to his fellow townsmen at the Concord Lyceum on January 26 and in February,

1848. It was first printed in Elizabeth Peabody's short-lived experimental magazine, *Aesthetic Papers,* in 1849.

Thoreau's interest in the lyceum had not been dormant. He delivered his first lecture, "Society," on April 11, 1838, and continued to lecture there regularly the rest of his life. At various periods he also served as secretary and as curator of the lyceum. In 1848 he was invited by Hawthorne to lecture in Salem, and in later years he lectured as far afield as Portland, Maine, and Philadelphia. Several attempts to arrange a western lecture tour did not materialize. It has been frequently remarked that Thoreau was not a success as a lecturer. The fact is that he was unpopular only when he was too Transcendental for his audience. His humorous lectures, particularly those on his excursions, were always well received, and his political lectures persuasive to many.

It was while Thoreau was at Walden that he made his first excursion to the Maine woods, to be followed by later excursions in 1853 and 1857. These expeditions were the basis for various magazine articles later combined into his posthumous book, *The Maine Woods.* He made similar excursions to Cape Cod in 1849, 1850, 1855, and 1857; an excursion to Canada in 1850; one to Vermont in 1856; and various trips to the White Mountains and Mount Monadnock, New Hampshire.

When in the fall of 1847 Emerson went to England on a lecture tour, he persuaded Thoreau to look after his house and family. It was in this period that Thoreau became best acquainted with the Emerson children, and the warmth of that friendship is reflected in the letters he wrote Emerson in England and in Edward Emerson's *Henry Thoreau as Remembered by a Young Friend.*

An amusing episode of this period was Thoreau's "romance" with Sophia Foord (or Ford, as it was sometimes spelled). A friend of the Alcotts and tutor of the Emerson children, Miss Foord thought Thoreau to be her "soul's twin" and proposed marriage. Thoreau fired back "as distinct a no as I have learned to pronounce after considerable practice." Rumors spread that she had committed suicide in her dejection, but she lived on to be eighty-two, carrying with her to the end an interest in Thoreau.

Sometime about this period Thoreau took up the profession of surveying, to add to his income while enjoying the woods and fields of his native town. At times it undoubtedly irked him to be tied to so routine an occupation, but most of the time he found it congenial. In later years he was often called upon by the town to walk its boundaries and to make offical surveys.

In the summer of 1848, on Emerson's return from England, Thoreau returned to live with his family at the Texas house. In 1850, with their pencil business prospering, the family purchased a more pretentious house on Main Street, and he lived there with them for the rest of his life.

Thoreau had always been a willing aid in the pencil business. Using knowledge he had gained from his college courses, he experimented with methods of preparing the graphite (lead) and perfected a pencil superior to any other then manufactured in the country. But he refused to capitalize on the invention and was satisfied to see his father's business quietly prosper as a result of his ingenuity. Later the family found it more profitable to abandon pencil making and concentrate on selling the graphite mixture wholesale to other manufacturers. At his father's death in 1859, Thoreau took over most of the responsibility for the business. Just how much effect working with the fine pencil and graphite dust had on his tendency toward tuberculosis is problematical. Unquestionably it did not help matters any.

Thoreau's first disciple was Harrison Gray Otis Blake, a Worcester schoolteacher who, like Emerson, had abandoned the Unitarian ministry. A frequent visitor to Emerson's home, he happened to reread Thoreau's paper on Persius in the *Dial* and was so impressed that he sent Thoreau a long letter in March, 1848. It was the beginning of Thoreau's longest and largest correspondence. Blake arranged almost annual lectures in Worcester for Thoreau and surrounded him there with a coterie of admirers. Years later Sophia Thoreau willed her brother's manuscripts to Blake, and from them he edited the four seasonal volumes of excerpts from the journal, *Early Spring in Massachusetts* (1881), *Summer* (1884), *Winter* (1887), and *Autumn* (1892).

*A Week* had been virtually completed before Thoreau left Walden in 1847, but it was two years before it was published. It wandered from one publishing house to another, always returning with a rejection slip, despite Emerson's forceful influence. After each rejection Thoreau revised it (the essay on "Friendship" in the "Wednesday" chapter, for example, was one of the late additions). Finally, in desperation, he guaranteed James Munroe and Company of Boston the cost of publishing it in an edition of 1,000 copies in the spring of 1849. It was one of the most complete failures in literary history. Only three reviews of any length appeared, and two of these were largely unfavorable. In 1853 the publishers wrote Thoreau complaining that only 219 copies had been sold and 75 given away. They asked him to take the remainder off their hands. The result of the failure was that the publication of *Walden,* which had been promised "soon" in the back pages of *A Week,* was postponed for five years.

In the late 1840s Thoreau's interest in natural history was rapidly growing. He collected specimens of various fish, reptiles, and small mammals for Louis Agassiz and his assistant, James Elliot Cabot, at Harvard. In 1850 Thoreau was elected a corresponding member of the Boston Society of Natural History, for contributing an American goshawk to their museum. In 1853 he was offered membership in the Association for the Advancement of Science but rejected it on the ground that his science was too Transcendental for them to appreciate. But to any careful reader of his *Journal* it is obvious that he was becoming more and more preoccupied with scientific data. It was a fact that did not please him; he often lamented in his *Journal* that he was taking a narrower view of the world of nature.

In July, 1850, Margaret Fuller was drowned in the wreck of the ship *Elizabeth* off the coast of Long Island. Thoreau was dispatched to the scene by her Concord friends to find her body and rescue her unpublished history of the Italian revolution of 1848. He was not successful in either endeavor. But he did recover the body of Charles Sumner's brother, lost in the same wreck, and thus established a friendship with Sumner that continued throughout the remaining years of Thoreau's life.

Thoreau and Margaret Fuller had long been acquainted through their common friendship with Emerson and through Ellery Channing's marriage to Margaret's sister. But there was little warm feeling lost between them. Miss Fuller was outspoken in her criticism of the articles he submitted to the *Dial,* and he found little charming in her personality.

*Walden* was finally published in August, 1854, thanks this time apparently to Emerson's good offices with the rising firm of Ticknor & Fields. Greeley gave the book a good send-off with the preliminary publication of large excerpts in his *New York Tribune.* The reviewers could not all agree as to its virtues, but it received enough praise to guarantee a comparatively good sale. It took five years to sell off the first edition of two thousand copies, but that was a marked improvement over the sale of *A Week.*

The fame of *Walden* attracted a number of disciples. The most persistent was the New Bedford Quaker, Daniel Ricketson. He read *Walden* as soon as it was published and wrote to Thoreau on August 12, 1854. Thoreau took nearly two months to reply, but the delay did not dismay Ricketson. They met the following Christmas Day, when Thoreau visited New Bedford on his way to lecture at Nantucket. (Ricketson drew an amusing little caricature of Thoreau at the time.) They visited each other and corresponded frequently (for Thoreau, that is) until Thoreau's death. Ricketson at one point even considered moving to Concord to be near him. Unlike some of the other disciples, Ricketson had a sense of humor that brought out the best in Thoreau. B. B. Wiley, a young Providence businessman, was another admirer attracted by *Walden.* He later moved to Chicago but continued to correspond at length, often asking Thoreau for guidance in planning his life.

Thomas Cholmondeley, a young Englishman, came to Concord in the fall of 1854 to visit Emerson. Meeting Thoreau, however, he neglected Emerson. When he returned to England he sent Thoreau a gift of forty-four rare Oriental works. Thoreau's interest in the Orient, at its height in the early 1850s when he had first had access to Emerson's library, had now largely subsided, but he nonetheless received the treasure with great joy. Cholmondeley frequently invited Thoreau to visit him in England and, when Thoreau failed to do so, came back to Concord to see him again in 1858. Their correspondence continued until Thoreau's death.

Throughout his adult life Thoreau was outspoken in his opposition to slavery. In 1844 he wrote a commendatory notice of the antislavery *Herald of Freedom* for the *Dial;* in 1845 he defended Wen-

dell Phillips's right to speak on the movement before the Concord
Lyceum; his antislavery opinions were a major motive in his refusal to pay his taxes; he aided runaway slaves on their way to
Canada; and from 1854 on he spoke out frequently against slavery,
though he never officially joined any of the antislavery organizations.

It is unfortunate that Thoreau's medical records—if they were
ever written down by the family physician—are not extant. Tuberculosis, or "consumption" as it was termed at the time, carried off
a number of his family. Concord town records indicate that it was
by far the leading cause of death in the town, as it was elsewhere.
Thoreau was ill enough in his late teens to withdraw from college
for several months. He was ill again at the time of his brother's
death, again just before he went to Staten Island, and also in 1851.
In 1855 he was ill most of the spring, and his legs felt weak for
many months. We cannot be certain that all these illnesses were
caused by lesions of the lung, but it is not unlikely.

In the fall of 1856 Marcus Spring, a then well-known abolitionist, invited Thoreau to survey the land for his experimental
community, Eagleswood, near Perth Amboy, New Jersey. This was
his only extensive association with any of those utopian experiments that dotted the landscape in the mid-nineteenth century. It
is obvious that he was not particularly impressed.

It was during this visit that Bronson Alcott led him to Brooklyn
to meet Walt Whitman. The two were ill at ease in the presence of
others, but they were mutually impressed, and Whitman gave
Thoreau *Leaves of Grass*. Shortly thereafter Thoreau wrote two letters to H. G. O. Blake, evaluating both Whitman and his work,
displaying a keen insight into Whitman's accomplishments and
refusing to join the mob in condemning Whitman's "indecency."
He later sent a copy of *Leaves of Grass* to his friend Thomas Cholmondeley in partial recompense for the "nest of Oriental books."

In 1855 Franklin Benjamin Sanborn, a recent graduate of Harvard, moved to Concord and established a private school. A wid-
ower, he took meals daily with the Thoreau family for some years.
He became involved in supporting John Brown's activities and in
1857 and again in 1859 introduced Brown to Thoreau. Thoreau
knew nothing of Brown's Harpers Ferry plans in advance. But no

sooner did news of the attack and its failure reach Concord than Thoreau came to Brown's defense.

In 1857 the long-projected *Atlantic Monthly* was started under the editorial guidance of James Russell Lowell. Thoreau was asked to contribute and submitted some chapters on his excursion to Maine. Lowell accepted them but without permission deleted a sentence that seemed to him sacrilegious. Thoreau wrote an angry letter denying Lowell's right of censorship and refused to submit any further work to the magazine.

In the late 1850s Thoreau's growing interest in scientific data led him to a study of tree growth. Although almost simultaneously several other scientists reached the same conclusions, he independently discovered the principle of "The Succession of Forest Trees" and read a paper on that subject before the Middlesex Agricultural Society in 1860. It was perhaps his major contribution to natural science. His "Succession" studies aroused further his botanical interests, and he embarked on a massive study of the dispersion of seeds and native wild fruits, accumulating hundreds of pages of rough drafts and notes that he never completed and most of which is still unpublished.

Thoreau acquired a severe cold while examining tree stumps on Fairhaven Hill on December 3, 1860. He had promised to deliver a lecture in Waterbury, Connecticut, on December 11. His friends attempted to persuade him to cancel the lecture, but he insisted on keeping the engagement. The strain was too much; the cold developed into bronchitis and eventually into acute tuberculosis. His illness gradually worsened. By late spring his doctor told him his only chance was to try another climate. He decided upon Minnesota and asked first Channing and then Blake to accompany him. When they both declined, he turned to the young botanist, Horace Mann, Jr. On May 11 they set out, stopping at Niagara Falls and Chicago on the way. But it was soon obvious that Thoreau was deriving no benefit from the excursion, and by July he was back in Concord.

Thoreau acknowledged his fate and faced it calmly. He began to assemble his manuscripts and to prepare them for publication, telling his friends that a man must leave some estate to his heirs. As he gradually weakened, he was forced to resort to dictating his

papers and correspondence to his sister Sophia. Ironically, he was
on the verge of the fame that had so long eluded him. Lowell had
resigned as editor of the *Atlantic Monthly* and had been succeeded
by James T. Fields, who eagerly requested essays. *Walden* had gone
out of print, and Fields assured him that a new edition was demanded and on the way. Not only that, but Ticknor & Fields
would purchase the remainder of the first edition of *A Week* and
reissue it. Bronson Alcott wrote a tribute entitled "The Forester,"
which appeared in the April *Atlantic*.

But it was too late. As Thoreau lay on his deathbed in the living
room of the Main Street house, friends, neighbors, fellow townsmen, and children streamed in to visit him. He greeted them all
cheerfully. When asked if he had thought of the other world, he
replied, "One world at a time." When asked if he had made his
peace with God, he replied, "I did not know that we had ever
quarreled." At nine on the morning of May 6, 1862, he died so
quietly that the moment of passing was not apparent.

He was buried from the First Parish Church with a eulogy by
Ralph Waldo Emerson. Concord schools were dismissed, and children strewed wild flowers on his coffin. He was buried in the Dunbar family lot in the New Burying Ground. Some years later his
body was transferred to nearby Sleepy Hollow Cemetery, where it
lies under a small stone marked simply "Henry," only a few steps
from the graves of his friends Alcott, Hawthorne, Channing, and
Emerson.

II

The first book-length biography of Thoreau appeared in 1873,
eleven years after his death. *Thoreau: The Poet-Naturalist* was written
by his most intimate friend and companion on many of his excursions, Ellery Channing. It has a curious bibliographical history.
Channing wrote it immediately after Thoreau's death and in 1863
made arrangements with F. B. Sanborn for it to appear in his
Boston *Commonwealth* serially. Publication began on December 25,
1863, and continued weekly until February 19, 1864. But Sanborn
then omitted an installment to give space to other literary matters,

and Channing, taking offense, withdrew the rest of the manuscript, leaving the book incomplete. However, in 1873 Roberts Brothers, the Boston publishers, offered to issue it. Channing completely rewrote it. But the text was not long enough to suit the publishers, and Channing used a unique device to enlarge it. In 1853 Emerson had hired Channing to compose a volume to be known as "Walks and Talks in Concord," or "Country Walking," to be made up of selections, arranged in conversational form, from the unpublished journals of Thoreau, Alcott, Emerson, and Channing. Although Channing completed the task, the book was never published. He now lifted two chapters from that volume and inserted them into the middle of the new volume, not bothering to assign the selections to the individual authors, but instead merely prefacing them with the comment, "To furnish a more familiar idea of Thoreau's walks and talks with his friends and their locality, some reports of them are furnished for convenience in the interlocutory form" (p. 120). These inserted chapters have little relation to the rest of the book and serve only to confuse the reader. He appended to the volume eight poems he had written about Thoreau, which he entitled "Memorial Verses."

The volume without these two curious additions is unusual enough in itself. In large part, it is made up of direct (but carelessly quoted) excerpts from Thoreau's published and unpublished writings. Channing had a keen ear for Thoreau at his best as a nature writer, but he made no attempt to identify the source of his quotations. There is very little biographical detail; the Walden experiment and the jail experience, for example, were hardly more than mentioned. Chronological order is almost completely abandoned. Most of the space is devoted to Thoreau as a naturalist or nature writer. But Channing does insert into the text many anecdotes that have become a standard part of the Thoreau legend, and his critical comments on Thoreau's writing are sharp and to the point. Thoreau once said that Channing's poetry was written in the sublime-slipshod style, and much the same could be said about the prose in this volume. It is a curious mélange of irrelevant material and very worthwhile information. The book is a gold mine to the biographer (and every biographer since Channing has used it), but it is otherwise of little value to the modern reader.

In 1902, after Channing's death, Sanborn reissued the volume. "In my new edition," states Sanborn (p. xii), "based upon a copy with the author's revision and notes, I have inserted here and there passages of no great length which I find in the original sketch, and which make the meaning plainer and the story more consecutive. At the end of this volume will be found some additions to the 'Memorial Poems' which evidently belong there." This later edition contains some material not in the earlier. But anyone familiar with Sanborn's methods of editing will approach it warily. The table of contents indicates that Sanborn felt free both to retitle some of Channing's chapters and to divide some. No one can say how much more he meddled with the text and how much of the editing was actually based on Channing's annotated copy, since its present location is unknown.

*Henry D. Thoreau,* by F. B. Sanborn, was issued in the "American Men of Letters" series in 1882. Sanborn lived in Concord during the last years of Thoreau's life, boarded in the Thoreau house, and knew all the members of the Concord group well. In later years he considered himself the official historian and biographer of the group. This firsthand acquaintance with Thoreau and his friends lends an authority to Sanborn's writings, and like Channing, he was able to put into print many details of Thoreau's life that would otherwise have been lost. Unlike the Channing volume, this biography records many factual details. Sanborn includes the texts of many otherwise unpublished letters (notably the correspondence between Thoreau and Greeley), essays (Thoreau's college writings in particular), and other important manuscripts. Unfortunately, Sanborn apparently considered himself a better writer than Thoreau and did not hesitate to take liberties with his manuscript materials. Thus, his text can never be completely trusted.

Sanborn, in speaking of Channing's biography, terms it "a mine of curious information on a thousand topics, relevant and irrelevant" (p. 11). No more appropriate description could be made of Sanborn's own book. He includes in it any material he happens to have on hand; for example, there are pages and pages on Daniel Webster that in no way could be said to pertain to Thoreau. But the book is important because it does contain primary source material unobtainable elsewhere. It is indispensable to the biographer of Thoreau, despite Sanborn's arbitrary editing and his careless handling of facts.

In 1890, *The Life of Henry David Thoreau*, by the British biographer and critic H. S. Salt, was published. Salt was a pacifist, a vegetarian, and a socialist. He delighted in calling himself "a compendium of cranks." A biography of Thoreau by such a man might not seem promising, but Salt kept his personal biases out of the volume and wrote what still is one of the most balanced biographies of Thoreau. His aim, which he adequately fulfills, is stated briefly in his "Prefatory Note": "To combine the various records and reminiscences of Thoreau, many of which are inaccessible to the majority of readers, and so to present what may supply a real want—a comprehensive account of his life, and a clear estimate of his ethical teaching" (p. vi). In writing this volume Salt was handicapped by the fact that he had never visited the United States. But one would never suspect it from the book. He writes with a clear and steady hand, basing his work on virtually all the material on Thoreau in print at the time and on extended correspondence with most of Thoreau's friends then still living.

The first two-thirds of the book are straightforward biography, displaying a sense of organization and insight lacking in all the earlier works. Salt has a sense of proportion in handling the details of Thoreau's life that all other biographers before and since might well have emulated. The concluding chapters are an evaluation of Thoreau's writings and philosophy. Salt approaches the problem objectively. He does not hesitate to point out Thoreau's weaknesses, but he is also effective in emphasizing and evaluating Thoreau's major contributions to both literature and ethics.

Annie Russell Marble, *Thoreau: His Home, Friends, and Books* (1902), is a difficult book to evaluate, and critics have generally been prone to dismiss it as insignificant. True, it is a highly sentimentalized approach to Thoreau, almost completely ignoring his salient, sturdier characteristics in favor of the sentimental nature lover. But as she says in her foreword: "Through the kindness of relatives and friends of the Thoreau family, there have been loaned for this volume some letters and diaries hitherto guarded from the public. Interviews have also been granted by a few surviving friends of Henry and Sophia Thoreau, who have now first given utterance to certain anecdotes and impressions" (p. viii). It is unfortunate that since many of these documents have disappeared, she did not quote from them more fully or identify them more particularly, but the important fact is that she did get many of these anecdotes and documents into print.

Her book is, in a strict sense, not a biography, even though it contains some new biographical information. Neither is it particularly successful in carrying out her aim "to estimate his rank and services as a naturalist and author" (p. viii). But because of the background information she presents in such chapters as "Thoreau's Concord and Its Environs," "The Thoreau Family," and "Thoreau and His Friends," her book cannot be ignored.

In 1917 a number of books and articles commemorating the centennial of Thoreau's birth appeared. One of the most delightful was Dr. Edward Emerson's little book, *Henry Thoreau as Remembered by a Young Friend.* Dr. Emerson, Ralph Waldo Emerson's son and for many years a Concord physician, had, as a boy, known Thoreau intimately as neighbor, friend, and housemate. "Troubled at the want of understanding, both in Concord and among his [Thoreau's] readers at large, not only of his character, but of the events of his life—which he did not tell to everybody—and by the false impressions given by accredited writers," Dr. Emerson "undertook to defend my friend" (pp. v–vi). Ironically, though it is on James Russell Lowell's shoulders that Dr. Emerson places most of the blame for the prevalent false conception of Thoreau, in actuality the blame can be placed as justly on Dr. Emerson's father. For it was Ralph Waldo Emerson's funeral sermon for Thoreau and his editing of Thoreau's letters that perhaps more than anything else created the concept of Thoreau as a cold, almost inhuman stoic. But Dr. Emerson, through this little book, did more than anyone else to correct the false impression.

*Henry Thoreau as Remembered by a Young Friend,* as its title implies, is not a formal biography. It is instead a brief memoir, supplemented by reminiscences Dr. Emerson solicited from other surviving acquaintances of Thoreau:

> I saw that I must at once improve my advantage of
> being acquainted, as a country doctor, with many per-

sons who would never put pen to a line, but knew much about him—humble persons whom the literary men would never find out, like those who helped in the pencil mill, or in a survey, or families whom he came to know well and value in his walking over every square rod of Concord, or one of the brave and humane managers of the Underground Railroad, of which Thoreau was an operative. Also I had the good fortune to meet or correspond with six of the pupils of Thoreau and his brother John, all of whom bore witness to the very remarkable and interesting character of the teachers and their school. (pp. vi–vii)

As a portrait of Thoreau the human being, this little volume has not been excelled. It refutes those who would dismiss Thoreau as a misanthrope, for the person who emerges from these pages is warm, friendly, kind, and genial.

It was also in 1917 that Sanborn published his final biography of Thoreau, *The Life of Henry David Thoreau.* This was a completely new and different book from his earlier biography. Unquestionably it is a great improvement. It is less discursive, more straightforward, and contains another invaluable hoard of otherwise unpublished Thoreau manuscripts, most notably a long series of Thoreau's college essays. Its appendix contains a catalogue of Thoreau's library, a partial list of his reading, and several documents pertaining to his ancestors. But Sanborn nonetheless remained Sanborn to the end. Francis H. Allen *(Thoreau's Editors,* pp. 15–16) tells us:

> As an editor for Houghton Mifflin Company I had the not unmixed pleasure of seeing this book through the press, and, finding that the author had followed his custom of using great freedom in the treatment of quoted matter, I asked him if he would not make some statement in his preface which would explain why his versions of matter already printed differed from the previous forms. To this he consented, apparently without reluctance and

in writing, but the statement never came, and he died on the very day when the proof of his preface was mailed to him—the preface, always the last of a book that the author sees in proof and now his last chance of keeping his promise.

Henry Seidel Canby's biography, *Thoreau* (1939), is an exceedingly difficult book to evaluate fairly; it has many good points, and yet at the same time is disappointing in many respects. Canby was the first to make extensive use of the large and hitherto chiefly unpublished correspondence of the Ward family. Two members of the Ward family boarded with the Thoreaus for many years. It was they who introduced the Thoreaus to the Sewall family, and they kept up a voluminous, gossipy correspondence filled with intimate details of the Thoreau family life. Canby made extensive and judicious use of this material, printing much of it verbatim. He was also the first biographer of Thoreau to have available such invaluable tools as Rusk's edition of Emerson's letters and Odell Shepard's edition of Alcott's journals, making wise use of both. Canby, himself a professional writer and editor, was primarily interested in this facet of Thoreau's life—"A life of Thoreau must chiefly emphasize the creative thinker" (p. xx)—and so included a more detailed discussion of Thoreau as a writer than had previously appeared. Finally, Canby created a very human portrait by placing greater emphasis on the emotional factors that made Thoreau the man he was.

However, the book appears to have been written too hastily. It is filled with factual errors (some of which were corrected in later impressions), and the vitally important Harvard period in Thoreau's life is very inadequately covered (granted that much new information has come to light since Canby wrote his book). But the major weakness, and one for which most of the scholarly reviewers of the book assailed Canby, was his handling of the relationship between Thoreau and Emerson's wife. It is Canby's thesis that "Thoreau was what the common man would call in love with Emerson's wife" (p. 163). Canby digs up a great deal of evidence in an attempt to support his thesis, but unfortunately most of it is weak, even though taken from Thoreau's own *Journal* and various unpublished writings, for Thoreau masked his identifications in pronoun references or such vague terms as "my sister," and we have only Canby's word that it was Mrs. Emerson of whom he was speaking. Indeed, to back up his statements, Canby at times is forced to change the sex of Thoreau's pronoun references from "he" to "she." To sum it up: Canby made many notable contributions to our knowledge of Thoreau, but his book must be read with care.

An important and much discussed study of Thoreau is Raymond Gozzi, "Tropes and Figures: A Psychological Study of David Henry Thoreau" (1957). Since Gozzi's work is based on a Freudian analysis of all Thoreau's writings and his conclusions have been reached only after a huge marshaling of evidence, it is unfair to summarize his findings without presenting his evidence. But that unfortunately is what must be done here. He believes that Thoreau had an insecure childhood because of his father's continued financial failures (pp. 3–4); that Thoreau had an unresolved Oedipus complex (p. 32); that his prevailing attitude was that sex was evil (p. 43); that he was colossally egotistic (p. 99); that his personality never matured (p. 102); that he had a compulsive, obsessional personality (p. 113); that his physical breakdown of 1855–57 was the response of his unconscious to the success of *Walden* (p. 141); that arrowheads, trees, and fungi were unconscious phallic symbols to him (pp. 175–90); that this love of nature was an unconscious expression of his fixation on his mother (p. 228); that he consciously expressed toward the state unconscious emotions of hatred toward his family (p. 263); that the unconscious feelings of love and hate he had toward his father became controlling by the process of transference in his relation to Emerson (p. 330); and that his death was brought about subsconsciously through a feeling of remorse and guilt after his father's death. Gozzi has raised problems that all serious future biographers of Thoreau must at least consider, if only to refute.

The most detailed factual account of Thoreau's life is Walter Harding, *The Days of Henry Thoreau* (1965). As its title implies, it gives an almost day-by-day account of the events of Thoreau's life. As is stated in its introduction:

I have not attempted to prove any particular thesis in this book, but rather to present the facts and let them speak for themselves. As a result, at times Thoreau not only appears inconsistent—he is inconsistent. At times, we can ascribe this inconsistency to a natural growth and development of his thought over a period of years. At other times, we can attribute it only to the fact that he was a very human human being. He, like most of us, could be sweet, gentle, and thoughtful one moment and a stubborn curmudgeon the next; I have tried to gloss over neither the thoughtfulness nor the stubbornness. . . .

As I have said, in writing this book I have had no thesis to present, no axe to grind. But I do think the wealth of new material that I have had the good fortune to use does modify at least the popular concept of Thoreau. It shows that while he was by no means lionized, he was more widely recognized in his own time than has been supposed; that he was more the townsman and neighbor and less the solitary and eccentric than he has been portrayed; that he was not the cold, unemotional stoic that some have believed, but a warm-blooded human being; and that rather than being bitter and disappointed in his last years, he was vibrant, creative, and happy to the very end. (pp. viii–ix)

The most recent biographical study of Thoreau is Richard Lebeaux's *Young Man Thoreau* (1977), an Eriksonian approach to an understanding of Thoreau's creativity. Arguing that Thoreau had a prolonged adolescence and a troubled young adulthood that included strained relations with his father, mother, and brother, Lebeaux asserts that at Walden Thoreau finally found himself. Lebeaux seems to overemphasize Thoreau's mother's domineering and his father's failure, and he is not entirely convincing that Thoreau's relations with his brother John were as openly hostile as he suggests, but these disagreements are chiefly only a matter of degree rather than of fact. His discussion of the development of Thoreau's creativity is both convincing and rewarding.

III

The problems of the biographer in handling Thoreau's life are many. Since he was not particularly famous in his own lifetime, there is a comparative dearth of reminiscences. Another difficulty is the wideness of the range of Thoreau's interests. Canby (p. xvi) did not overstate the case in the least when he said: "The truth is that there are a half-dozen possible biographies of Thoreau, depending upon the view the biographer takes of his subject. This is true of all complex characters, but seems to be particularly the case with this reserved researcher into the values of living."

Still another difficulty lies in the fact that because of the popularity of Emerson's funeral essay on Thoreau and James Russell Lowell's and Robert Louis Stevenson's essays, there is a widespread belief that Thoreau's philosophy was primarily negative. While most twentieth-century biographers disagree with this interpretation, they are almost automatically forced to assume a negative approach and state over and over again, "Thoreau was not this, but that." The result is that too often his biographers have appeared belligerent.

Very fundamental is the question of the success of Thoreau's life. Yet fundamental as it is, there has been anything but a basic unanimity among his biographers and critics. Mark Van Doren obviously considers Thoreau's life to have been a failure and Thoreau an embittered man in his last years. Brooks Atkinson, in *Thoreau, the Cosmic Yankee,* was not sure if Thoreau won happiness in the lifestyle he devised. Yet Canby and Harding both maintain that Thoreau was the happiest of the whole Concord group to the very end of his life.

There will never be a "definitive" biography of Thoreau to satisfy all times and all people. New factual material about his life continues to turn up with astonishing frequency for one now dead more than a century. Critical attitudes toward him continue to change making older biographies seem out-of-date. Someone has once said that a major figure needs a new biography for each new generation, and that is as undoubtedly true of Henry David Thoreau as of any other.

*Sources for Chapter One*

I

The major biographical studies of T are listed below in the notes for the second portion of this chapter. More specialized studies giving detailed information on particular phases of his life are listed here in an order approximating that of the text of the first part of the chapter. The T bibliography has expanded so greatly that it is impossible to include herein every article on the subject; only the more comprehensive ones are listed. The footnotes in Walter Harding, *The Days of HT* (New York, 1965), will guide the reader to even more specialized sources of information.

The best history of Concord is Ruth R. Wheeler, *Concord: Climate for Freedom* (Concord, Mass, 1967). Robert Stowell, *A T Gazetteer* (Princeton, 1970), is an invaluable collection of maps of the Concord of T's time and of all his major journeys. It includes the Herbert Gleason "Map of Concord, Mass.," which identifies nearly every Concord location T mentions in his *Writings*. For T's ancestry, see Raymond Adams, "A T Family Tree" *(TSB* 17). Before accepting the traditional harsh picture of T's mother, one should be careful to read Jean Munro Lebrun, "HT's Mother" *(Boston Advertiser,* February 14, 1883; frequently reprinted). For T's brother, see Max Cosman, "Apropos of John T" *(AL,* 12, 1940, 241–43), and Joel Myerson, "More Apropos of John T" *(AL,* 45, 1973, 104–6). For Sophia T, see S. G. Pomeroy, *Little-Known Sisters of Well-Known Men* (Boston, 1912); Walter Harding, "The Correspondence of Sophia T and Marianne Dunbar" *(TSB* 33); and Christopher McKee, "T's Sister in the White Mountains" *(Appalachia,* 23, 1957, 551–56). For reminiscences of the whole T family and their position in Concord, see Horace Hosmer, *Remembrances of Concord and the Ts,* edited by George Hendrick (Urbana, 1977), and Raymond Adams, "T and His Neighbors" *(TSB*

44). For the T family's religious vacillations, see H. H. Hoeltje, "T in Concord Church and Town Records" *(NEQ,* 12, 1939, 349–59).

For T's early schooling, see Hoeltje, "T and the Concord Academy" *(NEQ,* 21, 1949, 103–9), and Cameron, "Young HT in the Annals of the Concord Academy" *(ESQ,* 9, 1957, 1–42). For T's Harvard years, see Cameron, *T's Harvard Years* (Hartford, 1966), and his *T and His Harvard Classmates* (Hartford, 1965). For the details of his diploma, see Raymond Adams, "T's Diploma" *(AL,* 17, 1945, 174–75).

For a particularly detailed account of T's life from 1837 to 1847, see Emil Freniere, "HDT: 1837–1847" (Pennsylvania State Univ., Ph.D., 1961). The most detailed account of T's teaching experience is Anton Huffert, "T as a Teacher, Lecturer, and Educational Thinker" (New York Univ., Ph.D., 1951). For T's romance with Ellen Sewall, see Louise Koopman, "The T Romance" *(MR,* 4, 1962, 61–67). Edmund Sewall's experiences in the T school are recounted in Clayton Hoagland, "The Diary of T's 'Gentle Boy' " *(NEQ,* 28, 1955, 473–89). Harding has discussed the ramifications of T's relationship with Edmund in a forthcoming paper, "T and Eros." Most of the details of the T brothers' journey on the Concord and Merrimack is given in the book itself, but Christopher McKee, "T's First Visit to the White Mountains" *(Appalachia,* 31, 1956, 199–209), fills in the details of the one-week interlude when they wandered in the mountains. For details of T's 1844 trip to the Berkshires and the Catskills, see Thomas Woodson, "T's Excursion to the Berkshires and Catskills" *(ESQ,* 21, 1975, 82–92).

A thoughtful discussion of the Emerson-T relationship is Paul Hourihan, "The Inner Dynamics of the Emerson-T Relationship" (Boston Univ., Ph.D., 1967). Joel Porte, *Emerson and T* (Middletown, 1966), emphasizes T's impact on Emerson and the differences between them. There is much new information in Ralph Waldo Emerson, *The Journals and Miscellaneous Notebooks* (Cambridge, 1960–    ). For T's work on the *Dial,* see Clarence Gohdes, *The Periodicals of American Transcendentalism* (Durham, 1931); G. W. Cooke, *An Historical and Biographical Introduction to Accompany the Dial* (Cleveland, 1902); and especially Joel Myerson, "A History of the *Dial* (1840–1844)" (Northwestern Univ., Ph.D., 1971). For T's friendship with Hawthorne, see Edward Peple, "The Personal and Literary Relationship of Hawthorne and T" (Univ. of Virginia, Ph.D., 1970), his "The Background of the Hawthorne-T Relationship" (RALS, 1971, 104–12), and his "Hawthorne on T, 1853–1857" (TSB 119), and either of the twentieth-century editions of Hawthorne's American Notebooks (New Haven, 1932; Columbus, 1972). For T and Alcott, see Alcott, Journals (Boston, 1938) and Letters (Ames, 1969). For T and Greeley, see Helen Morrison, "T and the New York Tribune (TSB 77, 82); Walter Harding, "Horace Greeley on T" (TSB 116); and Michael Meyer, "The Case for Greeley's Tribune Review of A Week" (ESQ, 25, 1979, 92–94). The fullest account of T's Staten Island venture is Max Cosman, "T and Staten Island" (S.I. Historian, 6, 1943, 1–7). Both Frederick T. McGill, Channing of Concord (New Brunswick, 1967), and Robert Hudspeth, Ellery Channing (New York, 1973), devote much space to the friendship of Channing and T. For another Concord friendship, see Elizabeth Maxfield-Miller, "Elizabeth Hoar of Concord and T" (TSB 106). For T's friendship with the French-Canadian woodchopper, see Robert Bradford, "T and Therien" (AL, 34, 1963, 499–506). Jeanne Zimmer's "A History of T's Hut and Hut Site" (ESQ, 18, 1972, 134–40) is definitive.

The best account of T's arrest is S. A. Jones, "T's Incarceration" (TSB IV), but for the political background see John Broderick, "T, Alcott and the Poll Tax" (SP, 53, 1956, 612–26), and Walter Harding, "T in Jail" (AH, 26, 1975, 36–37). For T as a lecturer and lyceum participant, see Hubert Hoeltje, "T as Lecturer" (NEQ, 19, 1946, 485–94); Walter Harding, "T on the Lecture Platform" (NEQ, 24, 1951, 365–74), and his "A Check List of T's Lectures" (Bull. N.Y. Pub. Lib., 52, 1948, 78–87); and K. W. Cameron, "The Concord Lyceum—Its Surviving Records," in The Massachusetts Lyceum (Hartford, 1969, pp. 101–90).

T's misadventures with Sophia Foord are recounted in Walter Harding, "T's Feminine Foe" (PMLA, 69, 1954, 110–16). The standard sources on T as a surveyor are Albert McLean, "T's True Meridian" (AQ, 1968, 567–79); Marcia Moss, "A Catalog of T's Surveys in the Concord Free Public Library" (TSB XXVIII); Harry Chase, "HT, Surveyor" (Surveying & Mapping, June, 1965,

219–22); and K. W. Cameron, "Field Notes of Surveys Made by HDT Since November, 1849," in *Transcendental Climate* (Hartford, 1963, pp. 413–549). Ruth Frost has contributed a series of articles on T's Worcester friends to *Nature Outlook* (3–5, 1944–47), and fuller versions of these articles are gathered together in a special volume in the American Antiquarian Society in Worcester.

T's friendship with Daniel Ricketson is fully detailed in Anna and Walton Ricketson, *Daniel Ricketson and His Friends* (Boston, 1902). The best source of information on T's Plymouth friends is L. D. Geller, *Between Concord and Plymouth* (Plymouth, 1973). For T's friendship with Thomas Cholmondeley, see Joseph Jones, *"Walden* and *Ultima Thule:* A Twin Centennial" *(LCUT,* 5, 1954, 12–22). The fullest account of T's antislavery activities, including his relationship with John Brown, is Wendell Glick, "T and Radical Abolitionism" (Northwestern Univ., Ph.D., 1950). For T's visit to Eagleswood, see Maud Honeyman Greene, "Raritan Bay Union, Eagleswood, New Jersey" *(N.J. Hist. Soc. Proc.,* 68, 1950, 1–19). For T and Whitman, see Andrew Schiller, "T and Whitman" *(NEQ,* 28, 1955, 186–97). C. Carroll Hollis, "Whitman and William Swinton" *(AL,* 30, 1959, 425–49), adds further details. For T's various visits to Mount Monadnock, see Allen Chamberlain, "T's Camps," in *The Annals of the Grand Monadnock* (Concord, N.H., 1936, 70–80).

For T's study of tree growth, see Kathryn Whitford, "T and the Woodlots of Concord" *(NEQ,* 23, 1950, 291–306). T's unpublished papers on fruits and seeds are being edited for a forthcoming volume in the new Princeton Edition of T's *Writings.* For T's western journey, see Walter Harding, "T's Minnesota Journey" *(TSB* XVI), and Harriet Sweetland, "The Significance of T's Trip to the Upper Mississippi in 1861" *(TWA,* 51, 1962, 267–86). For T's editing in his final illness, see James Austin, *Fields of the Atlantic Monthly* (San Marino, 1953, pp. 302–5). For further information on his relations with his final publisher, see Ellen Ballou, *The Building of the House* (Boston, 1970). For an account of T's funeral, see Louisa May Alcott, *A Sprig of Andromeda* (New York, 1962), and for the correct details of his interment, see Raymond Adams, "T's Burials" *(AL,* 12, 1940, 105–7).

II

William Ellery Channing's biography first appeared serially as
"HDT" *(Commonwealth,* 1863–4), then in book form as *T: The Poet-
Naturalist* (Boston, 1873), and finally in an enlarged and revised
version edited by F. B. Sanborn (Boston, 1902). Sanborn gives a
detailed history of the vagaries of the book in "A Concord Notebook" *(Critic,* 47, 1905, 268–70).

F. B. Sanborn's first biography was *HDT* (Boston, 1882). *The
Life of HDT* (Boston, 1917) is a completely rewritten and far more
comprehensive volume. Francis H. Allen has discussed Sanborn's
techniques in *T's Editors (TSB* VII), and there are further details in
Walter Harding, "Franklin B. Sanborn and T's Letters" *(Boston
Pub. Lib. Quart.,* 3, 1951, 288–93).

Henry Salt's first biography was *The Life of HDT* (London,
1890), later revised and abridged as *Life of HDT* (London, 1896).
For information about Salt and his biographies, see George
Hendrick, *Henry Salt* (Urbana, 1977). An earlier English biography
is A. H. Japp ("H. A. Page"), *T: His Life and Aims* (London, 1878),
but it is little more than a sketch.

Annie Russell Marble, *T: His Home, Friends, and Books* (Boston),
appeared in 1902; Edward Emerson, *HT as Remembered by a Young
Friend* (Boston), in 1917. The latter is supplemented by further
reminiscences by Emerson that are included in Walter Harding,
*HDT: A Profile* (New York, 1971, pp. 73–90). A semifictional biography, and the first biography to appear in a foreign language, is
Leon Bazalgette, *HT, Sauvage* (Paris, 1924). It was translated by
Van Wyck Brooks as *HT: Bachelor of Nature* (New York, 1924).
Madeleine B. Stern, "Approaches to Biography" *(SAQ,·* 45, 1946,
362–71), evaluates most of the biographies of T up to this time and
particularly endorses Bazalgette's techniques.

Henry Seidel Canby, *T* (Boston), was published in 1939. Joseph
Wood Krutch, *HDT* (New York, 1948), while giving some atten-
tion to biographical details, is primarily a volume of criticism, as is
Mark Van Doren, *HDT: A Critical Study* (Boston, 1916).

Raymond Gozzi, "Tropes and Figures: A Psychological Study of

HDT" (New York Univ., Ph.D., 1957), is unpublished although
the two central chapters are included in Harding, *HDT: A Profile*
(Boston, 1971, pp. 150-87). Its thesis is summarized in Carl Bode,
"The Half-Hidden Thoreau" *(MR,* 4, 1962, 68-80). The Harding
volume is an anthology of studies of T's personality. Although
ostensibly an editing of a missing section of T's journal, Perry
Miller, *Consciousness in Concord* (Boston, 1958), contains a long introduction devoted in large part to a discussion of T's personality. For
a study of homoeroticism in T, see Jonathan Katz, *Gay American
History* (New York, 1976, pp. 481-94). Richard Lebeaux, *Young
Man T* (Amherst), was published in 1977. Another Eriksonian
study of T is Leonard Neufeldt, "The Wild Apple Tree: Possibilities of the Self in T" (Univ. of Illinois, Ph.D., 1966).

The only pictorial biography is Milton Meltzer and Walter
Harding, *A T Profile* (New York, 1962). Of a number of juvenile
biographies, by far the best is August Derleth, *Concord Rebel* (Philadelphia, 1962). Walter Harding, *T: Man of Concord* (New York,
1960), is a collection of more than one hundred reminiscences of T
by his contemporaries. Leon Edel, *HDT* (Minneapolis, 1970) can
only be described as unfortunate. Having no sympathy at all for,
and little understanding of his subject, Edel reverts to the un-
enlightened views of Lowell et al. and denounces T as querulous,
narcissistic, and humorless. The Emerson eulogy and the Lowell
and Stevenson essays may be found in their respective collected
works and in Walter Harding, ed., *T: A Century of Criticism* (Dallas,
1954).

# 2.

# Thoreau's Works

Although Henry Thoreau succeeded in publishing only two books and a handful of essays and poems in his lifetime, the standard collection of his works (the 1906 Manuscript or Walden Edition) fills twenty volumes and the now under way Princeton Edition projects approximately twenty-five volumes. Editors over the years have not been able to agree on any standard order of arrangement for his works but have tended instead to shift individual pieces from volume to volume to suit their whim or convenience. A strict chronological order would be ideal, for it would enable us to follow the development of both Thoreau's ideas and his style. But such an ideal is virtually unattainable, for Thoreau often worked on a number of writing projects simultaneously. He would start a project, drop it, and then pick it up later. He would publish a work and then later revise it heavily, and in the actual process of composition would often turn back to much earlier manuscripts to extract sentences or paragraphs he found appropriate. Thus his first book, *A Week*, was published in May, 1849, but he had completed a version of it as early as 1846. It tells the tale of a journey he took in 1839. It includes fragments from his *Journal* as early as 1837, at least one poem he wrote in 1839, and excerpts from works he had published in the *Dial* in the early 1840s. What is more, it includes the essay on "Friendship" that he did not write until 1848. And even after the book was published, he could not stop tinkering with it, so that after his death a "revised" version was published that contains many changes. Not all of Thoreau's works were as complicated in their composition as *A Week,* but to very few can there be given a specific date of composition.

It should be obvious by now that no final order of composition of Thoreau's works can be established. Hence, this chapter represents a compromise, in which the works are placed roughly in the order that he finished preparing them for first publication. Those works he was editing at the time of his death and that were published posthumously are arranged in the order of their first publication. Those essays that were later incorporated integrally into books, such as the individual chapters of *The Maine Woods* and *Cape Cod,* are treated as parts of those books, rather than separately, and assigned the date of book publication rather than of periodical publication, since most of them were heavily revised by Thoreau before incorporation into the book form. The letters, the poems, and the *Journal,* since they were worked on throughout Thoreau's adult life, are placed arbitrarily at the end of the chapter.

\*    \*    \*

"The Seasons" is Thoreau's earliest extant essay. A schoolboy essay, it was written when Thoreau was approximately eleven or twelve years old. Although it is by no means great literature, it does display remarkable facility for a child of that age and reflects his already keen interest in, and perception of, the world of nature. It should be noted, however, that its authenticity has been questioned because of the signature "Henry D. Thoreau," a form Thoreau is not known to have used elsewhere until more than ten years later. (He was baptized David Henry and did not regularly reverse the names until after his graduation from college.)

\*    \*    \*

The college essays include twenty-three themes and six forensic exercises Thoreau wrote in Edward Tyrrel Channing's rhetoric courses at Harvard. From his college days there are also a commencement exercise, a classbook autobiographical sketch, four book reviews or summaries (probably written for an undergraduate literary society), three fragmentary essays, an analysis of Milton's "L'Allegro" and "Il Penseroso," and a personal essay entitled "Musings." None of them shows any great merit, though the tradition that Channing rated many C has proven to be false. (The C on some of the manuscripts was placed there by F. B. Sanborn years after Thoreau's death simply to indicate he had made copies for his personal file!) They are read now only because Thoreau later went on to write his masterpieces.

Nonetheless, they are important to those who wish to study the development of Thoreau's thoughts and style. Joseph J. Kwiat says they may "be thought of as first attempts to integrate his formal Harvard studies, with their emphasis upon the Scottish philosophy, his efforts at self-culture, and the many contemporary influences, especially Emerson's, into some sort of personal expression, a major preoccupation with Thoreau during his entire mature life" (pp. 54–55). Moser adds: "Many a young Harvardite had been brought to a Transcendental position through the curriculum. The 'common sense' school had brought them to a rejection of the materialism of Locke, and by rejecting the Scottish school itself . . . budding Transcendentalists emerged" (pp. 18–19). All this is readily evident in these essays.

In examining the essays themselves, we find such typically Thoreauvian statements as: "So far as my experience goes, man *never* seriously maintained an objectionable principle, doctrine or theory. Error *never* had a sincere defender" (PE, 104). "The fear of displeasing the world ought not, in the least, to influence my actions" (PE, 106). "The majority of mankind are too easily induced to follow any course which accords with the opinion of the world" (PE, 10). "The civilized man is the slave of matter" (PE, 109). "The order of things should be somewhat reversed,—the seventh should be man's day of toil, wherein to earn his living by the sweat of his brow, and the other six his sabbath of the affections and the soul, in which to range this widespread garden and drink in the soft influences and sublime revelations of Nature" (PE, 117). "All of Thoreau's basic ideas are in the college essays, the seeds are all present, awaiting maturation" (Moser, p. 62). He needed but to develop his style to express them in the memorable phrasing of his later writing.

\*    \*    \*

"Died," the brief obituary for Anna Jones, which Thoreau published in the Concord *Yeoman's Gazette* for November 25, 1837 (p. 3), was his first writing known to have reached print. It adds little to our knowledge of Thoreau except to indicate his early interest in writing.

\*    \*    \*

*The Service,* apparently originally written for the *Dial* but rejected by Margaret Fuller, was not published until 1902. It was derived chiefly from his *Journal* from 1837 to 1840. Stylistically it is the young Thoreau in his most pompous and aphoristic vein, obviously influenced by the most vapid of his Transcendentalist contemporaries. While Thoreau's thoughts herein on the well-rounded or "spherical" man are important to an understanding of his later thoughts, he expressed most of the ideas more succinctly in his later works.

\*    \*    \*

The "Natural History of Massachusetts" was first published in the *Dial* for July, 1842. It was derived from the *Journal* for the years from 1837 to 1842. Nominally a review of *Reports—On the Fishes, Reptiles, and Birds; The Herbaceous Plants and Quadrupeds; The Insects Injurious to Vegetation; and the Invertebrate Animals of Massachusetts,* "published agreeably to an Order of the Legislature, by the Commissioners on the Zoological and Botanical Survey of the State" of Massachusetts, it is actually a nature essay drawn chiefly from the pages of Thoreau's own *Journal,* interspersed with much of his own poetry, and only in the last five brief paragraphs deals to any marked degree with the books reviewed. Although Thoreau chides the authors for their prosaic approach and points out a few errors in their texts, he welcomes their pioneer contributions to a systematic study of American flora and fauna. Thoreau continued to use the volumes for reference throughout his career.

But the modern reader will ignore those last few paragraphs and concentrate on the central theme: Thoreau's joy in the world of nature around him. It is his first published essay in the genre that was to make him famous. Best are the few brief paragraphs on muskrats and on fishing, which are almost worthy of a place in *Walden.*

\* \* \*

"A Walk to Wachusett" was first published in the *Boston Miscellany* for January, 1843, and Thoreau apparently never succeeded in obtaining payment for it. The essay is an account of a walking excursion with Richard Fuller, brother of Margaret Fuller, in July, 1842, to the solitary mountain just north of Worcester, Massachusetts. (He derived material, however, from his *Journal* for 1837, 1838, and 1841 in particular.) In quality it seems a slight retrogression from the "Natural History of Massachusetts." It is marred with the abstruseness characteristic of some of his earlier writings. But it improves in quality as he approachs and ascends the mountain, its literary peak coinciding with the mountain peak. The poem with which the essay opens was apparently written somewhat earlier and submitted to the *Dial,* but it was rejected by Margaret Fuller in her long, analytical letter of October 18, 1841.

\* \* \*

Thoreau did a number of translations for the *Dial.* "The Prometheus Bound" by Aeschylus first appeared in the January, 1843, issue. Little more than a literary exercise, it "is very literally and exactly and unimaginatively rendered; word order is sometimes painfully preserved" (Seybold, p. 18). Leo Kaiser, however, points out that it does include a few "unnecessarily free translations" (p. 69). C. C. Felton, Thoreau's Greek professor of Harvard, spoke of its having been "executed with ability." There have been long-standing rumors that it was reprinted and circulated among students at Harvard as a pony, but if it did, no copy of it is known. Thoreau's "Translations from Pindar" first appeared in the *Dial* for January and April, 1844. They display no great genius, but they are more poetically rendered. (Francis Allen points out that the version now included in the 1906 edition of Thoreau's works is marred by an omission and several errors.) Thoreau translated eleven poems of Anacreon for the April, 1843, *Dial* and later worked them into the text of his *Week*. He also translated "The Preaching of Buddha" from a French translation and included it in the January, 1844, *Dial*. A translation of *Seven Against Thebes* that he also apparently did for the *Dial* was not published there and did not reach print until 1959.

*    *    *

"Sir Walter Raleigh" is not one of Thoreau's masterpieces. It is of interest only as an apprentice piece. Apparently first written as a lecture and delivered before the Concord Lyceum on February 8, 1843, it was later revised for publication, possibly for the *Dial,* which suspended publication before it could have been included. Later he used a small portion of it in *A Week*. The essay adds nothing to our knowledge of Raleigh. In fact, it sheds more light on Thoreau's own youthful hero worship than on anything else. It is comparatively dull reading; none of Thoreau's later wit shows through.

*    *    *

"The Landlord," first published in the *Democratic Review* for October, 1843, was an attempt at the familiar essay in the style of Lamb and Hazlitt. It is poor Thoreau. It discusses the virtue of innkeepers, and obviously Thoreau's heart is not in the matter. He would rather be outdoors than in a tavern. In all probability, since it was written at Staten Island when Thoreau was making his first serious attempt to become a professional writer, it was an effort to please the general public. Thoreau himself described it as "a short piece that I wrote to sell" (W, VI, 111). Thoreau is at his best only when he is trying to be himself, not someone else.

*    *    *

[Note: PE includes in *Early Essays* seven essays Thoreau published in the *Dial:* "The Laws of Menu," "Sayings of Confucius,"

"Chinese Four Books," "Hermes Trismedistus," "Aulus Persius Flaccus," "Dark Ages," and "Homer. Ossian. Chaucer." The first four are Thoreau's editings of Eastern literature for the "Ethnical Scriptures" department of the *Dial.* The latter three Thoreau reworked and incorporated into the text of *A Week.*]

\*    \*    \*

"A Winter Walk," derived chiefly from the *Journal* for 1841 (although there are a few excerpts from the 1838 *Journal*), first appeared in the *Dial* for October, 1843, but only after Emerson had edited it severely. He not only cut from it an entire poem but also apparently edited many sentences, objecting to their *mannerism:* "for example, to call a cold place sultry, a solitude public, a wilderness *domestic* (a favorite word), and in the woods to insult over cities, armies, etc." (letter to Thoreau of September 8, 1843). Yet for the modern reader the essay is one of Thoreau's best. Welker terms it:

> perhaps the most evocative and lyrical short prose work Thoreau ever wrote. . . . Thoreau was beginning to transcend commonplace observations . . . and to look more deeply and react more subtly. . . . Here is the type of intimate and empathetic look into nature for which Thoreau is famous. He does not condescend, he does not go too far in personalizing his creatures, he does not moralize; instead he finds his way into their lives as far as his knowledge and understanding will permit. . . . Certainly Thoreau was saying nothing new; but he was foreshadowing . . . both the alienation from his time, and the compensating rapport with things of the wild, which would make *Walden* at once so somber and so heartening a book. (pp. 107–8)

Indeed the spirit of the whole essay is close to some of the best pages of nature description in *Walden.* The later book at times even echoes words and phrases from it, and probably the woodman's hut here so vividly described is that of Hugh Quoil, described again in *Walden.* Despite the fact that "The Landlord" and "A

Winter Walk" were first published in the same month, it is hard to
believe they were written by the same hand. The former is jejune,
almost puerile; the latter, Thoreau at his best.

\*    \*    \*

"Paradise (To Be) Regained" is a review of J. A. Etzler, *The
Paradise within the Reach of All Men, without Labor, by Powers of Nature
and Machinery. An Address to All Intelligent Men* (Part First, Second
English Edition, published in London in 1842). Thoreau wrote it
at the suggestion of Emerson, who wished to use it in the *Dial,* but
Thoreau instead submitted it to J. L. O'Sullivan, who published it
in the *Democratic Review* for November, 1843, although (according
to Thoreau's letter to Emerson of August 7, 1843) only after some
difficulties with the editor, who "could not subscribe to all the
opinions." Since the *Democratic Review* was primarily a political
organ, and Thoreau in his review advocates individual rather than
group reform, the difficulties are not surprising.

Etzler's pamphlet propounds the theory that would man only
unite, harness the wind, the tides, and the sun, live in community
apartments, and communize most of his productive activities, he
could produce a paradise on this earth that would relieve him of
all but the slightest necessity for labor. In many respects his ideas
closely parallel those of François Marie Charles Fourier, which at
that moment were inspiring the establishment of so many communities across the American countryside. Thoreau's review can be
considered his reply to the many Fourierists among his friends.

His rejection of Etzler's ideas is typically Transcendental and
Thoreauvian: "We will not be imposed upon by this vast application of forces. We believe that most things will have to be accomplished still by the application called Industry" (PE, 40). "The
chief fault of this book is, that it aims to secure the greatest degree
of gross comfort and pleasure merely" (PE, 45). "But a moral reform must take place first, and then the necessity of the other will
be superseded, and we shall sail and plow by its force alone" (PE,
45–46).

\*    \*    \*

"Herald of Freedom" was a brief notice of the New Hampshire antislavery journal edited by Nathaniel P. Rogers, published in the April, 1844, *Dial*. As Glick points out in "Thoreau and the 'Herald of Freedom' ": "For only three men, of the number whom Thoreau criticized in his works prepared for publication, is the quality of praise not strained: Nathaniel P. Rogers, . . . Wendell Phillips, . . . and John Brown" (pp. 194–95). Glick suggests that Thoreau's praise of Rogers was inspired in part at least by his objections to Garrison's dictatorial methods in leading the antislavery movement, for Rogers was one of the leaders of the opposition to Garrison. That Rogers was pleased with Thoreau's notice is indicated by his reprinting the article in his journal with a long "Introductory Note" (reprinted in Glick, pp. 198–200). In "Thoreau and Radical Abolitionism" Glick adds: "The significant thing about Thoreau's remarks about Rogers is that they marked his first departure from the ideal of the reformer who remains aloof and apart, in communion with the moral universe" (p. 181).

\*　　\*　　\*

"Wendell Phillips Before Concord Lyceum" was a letter written to William Lloyd Garrison, editor of the antislavery *Liberator* and first published in that journal in the issue of March 28, 1845. For some years there had been a quarrel within the ranks of the members of the Concord Lyceum between the conservative members who wished to avoid controversial issues and the liberals who in particular wished to have the antislavery problem discussed. The liberals finally won out and elected Thoreau and Emerson, among others, to the governing body of the lyceum. One of their first acts was to invite Phillips to speak, and the invitation was renewed in succeeding years. Thoreau's letter is a report on the third of Phillips's lectures. While the essay is filled with praise for Phillips, it is interesting to note that Thoreau singled out for particular praise Phillips's statement "that he was not born to abolish slavery, but to do right."

\*　　\*　　\*

"Thomas Carlyle and His Works" was written while Thoreau was at Walden. The few excerpts that appear in the extant *Journal* are chiefly of the period from 1845 to 1847. First used as a lecture before the Concord Lyceum on February 4, 1846, it was sent in August, 1846, to Horace Greeley, who acted as Thoreau's literary agent. A month later Greeley replied that the article had been accepted by *Graham's Magazine,* although it did not appear until the March and April, 1847, numbers, and Thoreau did not receive his pay (fifty dollars) for the article until Greeley, in desperation, wrote a draft on the publisher in May, 1848.

As one might expect from a Transcendentalist, it is a highly favorable review of Carlyle's life and works, perhaps one of the most understanding that Carlyle was to receive in his lifetime. Its importance to the modern scholar probably lies in its exposition of Thoreau's critical principles, and as the only extended essay by Thoreau on the literary work of a contemporary. When Carlyle received a copy of the essay, he wrote Emerson (May 18, 1847), "I like Mr. Thoreau very well, and hope to hear good and better news of him." Greeley later tried to persuade Thoreau to write a similar essay on Emerson. But Thoreau refused, apparently not wishing to presume on Emerson's friendship.

\* \* \*

In the summer of 1846 Thoreau was arrested and jailed for non-payment of his poll tax. That evening someone, probably his aunt Maria, paid the tax and the next morning he was released. But those few hours in jail resulted in his most famous and most influential single essay, "Civil Disobedience."

Thoreau had stopped paying his poll tax in 1842 or 1843 as a protest against slavery. (Despite Thoreau's implications to the contrary in his essay, the Mexican War was not a factor in his original protest, because it did not begin until 1845.) His protest was ignored for three or four years. His arrest in 1846 was due to a complex of political factors at the time, including the fact that Sam Staples, the jailor, would have had to pay the tax himself then had he not collected it. Oddly enough, Staples's arrest of Thoreau was in itself illegal, for the prescribed method was to seize sufficient property for auction to pay the taxes and fine—and Thoreau, with his large personal library, had more than sufficient property.

It was apparently Thoreau's intention to publicize his protest by going to jail, but Aunt Maria's intervention ruined this opportunity. Instead he turned to writing the essay to get his ideas before the people. In January and February, 1848, he gave a two-part lecture before the Concord Lyceum on "The Relation of the Individual to the State." The essay first reached print in May, 1849, in Elizabeth Peabody's short-lived periodical, *Aesthetic Papers* (pp. 189–213), under the title "Resistance to Civil Government." After his death it was included in his collected works under the title "Civil Disobedience," and it is sometimes entitled "On the Duty of Civil Disobedience."

Although the essay does tie itself down to specific political issues of Thoreau's time, it is basically more universal in its approach. When moral law and governmental law come into conflict, many argue that from expediency men should obey the government. But it is Thoreau's argument that "it is not desirable to cultivate a respect for the law, so much as for the right" (PE, 65). Having thus established his principle, he goes on to present the most effective method of defending it, that is, by practicing "civil disobedience," refusing to pay taxes, going to jail if necessary, and thus, by clogging the meshes of governmental gears and/or winning sympathy through martyrdom, making an aroused citizenry aware of the wrong and willing to right it.

It was not a new idea. Bronson Alcott had refused to pay his poll tax in 1843 and had been arrested. Emerson had theorized on the doctrine in his essay on "Politics." There had been frequent debates on the subject before the Concord Lyceum (in one of which, on January 27, 1841, Thoreau argued *against* the principle). A large segment of the abolitionist movement, that led by William Lloyd Garrison, espoused the doctrines of civil disobedience in their periodicals. And clergymen of the day were debating in their pulpits the merits of what they called the "higher law" controversy. Nor was the idea new in Thoreau's time. It can be traced back through the centuries as far at least as Sophocles' *Antigone* in the Western world and Mencius in the East.

Far more important than any study of its sources is the fact that

Thoreau's presentation of the idea has been the most influential in spreading the doctrine. It was Gandhi's textbook for his civil disobedience campaigns in Africa and India. It was published as a handbook of political action in the early days of the British Labour party in England, and was a manual of arms for the resistance movement under Nazi occupation in Europe in the 1940s. Martin Luther King, Jr., cited it regularly as the inspiration for his civil rights campaigns in the South. And during the "protest years" of the late 1960s and early 1970s, it appeared in popular paperback editions around the world. It has probably been more widely read than any other work by Thoreau. It is not unlikely that Thoreau is more widely known, particularly abroad, as the author of "Civil Disobedience" than of *Walden.*

\*   \*   \*

*A Week on the Concord and Merrimack Rivers* was Thoreau's first published book. It is based on a rowboat excursion he and his brother John took in the fall of 1839 as a vacation from their teaching. Although he had made sporadic earlier attempts to write about the voyage, it was his brother's tragic death in 1842 that led him to conceive of it as a memorial tribute. However, other duties kept him away from the task, and his decision to go to Walden in 1845 was inspired, in part at least, by the desire to write *A Week.* Work there progressed rapidly enough that by July 16, 1846, Emerson wrote to Charles King Newcomb, "In a short time, if Wiley & Putnam smile, you shall have Henry Thoreau's 'Excursion on Concord & Merrimack Rivers,' a seven days' voyage in as many chapters." However, Wiley and Putnam did not smile, nor did others that Thoreau tried at Emerson's behest, although several offered to publish it at Thoreau's expense. Thoreau took advantage of the extra time to revise and expand the book. As late as January, 1848, he added the "Friendship" essay to the "Wednesday" chapter. Sometime in 1848 Thoreau agreed to guarantee James Munroe of Boston the cost of publication in an edition of one thousand copies. Page proofs were probably in Thoreau's hands before the end of the year (they bear the copyright date of

1848), put perhaps because he asked for more than one thousand corrections, publication was delayed until May, 1849.

Its reception was a miserable failure. Even the printer failed him by accidentally omitting three lines of the text (p. 396 of the first issue). In four years only 218 copies were sold. Thoreau had to pay Munroe a total of $290 (J, V, 521). Munroe shipped the remainder to Thoreau on October 28, 1853, to clear his shelves, and that night Thoreau wrote in his *Journal,* "I have now a library of nearly nine hundred volumes, over seven hundred of which I wrote myself" (J, V, 459). Thoreau was not at all satisfied with the text and prepared a revised edition that included more than four hundred verbal changes and one thousand punctuation changes, but the revised edition was not published until 1868, six years after his death.

The basic plan of the book is a day-by-day account of the voyage. After the introductory chapter on "Concord River," there is a separate chapter for each day of the week from "Saturday" through "Friday." (Actually the excursion took two full weeks, but the period from Thursday to Thursday was used for a hike on foot to the top of Mount Washington.) The account of the voyage itself is smooth-flowing, vivid, and highly interesting. H. M. Tomlinson considered it the best of all travel books. But Thoreau inserted into the narrative many short essays on subjects as varied as Goethe and cattle shows, accounts of an excursion to western Massachusetts taken in 1844, incidents from his life on Staten Island in 1843, 48 original poems, and at least 126 quotations. Fifteen of these inserts were taken from material Thoreau had already printed in the *Dial.* Other pieces, such as one on Sir Walter Raleigh, were culled from his lecture manuscripts. But the great majority of the material was culled from his *Journal,* from its beginning in 1837 right up through 1848. Also, as became the pattern with his later "excursions," Thoreau, before he started on the journey, prepared himself by reading all the histories of the area he could place his hands on and then carried a gazetteer with him. He sprinkled liberally through his text references to, and quotations from, these works, including Fox's *History of the Old Township of Dunstable,* Mirick's *History of Havenhill, Massachusetts,* Johnson's *Wonder-Work-*

*ing Providence,* Gookin's *Historical Collections of the Indians in New England,* John Hayward's *New England Gazetteer,* and Alexander Henry's *Adventures.* In his commentary on the last-named, Thoreau remarks, "What is most interesting and valuable in it . . . is not the *annals* of the country, but the natural facts, or *perennials,* which are ever without date" (W, I, 231). Unfortunately, Thoreau sometimes failed to take his own advice, and it is the annals that he includes in this and his other volumes of excursions that date them more than anything else. It is the high proportion of perennials in *Walden* that make it his masterpiece.

Compared with his later books, *A Week* contains surprisingly little natural history other than a long essay on the fish of the Concord River in the first chapter. Yet in 1851, looking back at the book Thoreau himself was impressed with its *"hypoethral* character, to use an epithet applied to those Egyptian temples which are open to the heavens above." He trusted that it did not smell so much of the study and library "as of the fields and woods" (J, II, 275), but unfortunately we find the smell of the study there too often.

*A Week* is more typically Transcendentalist than his later volumes. There are frequent passages on the values of intuition and of the conscience. It often wanders into the abstract and occasionally into the vapid. But it was the section on religion (included in the "Sunday" chapter) that most disturbed the few of his contemporaries who read the book. And we need only glance at this to understand why the orthodox were frightened or angered by the book! "In my Pantheon, Pan still reigns in pristine glory" (W, I, 65); "It seems to me that the god that is commonly worshipped in civilized countries is not at all divine" (W, I, 65); "It is necessary not to be Christian to appreciate the beauty and significance of the life of Christ" (W, I, 68); "The reading which I loved best is the scriptures of the several nations, though it happens that I am better acquainted with those of the Hindoos, the Chinese, and the Persians, than of the Hebrews" (W, I, 72). Thoreau's willingness, even readiness, to tread on toes unquestionably was a factor in the book's poor sale.

But it is the large portion of digressions in the book that still distresses many readers. James Russell Lowell complained in his review, "We come upon them like snags, jolting us headforemost out of our places as we are rowing placidly upstream or drifting down." And there have been several editions of the book printed with many or most of the digressions deleted. Recent critics, however, have begun to argue that the structure of the book is not rickety as earlier critics claimed. They see the book as "organically" developed and look at the digressions as purposeful developments of an overall unifying theme. Unfortunately, no two of these recent critics have been able to agree on precisely what that unifying theme is nor just how each of the digressions fit into it. They see the book as a whole as "a search for the sacred" or "an exposition of the Transcendental experience" or "a defense of the American Indian" or "a paean to the Greek gods." Others argue that the book is unified by its structure and see it as based on the epic or the pastoral or the biblical story of creation or on circular imagery. But until these critics are able to agree upon what the unifying theme or the structural principle is, we must conclude that Thoreau did not wholly succeed in that unification. *A Week* remains one of Thoreau's least-read books.

*     *     *

In going through a miscellaneous collection of Thoreau manuscripts in the Widner Memorial Collection at Harvard College Library, Arthur Christy discovered what was apparently the manuscript of a hitherto unknown short work of fiction by Thoreau. However, upon further study he discovered that it actually was a translation from the French of *The Transmigration of the Seven Brahmans* from the *Harivansa* of Langlois, an anthology of Hindu literature published by the Oriental Translation Fund in Paris in 1834. Thoreau borrowed the *Harivansa* from Harvard College Library in 1849 and 1850 and apparently made the translation then. It is chiefly important as "the first extensive evidence ... of Thoreau's proficiency in French" (p. xvi). The "translation is not entirely literal, but occasionally an adaptation, and ... many sentences were omitted entirely" (p. 15).

*     *     *

The essay on "Love" was not published during Thoreau's lifetime. In September, 1852, on the occasion of his friend H. G. O. Blake's marriage Thoreau sent it and "Chastity and Sensuality" to Blake as a wedding gift of sorts. Like the "Friendship" essay imbedded in *A Week*, "Love" is highly Transcendental, condemning any physical basis for love, and shedding far more light on the author than on the subject.

\*    \*    \*

The essay on "Chastity and Sensuality" has a similar history. Even Thoreau had his doubts about it, for he wrote Blake, "I send you the thoughts on Chastity and Sensuality with diffidence and shame, not knowing how far I speak to the condition of men generally, or how far I betray my peculiar defects" *(Correspondence,* p. 288). But Thoreau, in word choice at least, was less inhibited than his friend Emerson, for when Emerson published the essay in *Letters to Various Persons* and was faced with the sentence, "In a pure society, the subject of copulation would not be so often avoided from shame," he prissily changed the word "copulation" to "marriage" and thus made nonsense of it.

\*    \*    \*

"An Excursion to Canada," earlier known as "A Yankee in Canada," based on a journey Thoreau took with Ellery Channing in the fall of 1850, was first published, in part, in *Putnam's Magazine,* beginning with the issue of January, 1853. But Thoreau disagreed with his old friend, George William Curtis, the editor, who insisted upon censoring certain passages, and withdrew his manuscript after only three of the proposed five chapters had appeared. Portions of the essay had been used as lyceum lectures in 1852. Most of the text is derived from his *Journal* for the summer and early fall of 1851, but he also made a few notations in his *Journal* just after his return from Canada in 1850 and a few more in the spring of 1852. After Thoreau's death the entire essay was issued with certain miscellaneous papers in a volume entitled *A Yankee in Canada, with Anti-Slavery and Reform Papers* (1866).

A railroad offered the eleven-hundred-mile, twelve-and-a-half-day trip for seven dollars, and fifteen hundred tourists responded. They visited both Quebec and Montreal, and Thoreau and Channing took the opportunity for a walking excursion along the banks of the St. Lawrence, visiting some of the notable waterfalls and observing the natives. It is one of Thoreau's least inspired "excursions." The opening sentence states, "What I got by going to Canada was a cold" (W, V, 3). The objective reader will have to agree that Thoreau found little else. Even the sentence structure and vocabulary of the essay are atypical, staccato, pedestrian journalese. As Edmund Berry has observed, "We learn that he is no abstracted, airy philosopher; he can on occasion be an extremely naive American tourist, with the self-righteousness, too, of the less attractive American tourists" (p. 74).

As usual with his excursions, Thoreau read all the history and travel books on the area he could find, referring in all to some forty-five different accounts by previous travelers to the region, although in this particular case he did most of his reading after his trip, rather than before. There is in the Morgan Library a mass of notes on the discovery and later history of Canada that Thoreau apparently compiled in preparation for writing this essay. But comparatively little of it was used. "An Excursion" is a fusion of the eighty-four-page account of his trip in his *Journal* for October, 1850, with seventy pages of the notes in his Canadian notebook. He quotes Kalm, Hontan, Cartier, Charlevoix, and others. And as soon as he arrived on the scene, he made haste to purchase two guidebooks and a map. But never did he succeed in adapting himself to the region or its inhabitants. French Canada was a holdover from "Europe and the Middle Ages," he thought. Its inhabitants were little better than savages, and ignoble savages at that. He resented the fact that few of them could speak English. And he spent pages denouncing the control that the Roman Catholic church exerted over them. Perhaps in this work more than in any other Thoreau displays the violent anti-Catholicism of the mid-nineteenth-century Yankee. He could appreciate cathedrals because they were like caves, but he wanted the priests omitted (W, V, 14). The shrine of St. Anne, to him, was nothing more than a fraud, and he suspected the crutches suspended on the walls "had been made to order by the carpenters who made the church" (W, V, 51).

The domination of the British military irked him even more. He visited the various fortifications, but thought the soldiers only "one vast centipede of a man, good for all sorts of pulling down" (W, V, 17). He suggested that were the soldiers to receive an education, they would immediately desert. And he could see no point to men standing guard duty in subzero weather when no enemy had approached the fortifications for centuries.

Even nature failed him here. The language difficulties with the natives were too great for him to learn the identity of certain botanical specimens that interested him, and in the whole essay there is only one brief list of the flowers he observed.

On the positive side, there are a few good pages devoted to the architecture of the region and an enlightening comparison of French and English colonial policies. On the whole, however, he is the superior Yankee looking down his long nose at an inferior race. The entire essay seems out of character. Even Thoreau himself cared little for it, for on February 27, 1853, he wrote Blake, "I do not wonder that you do not like my Canada story. It concerns me but little, and probably is not worth the time it took to tell it."

                              *    *    *


"Slavery in Massachusetts," delivered, in part, on July 4, 1854, at an antislavery convention at Framingham, Massachusetts, was first published in the *Liberator* on July 21 of that year. It was at this convention that William Lloyd Garrison publicly burned a copy of the Constitution to symbolize his protest against the protection it afforded slavery. But his act was hardly more violent than Thoreau's words, best summarized in one of his closing sentences, "My thoughts are murder to the State" (PE, 108).

Thoreau's protest was primarily against the recent arrest of the Negro Anthony Burns in Boston and his return to slavery in Virginia, and a large part of his essay is derived from his *Journal* entries at the time of Burns's arrest. But an almost equally large part of the essay is derived from his *Journal* entries from the early summer of 1851, at the time of the similar arrest of the Negro Simms. Thoreau was disturbed that his neighbors could protest slavery in the South or in Nebraska and yet overlook it in their own backyards, and he speaks out in some of his most violent language. As in "Civil Disobedience" (and the two essays are so similar in mood and tone that sentences could easily be exchanged between them), his appeal is based on obedience, not to governmental law, but to one's own innate sense of goodness. "They are the lovers of law and order who observe the law when the government breaks it" (PE, 98).

Wendell Glick points out that Thoreau here makes a two-way attack: (1) reform the individual, and (2) destroy those institutions that are corrupting mankind. Therefore Thoreau includes in this essay virulent attacks on both the press and the church as defenders of slavery. Despite the fact that the essay was inspired by a particular event, it is a timeless and universal appeal for a higher standard of morality.

* * *

*Walden* was Thoreau's second book, his last book to appear in his lifetime. It is based on his experiences at Walden Pond from July 4, 1845, to September 6, 1847, although it contains material from his *Journal* from as early as April 8, 1839, to as late as April 9, 1854. He completed a first draft of the book early enough to assure James Munroe, the publishers of *A Week,* that they could publish *Walden* soon after *A Week,* a fact they announced in the back pages of *A Week* in the late spring of 1849. But the failure of *A Week* led to cancellation of these plans, and *Walden* was not published until August 9, 1854, when it was issued in an edition of two thousand copies by Ticknor & Fields of Boston.

Thoreau used the intervening five years to revise, expand, and polish the work considerably, so that the book of 1854 was markedly different from the manuscript of 1849. Just how much the book was changed in those years has been revealed by J. Lyndon Shanley. Although the final "fair copy" of *Walden* apparently went into the printer's wastebasket as soon as the book was published, Huntington Library owns a large collection of miscellaneous manuscripts that are obviously parts of earlier drafts of the book. Shanley, by examining carefully the various types of paper and the variations in handwriting, found the manuscripts to consist of portions of seven different drafts of *Walden,* including an almost complete version of the first draft. In *The Making of Walden* he published that first draft with a detailed analysis of the changes that came about in succeeding drafts.

"The essential nature of *Walden* did not change from first to last" (Shanley, p. 6). "It was as if after having built a modest six- or seven-room house and living in it for a time, he found that it was not large enough, and then, as he did so, he decided to add new rooms and still later he found he could improve the proportions and disposition of the various parts of the house. But he did all this work from the inside out, cutting apart and spreading the foundations, walls and roof wherever necessary to accommodate the changes within, without destroying the fundamental character of any considerable portion of the original" (p. 6). Most of the quotations were not added till the later versions (p. 25). The chapter divisions were not made until 1853 (p. 4). Details were corrected from version to version as, for example, the price of a railroad ticket being changed from one dollar, to 70 cents in the page proof (p. 36).

Since Shanley made his studies, Ronald Clapper has investigated the Huntington manuscripts further. His doctoral dissertation, "The Development of *Walden:* A Genetic Text" (1967) is one of the most important doctoral dissertations of recent years. No serious student of *Walden* can afford to ignore it. It "provides a complete transcript of the additions, cancellations, and revisions contained in the seven manuscript versions of *Walden* and traces the development of Thoreau's masterpiece from the time he left the pond in 1847 until just before he prepared the copy for the printer in 1854" (p. viii). "One of the insights to be gained from a study of the Genetic Text is that many of the book's inconsistencies can be traced to a difference in their period of composition" (p. 5). "During the seven years that elapsed between the time he left the pond and the year his book was published Thoreau matured far beyond the confines of Emerson's Transcendental optimism and achieved a rich intellectual and poetic subtlety and complexity . . . ; what had begun as a fairly straight-forward account of his life in the woods . . . became by the time of its publication a remarkably suggestive book that reflected the intellectual problems of its age" (p. 7).

Although Thoreau spent two years, two months, and two days at Walden Pond, he has condensed these experiences into one year, and therein lies the chief unity of the book. Early critics were prone to claim that *Walden* had no unity. Francis H. Allen, for example, complained in 1910, in the introduction to his edition of *Walden*, "It is not an artistic composition. It lacks form. It cannot be taken as a model for the building of a book. It disregards the rules of essay construction" (p. xix). But more recent critics speak differently. Richard P. Adams, for example, in "Romanticism and the American Renaissance" *(AL,* 22, 1952, 425) says, "The basic structure of the book may be most clearly understood in the fact that Thoreau, 'for convenience,' condenses his two years' experience at Walden into one, and describes it beginning with summer and proceeding through fall and winter to spring. The turning seasons thus define a process of symbolic death and rebirth which, for Thoreau as for other romantics, represents the character of personal development." Not only does he use the symbolism of the year throughout the book, but he also uses the symbolism of the day (the epitome of the year) in the individual chapters. Thus, "Sounds" begins with the sounds of the afternoon, continues through the evening, the night, and ends with the cockcrowing of dawn. "A survey of Thoreau's use of the related imagery of morning and spring in *Walden* reveals remarkable variety; he has used the imagery to criticize contemporary life, to reveal aspects of his theory of expression, to celebrate his aims in life, to emphasize the importance of man's correspondence with nature, and to argue the almost limitless possibilities of individual inspiration and achievement" (Broderick, p. 89). *Walden* may seem to begin in despair, but it ends in ecstasy.

The early critics thought that, as Carlyle had said of Emerson's essays, *Walden*, organizationally speaking, was a collection of duck shot in a bag. It could be read backward as easily as forward, or the pages could be shuffled and it would not be materially harmed. But Shanley has demonstrated that Thoreau had a carefully formulated blueprint of the book as a whole and that each chapter, paragraph, and sentence was put in its particular place for a precise reason. There is not space to demonstrate that fact at length here, but one need only look at the beginning sentence of each chapter to see its truth. Thus, the transition sentence from "Reading" to "Solitude" begins, "But while we are confined to books . . ." and the transition sentence from "The Bean-Field" to "The Village" begins, "After hoeing. . . ." "Solitude" and "Visitors" are set up in direct antithesis to each other. And so on.

> There are four related but distinct "matters" with which the book concerns itself, and they might be enumerated as follows: (1) The life of quiet desperation which most men lead. (2) The economic fallacy which is responsible for the situation in which they find themselves. (3) What the life close to nature is and what rewards it offers. (4) The "higher laws" which man begins, through some transcendental process, to perceive if he faithfully climbs the stepladder of nature whose first rung is "wildness," whose second is some such gentle and austere but not artificial life as Thoreau himself was leading, and whose third is the transcendental insight he only occasionally reached. (Krutch, p. 108)

Reginald Cook finds three literary archetypes for *Walden: Robinson Crusoe* ("Man's skill in solving self-imposed economic problems" [p. 3]), *Gulliver's Travels* ("A critical arraignment of so-called civilization" [p. 4]), and *Pilgrim's Progress* ("An autobiographical narrative of . . . spiritual wayfaring" [p. 5]). Cook might have added a fourth: *The Natural History of Selborne,* for many there are who still ignore *Walden*'s philosophical content and think of the book as primarily a report on the flora and fauna of Concord.

Certain it is that many of Thoreau's contemporaries thought of the book primarily as a volume of natural history. Some even went so far as to suggest to the reader that he skip the more philosophical chapters—"Economy," "Higher Laws," and "Conclusion." Paradoxically, it is just those chapters that have best stood the test of time.

It is well to remember that on the title page of the first edition

Thoreau quoted from his chapter on "Where I Lived and What I Lived For," saying, "I do not propose to write an ode to dejection, but to brag as lustily as chanticleer in the morning, standing on his roost, if only to wake my neighbors up." Unfortunately, many modern publishers omit this epigraph. The book is "the most delicious piece of brag in literature" (Burroughs, *Indoor Studies,* p. 33), and unless the reader keeps this in mind, he is likely to miss the point of the book. And finally, it is important to remember that Thoreau wrote with a sense of humor. It may seem like belaboring the obvious to point this out, but many readers have failed to see it.

Thoreau's purpose in writing *Walden* is all too frequently misunderstood. He states explicitly several times in the volume that he is writing for a limited audience. For example:

> I do not mean to prescribe rules to strong and valiant natures, who will mind their own affairs whether in heaven or hell, and perchance build more magnificently and spend more lavishly than the richest, without ever impoverishing themselves not knowing how they live,—if, indeed, there are any such, as has been dreamed; nor to those who find their encouragement and inspiration in precisely the present condition of things, and cherish it with the fondness and enthusiasm of lovers ... ; I do not speak to those who are well employed, in whatever circumstances, and they know whether they are well employed or not;—but mainly to the mass of men who are discontented, and idly complaining of the hardness of their lot or of the times, when they might improve them. ... I also have in my mind that seemingly wealthy but most terribly impoverished class of all, who have accumulated dross, but know not how to use it, or get rid of it, and thus have forged their own golden or silver fetters. (PE, 16)

Or, to recapitulate briefly, if you are satisfied with your own way of life, this is not a book for you. But if you are leading a life of "quiet desperation," Thoreau here offers you a way out.

Second, Thoreau is not advocating that we all abandon our

cities and homes and our families and go out into the wilderness to live in huts and meditate on nature:

> I would not have any one adopt *my* mode of living on any account; for, besides that before he has fairly learned it I may have found out another for myself, I desire that there may be as many different persons in the world as possible; but I would have each one be very careful to find out and pursue *his own* way, and not his father's or his mother's or his neighbor's instead. (PE, 71)

Third, Thoreau is not advocating that we abandon civilization. To be sure, he was discouraged at times, as all thinking people are, with some of the dark spots in modern life. He simply bewails the fact that so many of our so-called improvements of civilization are but "improved means to an unimproved end." We are in great haste to get nowhere to do nothing. Since we have invented time-savers, let us make the most of them, he suggests. But let us improve our spiritual natures as well as our material world.

Thoreau had talked of going to Walden Pond for a number of years before he actually moved there to live in his twenty-eighth year. He tells us that when he first saw its crystal-clear waters as a child, he wanted to live on its shores. After graduating from Harvard in 1837 and trying his hand at schoolteaching for several years, he more and more frequently talked with his friends of going off by himself for awhile to experiment with life. At first he tried unsuccessfully to obtain teaching positions in distant Virginia and Kentucky, but then he thought of living independently nearer home. His college classmate Charles Stearns Wheeler had lived in a hut in the woods in nearby Lincoln, and Thoreau had visited him there. Ellery Channing had lived for a time alone on the Illinois prairie. From 1840 on we find constant reference in Thoreau's *Journal* and letters to a desire to settle down in solitude for a time.

In 1845 Thoreau found the opportunity. Emerson purchased fourteen acres of woodland at Walden Pond, wishing to preserve the quiet beauty of the woods and lake. Soon after, Thoreau entered into an agreement with him. There was a small field on the land and Thoreau would render it arable. In return he would have the privilege of "squatter's rights" on the land.

Thoreau purchased the remains of a railroad shanty from an Irish immigrant named James Collins and carried its timbers to the pond to build his cabin. Most of the work on the building was his own, although he did call in a few friends for the frame-raising. The cabin was a well-built structure, fifteen feet by ten, with one room, one door, one window in each side, a cellar hole, a garret, and a closet. A few months after he moved in, he plastered the walls for winter weather and built a fireplace. The second winter he added a stove.

Explaining why he went to the pond to live, he wrote: "I went to the woods because I wished to live deliberately, to front only the essential facts of life, and see if I could not learn what it had to teach, and not, when I came to die, discover that I had not lived" (PE, 90). There is the essence of Thoreau's experiment. He was not an escapist from civilization. His cabin was only two miles from town and twenty from "the hub of the universe." The railroad rattled by one end of the pond, and the highway passed within sight of his garden. Rarely a day went by that he did not hike into town on an errand or that visitors did not come out to call on him.

His life at Walden Pond was quietly devoted to living. Each morning he took his bath in the pond and then hoed in his garden, "making the earth say beans instead of grass" (PE, 157). Stormy days or winter mornings he read or wrote. Afternoons he spent in wandering through the Concord woods or boating on its ponds and rivers, pursuing assiduously his studies of the world about him. Evenings he devoted to his friends, with either a trip to the village for a conversation or a few guests in his cabin. After two years he had accomplished his set task and "left the woods for as good a reason as I went there. Perhaps it seemed to me that I had several more lives to live, and could not spare any more time for that one" (PE, 323).

\* \* \*

"A Plea for Captain John Brown" is the first of Thoreau's three essays on Brown. Through F. B. Sanborn, who acted as Brown's agent in Concord, Thoreau met Brown twice and was greatly impressed. Although he knew nothing in advance of Brown's plans at Harpers Ferry, and although the press and even many of the abolitionists hastened to disavow and denounce Brown when word of the attack reached the North, Thoreau, almost alone, came quickly to his defense. He called a meeting in Concord Town Hall on October 30, 1859, and when the selectmen refused to ring the bell to announce the meeting, he rang it himself. The local Republicans sent him word that they thought such a meeting at the moment inexpedient, and he replied that he was not asking for advice but announcing a meeting. According to Emerson, many came who were opposed to Thoreau's opinions but found themselves listening with a surprising sympathy. Two nights later he repeated the speech at Theodore Parker's Temple in Boston, a last-minute substitute for Frederick Douglass. On November 3 the lecture was delivered in Worcester under the auspices of his friend Blake. Although he originally hoped to have the lecture printed as a pamphlet to be "sold for the benefit of Captain Brown's family," Thoreau abandoned that plan and it was printed in James Redpath's *Echoes of Harper's Ferry* in 1860.

To many people the John Brown essays have seemed to embody a complete reversal of all the principles for which Thoreau had once stood. And some, such as John Burroughs, who thought of "Civil Disobedience" as savoring of "a little bit of the grotesque and the melodramatic" *(Indoor Studies,* p. 9), found his defense of John Brown "the most significant act of his life" (p. 8). As Wendell Glick asserts: "To the impartial student of Thoreau, it is obvious at the very outset that there was much in John Brown which not only did not conform to Thoreau's fundamental theories of reform but was in direct contradiction to them" (p. 159). "The championing of John Brown was tantamount to Thoreau's categorical rejection of his early faith in the omnipotence of the 'natural' forces for good in the universe" (p. 167). "Yet . . . in championing Brown Thoreau did not feel guilty of compromising his earlier beliefs. Instead, he saw in Brown the fulfillment of them. He made every attempt to reconcile Brown's method of reform with his own earlier theories" (p. 159). It was true that Brown was using political (i.e., external) reform rather than the inward reform of the individual. But Thoreau did find that Brown "fulfilled three of his principles—he woke man up out of his lethargy; he showed contempt of government; and he set a great personal example" (p. 168).

It was perhaps this last aspect that so much impressed Thoreau. In "Civil Disobedience" he had stressed that one *good* man could reform a nation. And in Brown, Thoreau found a man who was willing to practice that principle. Thus, Brown was a major hero, on a level with Christ: "Some eighteen hundred years ago Christ was crucified; this morning, perchance, Captain Brown was hung" (PE, 137). In deifying Brown, Thoreau called him "a transcendentalist above all, a man of ideas and principles" (PE, 115), thus apparently rationalizing for the disparity in Brown's views and Thoreau's own.

One will find many ideas in Thoreau's essay that are not contradictory to his earlier writings: "He had the courage to face his country when she was in the wrong" (PE, 113). "The only government that I recognize . . . is that power that establishes justice" (PE, 129). "When were the good and the brave ever in a majority?" (PE, 131). "Is it not possible that an individual may be right and a government wrong?" (PE, 136). Any of these sentences would be appropriate in "Civil Disobedience" or "Slavery in Massachusetts." The fundamental distinction of the John Brown essays is that they apply the principles of the earlier essays to a particular man and a particular situation, even though some significant elements of that man's character and action were in conflict with some of Thoreau's principles.

Thoreau apparently wrote the essay under great emotional pressure. As he himself says, "I put a piece of paper and a pencil under my pillow and when I could not sleep I wrote in the dark" (PE, 118). The *Liberator* (November 4, 1859) was moved to comment, "This exciting theme seemed to have awakened 'the hermit of Concord' from his usual state of philosophic indifference, and he spoke with real enthusiasm." The essay is filled with memorable epithets, such as Brown "was a volcano with an ordinary chimney flue" (PE, 115). And, as usual in his later polemical writings, Thoreau expressed his indignation with the church and press for opposing rather than supporting the right.

\* \* \*

"Martyrdom of John Brown" (also known as "After the Death of John Brown") was delivered by Thoreau at the memorial services, which Thoreau himself was chiefly responsible for arranging, held in Concord the day Brown was hanged, December 2, 1859. Except as a further indication of Thoreau's interest in Brown, the essay has little value. The closing passages are a few paragraphs from Thoreau's own translation of Tacitus.

\* \* \*

"The Last Days of John Brown" was written for the memorial services held in North Elba, New York, on July 4, 1860, at the time of John Brown's burial there. It was derived almost entirely from Thoreau's *Journal* for November and December, 1859. Thoreau was unable to make the trip to North Elba, and the paper was read for him by R. J. Hinton. It was printed in Garrison's *Liberator* for July 27, 1860. Like the earlier "Plea," it is a passionate defense of John Brown and his actions. It is of interest to students of Thoreau's mind because for the first time he publicly abandoned his Transcendentalist belief that all men are innately good, with the remark, "I have known many a man who pretended to be a Christian, in whom it was ridiculous, for he had no genius for it" (PE, 149). As Wendell Glick has pointed out, with the John Brown episode Thoreau adopted the principles William Lloyd Garrison had argued for in his war against slavery some years before.

\* \* \*

"The Succession of Forest Trees" was first delivered as an address before the Middlesex Agricultural Society in Concord in September, 1860, and first printed in the *New York Tribune* for October 6, 1860. It is derived from the *Journal* for the period from 1852 to 1860. As Thoreau tells us, "I have often been asked, as many of you have been, if I could tell how it happened that when a pine wood was cut down an oak one commonly sprang up, and *vice versa*" (W, V, 185). His answer is his major contribution to scientific knowledge. "While Thoreau can not be said to have introduced the subject to science, it appears that no important studies of ecological succession were made in America for more than thirty years after his memorable lecture" (Deevey, p. 8). And when Kathryn Whitford compared his findings with a modern study made with the benefit of the development of the science of ecology in the intervening years, she found, "The similarities are too great to be obscured even by the changes which more than eighty years have made in the vocabulary of science" (p. 299). Thoreau did not discover the principle of tree succession. He himself in his essay does not hesitate to give credit for some of his ideas to William Bartram and to Loudon. (Although Thoreau does not mention it, despite the fact that he was familiar with the book, there is a further suggestion of the principle in Timothy Dwight's *Travels in New England and New York*, II, 440). Thoreau's was the first well-formulated presentation of the idea, yet it took modern science eighty years to recognize his contribution.

The ideas behind Thoreau's "Succession of Forest Trees" grew out of his almost daily contact with woodlots as a professional surveyor. In serving as a surveyor, Thoreau "had so far yielded to expediency as to become an important instrument in the very destruction [of Concord's forests] which he necessarily regretted" (Stoller, p. 93), for surveyors were most frequently called in when a farmer was about to cut his woodlot. But "the significance of Thoreau's silvical investigations is that they led to a reconciliation of these contradictory strains in his attitude to the forest. His discovery of the mechanism of succession pointed to a system of forest management which would yield lumber and profit to satisfy man's grosser instincts and at the same time preserve nature for the disciplining of his spirit" (p. 96).

Although the essay is scientifically accurate, it is filled with witticisms and sly humor. Thoreau admits to his neighbors that he is a man "distinguished for his oddity" (W, V, 184). And he closes with an amusing tale of his squash that had won first prize at the Agricultural Society fair in 1857. But his audience recognized its value and the society's president congratulated him on "an address so plain and practical, and at the same time showing such close observation, and careful study of natural phenomena." The society printed the essay in its *Transactions* for 1860, and it was reprinted (in "expurgated" form) in the *Eighth Annual Report of the Secretary of the Massachusetts Board of Agriculture* for the same year.

\* \* \*

Although "Walking" was not published until June, 1862, in the *Atlantic Monthly,* a month after Thoreau died, most of the material in it was taken from his *Journal* of the years 1850–52. He used it frequently as a lecture in 1851 and 1852 and again in 1856 and 1857, although by the time of the latter lectures, according to his letter to Blake of December 31, 1856, he had split it into two. He then apparently revised it in the last months of his life and submitted it to the *Atlantic* on March 11, 1862, suggesting that it could, if necessary, be again split into two papers.

It is the least organized of his shorter works and might well have been improved by having been split. The first portion is a delightful essay on the joys of walking, beginning with a fanciful etymology of the term and then extolling the virtues of spending a goodly portion of each day exploring the countryside. At times it becomes almost chauvinistic in boasting the superiority of the American landscape to the European. Thoreau discovers that he inevitably settles upon a southwestward course for most of his walks and looks upon it as a subconscious vindication of "Westward the star of empire takes its way." (But, as Raymond Adams has suggested, it is more simply explained by the fact that in Thoreau's native Concord all the best walking territory is southwest of the town.)

The second part of the paper is an essay on "the Wild," in which Thoreau expounds on the need of civilized men to return to nature now and then for "nourishment and vigor." The last few pages are a highly miscellaneous conglomeration of barely related paragraphs, but he closes with the same image he uses in the final paragraphs of *A Week, Walden,* and "Civil Disobedience": this is the dawn of a new morning. There will be "a great awakening light, as warm and serene and golden as on a bankside in autumn" (W, V, 248). Perhaps next to "Life Without Principle," "Walking" is the best brief exposition of Thoreau's philosophy, although it lacks the trenchancy of the former essay.

\* \* \*

"Autumnal Tints," though used as a lecture as early as 1859 and derived from the *Journal* for 1851–58, was not published until October, 1862, in the *Atlantic Monthly*. It is another of the essays Thoreau revised for publication in the last months of his life and, in this case, according to his March 11, 1862, letter to Ticknor & Fields, he was able to correct the proofs before his death. In the *Atlantic* the essay was illustrated with an engraving of a scarlet oak leaf that Thoreau submitted to the editors; this was omitted in book publication.

In his own words, it is an attempt "to describe all these bright tints of [autumn foliage] in the order in which they present themselves" (W, V, 251). In his *Journal* (XI, 457) he complained that his audience thought he had assumed that "they had not seen so much of them [the autumnal colors] as they had." And the essay does at times have a somewhat superior air. Along with "Night and Moonlight," "Wild Apples," "Life Without Principle," and "Walking," this essay was culled from his *Journals* of the early 1850s, but in revising them he changed the tone from discouragement to satisfaction (Seybold, pp. 86–87).

\* \* \*

"Wild Apples" is Thoreau's most successful attempt at the familiar essay. It was delivered originally as a lecture before the Concord Lyceum on February 8, 1860, with exceptional success. It was considered the best lecture of the season and was followed by "long, continued applause" (Marble, p. 155). Most of it was derived from the *Journal* for 1850–52, although there are also excerpts from the *Journal* for 1857–60. He continued to revise it, however, as is indicated by his mentioning seeing the wild crab apple in Minnesota in 1861, and it was not published until November, 1862, in the *Atlantic Monthly*.

He traces the history of the apple from the Garden of Eden to his own backyard, and from the seed to the fruit, and he launches into a facetious catalogue of imaginary species that includes some of his best wordplay. The whole essay is marked by a whimsical humor, and his description of the fight of the wild apple for survival from the browsing of the cows is not only vivid writing but good natural history. Underlying the whole essay is Thoreau's basic philosophy: we get from nature only what we give. Although (or perhaps because) it lacks the sturdiness of most of his best writing, it has been one of his most frequently anthologized essays.

\* \* \*

"Life Without Principle" was published October, 1863, in the *Atlantic Monthly,* more than a year after Thoreau's death. It was another of the essays he readied for publication in his last months. But the nucleus of the paper was written many years before in his *Journal* for 1851–55, and a version of it was delivered as a lecture, under the title "Getting a Living," at least as early as 1854. He also occasionally entitled it as a lecture, "What Shall It Profit [a Man If He Gain the Whole World But Lose His Own Soul]?"

It is perhaps the most central to Thoreau's philosophy of all his shorter essays and contains virtually all the fundamental principles upon which he based his life. It is too highly concentrated to be accurately condensed, but basically it is his essay on "Self-Reliance." He asks us to get down to fundamental principles in life and not to be led astray by our neighbors, our nation, our churches, public opinion, the desire for wealth, or any other diverting influence. It is pure Transcendentalism, advocating that the good life be discovered within oneself. Like his other major writings, it ends with the morning symbol that we are at the dawn of a new day.

In this essay Thoreau is writing at his highest level, not only in content, but also in style. It is filled with some of his most memorable phrases. Perhaps it is too highly concentrated to make a good introduction to his writings, but it ties together all his fundamental principles better than any other brief work.

\* \* \*

In the summer of 1854 Thoreau apparently started work on an "intended Course of Lectures" on "Moonlight." He went back through his *Journal* of recent years, excerpting and rewriting passages on the subject, and on October 8, 1854, read a portion of the manuscript at Leyden Hall in Plymouth to a small informal gathering of Marston Watson's friends. Later that winter he abandoned the project, only to revive it once more in 1859 or 1860, and again abandon it. When the volume *Excursions* was being prepared for publication in 1863, the publishers were faced with a nearly empty signature at the back of the book; they printed just enough excerpts from this unfinished manuscript to fill the signature and entitled it "Night and Moonlight." Later, in 1927, Francis Allen published another series of excerpts as *The Moon.* Neither version is particularly remarkable as a whole, although each contains a few sentences of effective nature writing. Basically they are effusions on the beauties of a moonlit night. Recently William L. Howarth has made a further study of the "Moonlight" manuscripts (unfortunately, they have been scattered to the four winds), and the Princeton Edition will eventually include a much more accurate and complete version.

\* \* \*

*The Maine Woods* was the second book to be published after Thoreau's death. *(Excursions,* a collection of his travel essays, had appeared in 1863.) Edited by his sister Sophia and his friend Ellery Channing, it appeared in 1864. Its text was derived from two magazine articles, "Ktaadn and the Maine Woods," which had appeared serially in the *Union Magazine* from July through November, 1848, and "Chesuncook," which had appeared serially in the *Atlantic Monthly* from June through August, 1858, and an unpublished manuscript, "The Allegash and the East Branch," which Thoreau had been working on at the time of his death. "Ktaadn" was derived chiefly from the *Journal* for 1847, which, although still extant, has never been published. (It will eventually be included in the

Princeton Edition.) "Chesuncook" follows the *Journal* of 1853 so closely that it has been omitted from the printed version (see J, V, 424, 456), but it also includes selections from the *Journal* as early as 1850 and as late as 1858. "Allegash" follows the *Journal* of 1857 so closely that it too has been omitted from the printed version (J, IX, 485; X, 53). Thoreau had used some of this material for lectures: a portion from "Ktaadn" in January, 1848; from "Chesuncook" on December 14, 1853; and a portion of "Allegash" on February 25, 1858.

That *The Maine Woods* is not a well-integrated book but a collection of three separate essays is obvious. The essays are frequently repetitive, and Thoreau makes explanations in the latter two that are not necessary after reading the first. But it should be remembered that Thoreau died before he completed the task of editing these Maine papers, and there are strong indications that the "Allegash" essay was never completed in itself.

The book is based on three separate expeditions to the Maine woods by Thoreau with various companions: "Ktaadn" on one taken in August and September, 1846 (while he was at Walden), with his cousin George Thatcher, two friends from Bangor, and two boatmen; "Chesuncook," September, 1853, with Thatcher; and "Allegash and East Branch," with Edward Hoar of Concord, July and August, 1857. The basic form is a series of travel letters such as frequently appeared in the periodicals of Thoreau's time. In the "Allegash" section each separate day's excursion is headed by its date, but the dates have been omitted in the first two chapters, perhaps because, as Thoreau suggested in his letter to James Russell Lowell of January 23, 1858, when he submitted "Chesuncook" for publication in the *Atlantic Monthly,* the essays would otherwise appear out-of-date for periodical publication.

As Thoreau states in "Chesuncook," he went to the Maine woods primarily to study at first hand the "ways" of the Indian. The Indian community at Oldtown, Maine, was well known, and the fact that Thoreau's cousins lived in nearby Bangor gave him a convenient base for operations. Although on his first expedition the Indian Louis Neptune failed to keep his promise to act as a guide and Thoreau had to turn to a white man, on the second and third

trips he had able Indian guides in the persons of Joe Aitteon and
Joe Polis, respectively. And as Emerson pointed out in his funeral
address, Polis made a particularly strong impression on Thoreau.
With Polis, Thoreau made an agreement. "I would tell him all I
knew, and he should tell me all he knew" (PE, 168), and apparently he made a similar agreement with Aitteon, for the book is a
gold mine of Indian lore and terminology, and he includes a six-
page appendix of Indian words.

As usual, Thoreau read carefully in the literature of the area
both before and after making his expeditions. The book is filled
with allusions to, and quotations from, such volumes as John
Springer's *Forest Life and Forest Trees* (New York, 1851) and C. T.
Jackson's various reports on the public lands of Maine; from naturalists such as F. André Michaux and such early historians as John
Josselyn. His quotations, however, are far more carefully integrated into his text than they are in *Cape Cod.*

Thoreau records much about the natural history of the area and
includes in his appendix lists of the trees, flowers and shrubs,
plants, birds, and quadrupeds. However, these lists are somewhat
inaccurate (Eckstorm, pp. 245–46).

Although this volume is supposedly one of those upon which
Thoreau worked in the last years of his life to remove the humor
because he could not "bear the levity" he found, there is still much
punning, exaggeration, and even slapstick comedy.

There is comparatively little social criticism in the volume, although Thoreau does make a few remarks about the carelessness
with which forests are harvested by the lumberers and sets up an
ideal for conservation. As usual, he cannot resist making a few
gibes at the religiously orthodox and is a little irritated when his
Indian guide wishes to rest on Sundays. One particular sentence
about a pine tree ("It is an immortal as I am, and perchance will
go to as high a heaven, there to tower above me still" [PE, 122]) so
offended James Russell Lowell that he deleted it before "Chesuncook" appeared in the *Atlantic Monthly,* and so brought Thoreau's
wrath down upon his head. But the sentence was restored in the
book.

Most surprising to those who think of Thoreau as an escapist from civilization are his numerous comments on the loneliness of the wilderness and his remark at the end of "Chesuncook," in which he said, "It was a relief to get back to our smooth but still varied landscape. For a permanent residence, it seemed to me that there could be no comparison between this and the wilderness" (PE, 155).

Altogether, *The Maine Woods* is by no means Thoreau's best book, even though Canby (p. 373) describes it as his "most normal"; yet certainly it does not deserve Robert Louis Stevenson's curt dismissal of it as "not literature." Thoreau captures the atmosphere of the coniferous forest, tells his story vividly (even though not very profoundly) and with a sense of humor, and rarely bogs down in detail, as he does in some of his other works.

\* \* \*

*Cape Cod* is Thoreau's sunniest book—and least profound. It provides perhaps the best introduction to his writings for those who are frightened by the "chanticleer crowing" of *Walden*. Like *The Maine Woods*, it was posthumously edited (by Ellery Channing and Sophia Thoreau) and published in 1864. It was based on excursions he had made to Cape Cod in October, 1849; June, 1850; and July, 1855; the first and last times with Ellery Channing and the second time alone. A fourth excursion, alone, in June, 1857, is recounted in his *Journal* but is not included in *Cape Cod*.

Comparatively little of *Cape Cod* still shows up in the *Journal*, although there are occasional extracts from 1850 to 1855. Thoreau had used his first excursion (and possibly his second) as the basis for lectures on Cape Cod before the lyceums in Concord, Danvers, and Clinton in 1850 and 1851. They were among his most successful lectures, and Emerson (in his February 6, 1850, letter to Thoreau) reported of one that he heard "that Concord people laughed till they cried, when it was read to them." Portions of *Cape Cod* appeared in *Putnam's Monthly Magazine* for June, July, and August, 1855, and more was to have appeared, but the editor objected to "its tone towards the people of that region" (Francis Allen, *Bibliography*, p. 71). Still later, after Thoreau's death and immediately before its book publication, two chapters appeared in the *Atlantic Monthly* for October and December, 1864.

Basically it is a much better integrated book than *The Maine Woods*. Using the first excursion as an outline for his book, Thoreau inserts into the narrative incidents from the two later ones so skillfully that one is hardly aware of the transition. Nonetheless, as the editors of the Walden Edition point out (p. ix), "It should be borne in mind by the reader that a considerable part of this book never received its final revision at the hands of its author." Its greatest weakness is that it contains too much undigested historical source material, particularly in the final chapter, where there are pages and pages of quotations from early histories of Cape Cod. Thoreau evidently recognized this weakness, for when portions of the book were serialized in *Putnam's,* he wrote the editor, George William Curtis, on November 16, 1852, that he was "in doubt about the extracts" and advised Curtis he could omit them or print them in smaller type. Another weakness is that Thoreau felt impelled to intersperse the narrative with quotations in Greek. He excuses himself with the statement, "I put in a little Greek now and then, partly because it sounds so much like the ocean" (W, IV, 67). The reaction of the modern reader is more likely to be that it was ostentation that motivated Thoreau—a charge that can rarely be brought against him.

But despite these weaknesses, *Cape Cod* is a delightful book. The humor fairly bubbles over in puns and anecdotes. A primary value lies in its depiction of Cape Cod before the present-day tourist invasion. Here we meet the retired sea captains, the widows, the village characters. We see the men sailing out to catch mackerel, the wives drying fish in their yards. We get accurate descriptions of the flora and fauna of the area, usually better integrated than the catalogues in *The Maine Woods*. The account of the dwarf forests on the sand dunes on the tip of the Cape is particularly memorable. His note that he discovered broccoli in the Wellfleet oysterman's garden is often cited as the earliest incidence of that plant in North America.

Although there is comparatively little social criticism, Thoreau does not miss the opportunity to take an occasional crack at the otherworldliness of the clergy, at the proneness of the natives to make an extra dollar at the expense of shipwrecked mariners, and at the habits of the men wasting their time in barrooms and taverns. But there is a saving grace in his seeing the funny side of his own appearance, and he is greatly amused when he is mistaken for a robber who had recently raided a bank in Provincetown. He even laughs at the dullness of one of his chapters and ends it with the comment, "There was no better way to make the reader realize how wide and peculiar that plain [Nauset Plain] was, and how long it took to transverse it, than by inserting these extracts in the midst of my narrative" (W, IV, 56). But despite its sunniness and good humor, *Cape Cod* also has its somber side. Death stalks its pages from the description of the wreck of the *St. John* in the first chapter, right through to the end. It is a subject worthy of study. Emory Maiden, Jr., sees in *Cape Cod* "a precocious intuition of the forces which shape the work of American naturalistic writers of thirty years later" (p. 3).

Thoreau, as usual, prepared himself well in advance with a reading of all the literature on the area he could discover. In fact, he carried along with him in his pack a gazetteer and a volume of historical collections. As we have already indicated, the book is filled with references to most of the histories of the area, from the accounts of the Norse explorers, Champlain, John Smith, the Pilgrims, and Timothy Dwight. He also reread the Cape Cod portions of the various Massachusetts natural history reports that he had reviewed some years earlier in the *Dial*.

But it is when he weans himself from these source books that Thoreau is at his best in *Cape Cod*. He writes pungent, trenchant prose in which you can "hear the sea roar, as if I lived in a shell" (W, IV, 269). A vivid indication of the memorableness of his prose was pointed out by the *New Yorker* some years ago when it demonstrated that Robert Lowell in his Pulitzer Prize-winning "Quaker Graveyard in Nantucket" echoes word for word a lengthy passage from Thoreau's description of the wreck of the *St. John*.

Thoreau "did not intend this for a sentimental journey" (W, IV, 78). He portrayed Cape Cod as he saw it, omitting none of its barrenness in its physical features or in the lives of its inhabitants, but always describing it with a sense of humor. It stands, and long will continue to stand, as *the* book about Cape Cod.

\* \* \*

Shortly after Thoreau's death, his sister Sophia asked his Worcester friend, H. G. O. Blake, to collect and edit an edition of his letters *(Daniel Ricketson and His Friends,* p. 159). When Blake refused, Emerson was asked. *Letters to Various Persons* (Boston, 1865), the resulting volume, is far from satisfactory. Since Emerson wished to emphasize Thoreau's stoic qualities, he was highly selective. He deleted many personal references and those portions of the letters that would have shown Thoreau's warmth and friendliness. When Sophia Thoreau saw the manuscript, she protested to the publisher and insisted certain passages be restored. A compromise was worked out that satisfied neither. Emerson complained that the "perfect Stoicism" of the volume had been marred, and Sophia Thoreau felt that her brother had been misrepresented.

In 1894 Sanborn brought out a new edition entitled *Familiar Letters.* Although in his preface he denounced Emerson's editing, Sanborn committed even greater outrages himself. He included many more letters and restored the names and many of the expurgated passages of the Emerson edition, but he revised the punctuation, spelling, and even the wording to suit his own taste and was extremely careless in dating and annotating the letters.

It was not until 1958 that a comprehensive edition of Thoreau's letters was published and that was the first to include letters written to him as well as by him. While Thoreau was by no means a Horace Walpole in the quality of his letter writing, he does at times, particularly in his letters to H. G. O. Blake (although in not all of them), reach the levels of his better formal prose. But the letters are important for an understanding of Thoreau the man and his times.

\* \* \*

Thoreau can hardly be considered a major poet. His *Collected*

*Poems* contains more than two hundred, yet the number of significant poems he wrote can be numbered on the fingers of both
hands, if not of one. And rare is the anthology of American poetry
that bothers to include more than two or three.

Early in his writing career Thoreau apparently thought of himself primarily as a poet. But as the years passed, he turned more
and more consistently to prose. One major factor was undoubtedly
Emerson's negative criticism of some of his verse, which led him at
one point to burn many of his manuscript poems—an act he was
later to regret. But he is joined in this regret by few others, for the
simple fact is that most of his poetry is bad poetry. Much of it
deserves no better name than doggerel. When it is regular, it is
singsong; when it is free verse, there seems little point to the freedom. His diction is often archaic. He can commit such atrocious
rhymes as "Venice" and "fen is" (p. 8), or, even worse, such a
couplet as

> *I love a life whose plot is simple,*
> *And does not thicken with every pimple.* (p. 42)

But there is little point to belaboring his bad poetry. It must also
be acknowledged that he did write a few good poems. The best of
these are probably the nature odes, "Smoke" (p. 27), "Fog" (p. 56),
and "Haze" (p. 59), all of which he himself felt worthy of including in either *A Week* or *Walden*. They are Grecian in form and
mood. Emerson said of the first that it "suggests Simonides, but is
better than any poem of Simonides," and the same praise might
well be given to the others.

Other notable and popular poems include "My Prayer" (p. 10),
"Gentle Boy" (pp. 64–66) (written about Edmund Sewall and not
his sister Ellen, as some have suggested), "Sic Vita" (pp. 81–83),
and "Inspiration" (pp. 230–33). The last, especially in its central
stanzas beginning

> *I hearing get who had but ears,*
> *And sight, who had but eyes before,*

is one of the best expositions of the Transcendental experience in all Thoreau's writings.

Henry Wells discerns the influence of many schools of poetry from medieval times to Thoreau's own, and even anticipations of twentieth-century poetry. Strangely enough, Thoreau imitated most frequently either Skelton or the seventeenth-century metaphysical poets, none of whom was popular in his day. "Scarcely a single poem from his hand can be associated with American fashions soon to be securely established by Longfellow, Whittier, and Lowell" (p. 100).

Perhaps the greatest value of his poetry is that it often presents in epitomized form those ideas he expounded at greater length in his prose. Thus,

> *Tell Shakespeare to attend some leisure hour,*
> *For now I've business with this drop of dew.* (p. 76)

or

> *He's governed well who rules himself,*
> *    No despot vetoes him.* (p. 199)

Thoreau's best poetry, paradoxically enough, is in his poetic prose.

\*    \*    \*

In 1905 the Bibliophile Society of Boston issued *The First and Last Journeys of Thoreau* in a limited edition edited by Sanborn. Its source was described as some unpublished fragments "lately discovered among his unpublished journals and manuscripts." (At least some of the material Sanborn used is now part of HM 13182 in Huntington Library.) The book shows every sign of Sanborn's tampering and revision. A highly miscellaneous group of manuscripts is included, and these are tossed about with little regard for chronological (or any other) order. Because the volumes give hitherto unpublished portions of early drafts of *A Week* and the only detailed account of Thoreau's journey to Minnesota, they could have been invaluable source material. But Sanborn's high-handedness puts all scholars into a quandary, and his editions can be used only with the greatest caution.

The first volume is made up of excerpts from the Ward family correspondence of 1839 (pp 1–7); Thoreau's diary of his voyage on the Concord and Merrimack rivers (pp. 7–62); excerpts from his *Journal* while on Staten Island in 1843 (pp. 63–113); a fragmentary essay on "Conversation" (pp. 113–17); and an appendix of *Journal* fragments and poems accompanied by facsimile reproductions of the manuscripts (pp. 121–46). The second volume is devoted to the trip to Minnesota and includes excerpts from his journey notebook, fragments of the Mann family correspondence, Thoreau's botanical lists for the journey, and excerpts from letters Thoreau wrote while in the West. The many faults and errors of this volume have been adequately pointed out by Evadene Burris Swanson. The Minnesota material has since been edited by Walter Harding.

\*    \*    \*

On October 22, 1837, just a few months after Thoreau graduated from Harvard, he purchased a blank notebook and entered on the first page, " 'What are you doing now?' he asked, 'Do you keep a journal?' So I make my first entry to-day" (J, I, 3). Thus, probably at Emerson's suggestion, he began a task that was to last a lifetime, for nearly every day until a few months before his death he faithfully entered his thoughts into his journal, occasionally only a brief entry, such as "Went to Boston," but more frequently a page or two pages, or even five or six, recording his thoughts, beliefs, and aspirations, to a final total of about two million words.

Thoreau, originally at least, had no intention of publishing his *Journal.* " 'Says I to myself' should be the motto of my journal," he wrote in it on November 11, 1851 (J, III, 107). Like Emerson's journal, its major function was to be a source book for other, more formal writings, but as the years passed it became more and more obvious that Thoreau was thinking of it as a work of art in itself. In 1853 Emerson hired Ellery Channing to compile a volume of excerpts from the journals of Emerson, Channing, and Thoreau, to be entitled *Country Walking.* But that effort died aborning. Sometime after Thoreau's death, when Thomas Wentworth Higginson "endeavored to enlist Judge Hoar, the leading citizen of Concord, in an effort to persuade Miss [Sophia] Thoreau to allow her brother's journals to be printed, he heard me partly through, and then quickly said, 'But you have left unsettled the preliminary question, Why should any one care to have Thoreau's journals put in print?' " *(Cheerful Yesterdays,* p. 170).

As early as 1872 Bronson Alcott suggested (in his *Concord Days,* p. 264) that "A delightful volume might be compiled from Thoreau's Journals by selecting what he wrote at a certain date annually, thus giving a calendar of his thoughts on that day from year to year." And it was this plan Thoreau's Worcester friend, H. G. O. Blake, who had inherited the manuscript journals from Sophia Thoreau, followed when he issued *Early Spring in Massachusetts* (Boston, 1881). So immediate was the success of this volume that he followed it with *Summer* in 1884, *Winter* in 1888, and *Autumn* in 1892. Unfortunately, Blake's selections gave no really adequate indication of the content of the *Journal* as a whole, since they concentrated almost entirely on Thoreau's nature writing. Nonetheless, they served their purpose in stimulating interest and paved the way for publication of the full *Journal.*

It was in 1906 that Houghton Mifflin issued the so-called complete *Journal,* in an edition of fourteen volumes, as part of the twenty-volume Manuscript or Walden Edition of Thoreau's work. Although the title page assigns the credit for editing the *Journal* to the then well-known nature writer Bradford Torrey, most of the work was done by Francis Allen, of the Houghton Mifflin staff. (When the *Journal* was reissued in 1949, Allen at long last received the credit he deserved of having his name appear on the title page.) The work of transcription and editing was no easy task, as anyone who has worked with Thoreau's manuscripts will quickly concede. But the editors proceeded carefully and conscientiously. The editorial practices they followed are stated in their preface (J, I, vii–ix).

The printed *Journal* as it now stands is, however, not complete. The editors have omitted long quotations; certain of the Maine woods material, which was incorporated into *The Maine Woods;* some extended lists of plants; and many tables and charts of the river's depth made by Thoreau for the dam controversy of 1859. And occasionally they omit a proper name "out of regard for the feelings of possible relatives or descendants of the persons mentioned" (J, I, vii–viii). More questionable is the fact, pointed out by Perry Miller in *Consciousness in Concord,* that they were lamentably inconsistent in recording Thoreau's editorial revisions.

More important, however, is the fact that two early volumes of the *Journal* were not available to the editors. The first of these covers the period from July 30, 1840, to January 22, 1841, and consists of more than 16,000 words. This volume was available to Blake, and he used nearly two-thirds of it in his seasonal volumes. However, he omitted important material shedding further light on Thoreau's romance with Ellen Sewall. Fortunately this volume was acquired by the Morgan Library and edited by Perry Miller as *Consciousness in Concord.* The second volume, covering part of the year 1846, consists of more than 42,000 words. It is devoted chiefly to the first trip to Maine. This volume is now in the New York Public Library. Also omitted are many pages of the *Journal* of the 1830s and 1840s, which Thoreau himself scissored out to use in *Walden, A Week,* and other writings. Thanks chiefly to the ingenious detective work of Thomas Blanding, many of these pages are now being recovered and thus the new Princeton Edition will include a great deal of early material not included in the 1906. The great majority of rough drafts of *Journal* material that are extant in various collections have proved to be not pre-*Journal* drafts, as once commonly thought, but post-*Journal* drafts—that is, material transcribed and reworked from the *Journal* (after Thoreau gave up the habit of scissoring such material out) for use in essays and books.

It is virtually impossible in a few words to summarize the contents of the *Journal.* As Thoreau himself said, the ideas for it came "from all points of the compass, from the earth beneath and the heaven above" (J, I, 413). The first volume is in large part simply a commonplace book, filled with favorite quotations from his reading, alternated with Transcendental aphorisms in the vein of Bronson Alcott's "Orphic Sayings." William Drake says: "The striking thing about his own early work is the preponderance not of observed fact but of highly generalized speculation" *(A Formal Study of Thoreau,* p. 4). There is comparatively little nature writing in these pages, although what there is occasionally equals the best writing of his later years. Here too are imbedded many of his poems and drafts of some of his early lectures for the Concord Lyceum. Thoreau's scissoring from the early *Journal* may account for the lack of lists of species of flora and fauna before 1850, but another possible explanation is that he had not yet begun compiling such lists.

From 1850 on we find a quite different work. It is "one of the most complete records extant of the inner life of an individual" (Canby, p. 79). Late in 1857 Thoreau wrote: "Is not the poet bound to write his own biography? Is there any other work for him but a good journal? We do not wish to know how his imaginary hero, but how he, the actual hero, lived from day to day" (J, X, 115). Such a record of himself Thoreau presents in his *Journal*. It reports "all his joy, his ecstasy" (J, IV, 223). There are still occasional quotations from his reading, a few aphorisms, and numerous lists of natural phenomena (these latter increasing noticeably as the years progress), but there are also added many character sketches of his neighbors and, most important of all, a remarkably full record of his thoughts on man, life, society, and government. When the full *Journal* was published in 1906, many critics expressed their amazement that so large a portion of the work was thus devoted to his thoughts. They had considered him primarily a nature writer; now they discovered that he was more fundamentally a thinker.

\* \* \*

In the last years of his life Thoreau began work on a series of interrelated manuscripts growing out of his work on "The Succession of Forest Trees." There was to be a series of essays on "Wild Fruit," another on "The Dispersion of Seeds," and still another on "The Fall of the Leaf." He also began construction of a series of phenological charts of Concord's flora and fauna. But unfortunately his ill health precluded his completing any of these projects. After a great deal of study, Leo Stoller succeeded in extracting a charming essay on "Huckleberries" from this mass of manuscripts, and the Princeton Edition hopes eventually to cull out several more, or at least fragments thereof for their edition. Portions of this material contain some of Thoreau's best nature writing, but because he did not have the opportunity to complete and polish any of it, it is all necessarily fragmentary.

The various editors of the Princeton Edition have also succeeded in putting together from fragmentary manuscripts several other essays Thoreau never completed. Wendell Glick has published "Reform and the Reformers," apparently a lecture manuscript from which Thoreau later drew material to use in *Walden*. Thomas Blanding has isolated drafts of essays on "Life Misspent," "The Reformer," "On Government," "Places to Walk To," and "New England Native Fruits." There are also a number of short essay fragments from Thoreau's earlier years on such topics as "Gratitude," "The Best Criticism," "The Devil," "The Sphinx," "Hindoos," and "Conversation." Some or all of these will eventually be included in the Princeton Edition.

*    *    *

Thoreau also kept a series of notebooks in which he jotted down favorite quotations, excerpts from his reading, and related material. The most significant of these are some commonplace books, which became source books for the quotations he used in many of his books and essays, and a series of twelve Canadian and Indian notebooks. While Thoreau occasionally inserted brief comments of his own into these books, they are chiefly made up of quotations from other writers, and they are primarily of interest to the researcher into Thoreau's sources rather than to the general reader.

*Sources for Chapter Two*

The standard edition of T's works is *The Writings of HDT* (referred to herein as "PE"), published by Princeton University Press (1970–    ) under the sponsorship of the National Endowment for the Humanities and the Modern Language Association. As of this writing only four volumes have appeared, but there are plans eventually for approximately twenty-five. PE has been edited by a team of T scholars under the direction first of Walter Harding then of William L. Howarth and now of Elizabeth K. Witherell. Each volume "provides for the scholar and the general reader authoritative texts, edited according to the most advanced bibliographical principles." Each volume has extensive editorial apparatus that lists all known textual variants and gives a rationale for the present choice of text. In some volumes there is also an historical introduction. Robert Stowell, *A T Gazetteer* (Princeton, 1970), edited by William L. Howarth and published to accompany PE, has many maps and photographs that are extremely useful in understanding T's travels both in and out of Concord.

For those works which have not as yet appeared in PE, the Manuscript or Walden Edition (they were printed from the same plates) of *The Writings of T* (Boston, 1906, 20 vols.) is standard. There are several other collected editions, a number of volumes of selections from T's writings, and almost innumerable editions of his more popular works that vary greatly in textual accuracy and scholarship.

The most comprehensive critical study of T's works is Sherman Paul, *The Shores of America* (Urbana, 1958), which analyzes, in chronological order, all but a few of the minor works and thus gives a comprehensive view of the development of T's thought and artistry, though it is weak on the political essays. William Drake, "The Depth of Walden: T's Symbolism of the Divine in Nature" (Univ. of Arizona, Ph.D., 1967), also concentrates on the development of T's ideas but is limited to the *Journal* from 1837 to 1845 and *Walden* and *A Week*. Textual and critical studies of individual works are cited below. There are a number of collections of critical articles on T. They include:

Wendell Glick, *The Recognition of HDT* (Ann Arbor, 1969)
Walter Harding, *T: A Century of Criticism* (Dallas, 1954)
John Hicks, *T in Our Season* (Amherst, 1966)
Joseph McElrath, Jr., *T: A Symposium (ESQ,* 19, 1973, 131–99)
Sherman Paul, *T: A Collection of Critical Essays* (Englewood Cliffs, 1962).

\*    \*    \*

In each case the best text of each work is cited first. In those cases where a PE version has not yet appeared, the volume it is scheduled for is indicated.

"The Seasons" (PE, *Early Essays,* p. 3).

The college essays (PE, *Early Essays,* pp. 4–118). Facsimile reproductions and annotations on many of T's college writings are included in "T's Notes on Harvard Reading," in Kenneth Cameron, *The Transcendentalists and Minerva* (Hartford, 1958, pp. 130–358). See also Joseph Kwiat, "T's Philosophical Apprenticeship" *(NEQ,* 18, 1945, 311–20), and Edwin Moser, "HDT: The College Essays" (New York Univ., M.A., 1951).

"Died" (PE, *Early Essays,* p. 121).

"The Service" (PE, *Reform Papers,* pp. 3–17). The manuscript and Sanborn's notably corrupt transcription (Boston, 1902) are reprinted in Kenneth Cameron, *The Transcendentalists and Minerva* (Hartford, 1958, pp. 935–70). (The text given in W, IV, 277–9, is only a fragment.) F. O. Matthiessen gives a detailed analysis in *American Renaissance* (New York, 1941, pp. 83 ff.) Kenneth Harris, "T's 'The Service': A Review of the Scholarship" *(ATQ,* 11, 1971, 60–63), is a helpful survey of virtually all scholarly comments on the essay.

"Natural History of Massachusetts" (W, V, 103–31; PE, *Excursions).* A good discussion will be found in Robert Welker, *Birds & Men* (Cambridge, 1955, p. 106).

"A Walk to Wachusett" (W, V, 133–52; PE, *Excursions).* Lauriat Lane, Jr., "T at Work: Four Versions of 'A Walk to Wachusett' " *(Bull. N.Y. Pub. Lib.,* 69, 1965, 3–16), is not only an enlightening comparison of the varying versions of this essay but a thoughtful study of the artist at work. For a structural comparison of this essay and "A Winter Walk," see Lane, "T's Two Walks" *(TSB* 109). For Richard Fuller's account of their journey, see his "Visit to Wachusett" *(TSB* 121).

"Prometheus Bound" (W, V, 337–75; PE, *Translations).* For the background of this translation, see Ethel Seybold, *T: The Quest and the Classics* (New Haven, 1951); Leo Kaiser, "Remarks on T's Translation of the Prometheus" *(Classical Weekly,* 46, 1953, 69–70); and Walter Harding, "T's Professor Has His Say" *(TSB* 46).

"Translations from Pindar." *(TSB* 26) points out the errors and omissions in the Walden Edition transcription. "The Origin of Thera," included in the *Dial* (IV, 385), was inexplicably dropped. "The Seven Against Thebes," edited by Leo Kaiser *(ESQ,* 17, 1959, 1–30; PE, *Translations).* The "Anacreontics" (PE, *Translations)* have not been separately published, nor has "The Preaching of Buddha" (PE, *Translations).* For a discussion of the latter, see Roger Mueller, "A Significant Buddhist Translation by T" *(TSB* 138). Kevin Van Anglen is working on a new edition of the *Translations* for PE.

"Sir Walter Raleigh" (PE, *Early Essays,* pp. 178–218). Details of the complicated history of its composition are given in PE, *Early Essays,* pp. 391–93. T's literary criticism therein is discussed at length in Raymond Adams, "HT's Literary Theories and Criticism" (Univ. of North Carolina, Ph.D., 1928, chap. XII). For an interesting contemporary review of it as a lecture, see Walter Harding, *The Days of HT* (New York, 1965, pp. 142–44). The Metcalf-Sanborn version of the essay (Boston, 1905) is completely unreliable.

"The Landlord" (W, V, 153–62; PE, *Excursions).* For a lengthy analysis and defense of the artistry of the essay, see Joseph DeFalco, " 'The Landlord': T's Emblematic Technique" *(ESQ,* 56, 1969, 23–32).

"Aulus Persius Flaccus," "The Laws of Menu," "Sayings of Confucius," "Dark Ages," "Chinese Four Books," "Homer. Ossian. Chaucer," "Hermes Trismedistus" (PE, *Early Essays,* pp. 122–77).

"A Winter Walk" (W, V, 163–83; PE, *Excursions).* Emerson's criticism will be found in his letter to T of September 8, 1843. Welker's observations are in *Birds & Men.* See also the Lane article listed under "A Walk to Wachusett" above.

"Paradise (to Be) Regained" (PE, *Reform Papers,* pp. 19–47). Note that the essay exists in two quite different versions, the periodical version of 1843 (given in PE) and a much briefer posthumous version. For a good discussion of the philosophical differences between T and Etzler, see Robin Linstromberg and James Ballowe, "T and Etzler" *(Midcontinent Amer. Studies Jour.,* 11, 1970, 20–29). For T's misquoting of Etzler's text, see Wendell Glick, "T's Use of His Sources" *(NEQ,* 44, 1971, 101–9).

"Herald of Freedom" (PE, *Reform Papers,* pp. 49–57). The history of the text is a particularly complicated one (see PE, *Reform Papers,* pp. 287–97), but PE may have erred in adding the last several paragraphs from the Houghton Library manuscript to the text since they appear to have been part of an abandoned reworking of the essay for possible inclusion in *A Week.* For discussions of the essay, see Wendell Glick, "T and Radical Abolitionism" (Northwestern Univ., Ph.D., 1950), and his "T and the 'Herald of Freedom' " *(NEQ,* 22, 1949, 193–204).

"Wendell Phillips Before Concord Lyceum" (PE, *Reform Papers,* pp. 59–62).

"Thomas Carlyle and His Works" (PE, *Early Essays,* pp. 219–67). Note that the text exists in two versions, the periodical version (given in PE), and a much briefer posthumous version. The vicissitudes of publishing the essay are given in PE (pp. 406–9). A detailed analysis of the essay may be found in Raymond Adams, "H's Literary Theory and Criticism" (chap. XI) and in Frederick W. Lorch, "T and the Organic Principle in Poetry" *(PMLA,* 53, 1938, 300–2).

"Civil Disobedience" (W, IV, 356–87; PE, *Reform Papers,* pp. 63–90). The argument as to whether the 1849 "Resistance to Civil Government" or the 1866 "Civil Disobedience" text is the better is a long one. We opt for the latter. We see every indication that the changes in the 1866 version are T's own. For arguments on both sides see Thomas Woodson, "The Title and Text of T's 'Civil Disobedience' " *(Bul. of Research in the Humanities,* 81, 1978, 103–12), and Wendell Glick, "Scholarly Editing and Dealing with Uncertainties: 'T's Resistance to Civil Government' " *(AEB,* 2, 1978, 103–15). For a typographical error in spacing common to most editions, see Lauriat Lane, Jr., " 'Civil Disobedience': A Bibliographical Note" *(PBSA,* 63, 1969, 295–96). Raymond Adams, " 'Civil Disobedience' Gets Printed" *(TSB* 28), gives the publishing history of the essay. John C. Broderick, "T, Alcott, and the Poll Tax" *(SP,* 53, 1956, 612–26), gives the historical background, but see Walter Harding, "T in Jail" *(AH,* 26, 197, 36–27), on the illegality of T's arrest. Samuel Arthur Jones, "T's Incarceration" *(TSB* IV), gives the fullest account of the jailing incident. Raymond Adams, "T's Sources for 'Resistance to Civil Government' " *(SP,* 42, 1945, 640–53), discusses some influences on T's thinking, but it is challenged by Wendell Glick, " 'Civil Disobedience': T's attack upon Relativism" *(WHR,* 7, 1952, 35–42). For a suggestion that the essay was written in a revolt against Emerson's domination, see Paul Hourihan, "The Inner Dynamics of the Emerson-T Relationship" (Boston Univ., Ph.D., 1967). For details of the "higher law" controversy, see Edward Madden, *Civil Disobedience and Moral Law in Nineteenth-Century American Philosophy* (Seattle, 1968). A tremendous body of literature discussing the moral and philosophical pros and cons of the idea of civil disobedience has grown up over the years, particularly during the late 1960s and the early 1970s. The best collection of such essays is Hugo Adam Bedau, ed., *Civil Disobedience: Theory and Practice* (New York, 1969), and particularly the editor's own introduction. For a strongly negative appraisal, see Heinz Eulau, "Wayside Challenger: Some Remarks on the Politics of HDT" *(Antioch Rev.,* 9, 1950, 509–22). John A. Christie, "T on Civil Resistance" *(ESQ,* 54, 1969, 5–12), presents a moderate's analysis. For a discussion of the rhetorical devices used in the essay, see Michael Erlich, "T's 'Civil Disobedience': Strategy for Reform" *(Conn. R.,* 7, 1973, 100–10). For an argument that T himself was more of a conscientious objector than a civil disobedient, see William Herr, "T: A Civil Disobedient?" *(Ethics,* 85, 1974, 87–91). For T's place in American anarchism, see Richard Drinnon, "T's Politics of the Upright Man," in John Hicks, *Thoreau in Our Season* (Amherst, 1966, pp. 154–68).

*A Week on the Concord and Merrimack Rivers* (PE). One should note that there are between 1,200 and 1,300 changes (mostly minor) between the first edition and the revised 1868 edition. For a full concordance, see James Karabatsos, *A Word-Index to A Week* (Hartford, 1971). A shortened version, edited by Dudley Lunt *(The Concord and the Merrimack,* Boston, 1954), drops many of the "digressions," but has helpful notes and a detailed map. See also the maps in Robert Stowell, *A T Gazetteer* (Princeton, 1970). Carl Hovde, "The Writing of HDT's *A Week on the Concord and Merrimack Rivers"* (Princeton Univ., Ph.D., 1956), has been published in part as "Nature into Art: T's Use of His Journals in *A Week" (AL,* 30, 1958, 165–84), and "Literary Materials in T's *A Week" (PMLA,* 80, 1965, 76–83). Mary Suzanne Carroll, "Symbolic Patterns in HDT's *A Week"* (Indiana Univ., Ph.D., 1975), gives an almost paragraph-by-paragraph explication of the text, discussing in particular the symbolism therein. Gail Baker, "The Organic Unity of HDT's *A Week on the Concord and Merrimack Rivers*" (Univ. of New Mexico, Ph.D., 1970), is a lengthy rationale for the unity of the book. Rosemary Whitaker, *"A Week on the Concord and Merrimack Rivers:* An Experiment in the Communication of the Transcendental Experience" (Univ. of Oklahoma, Ph.D., 1970), in one of the more convincing of expositions, sees the book as unified in an expression of the Transcendental experience. Paul David Johnson, "T's Redemptive *Week" (AL,* 49, 1977, 22–33), discusses the book as "carefully structured around the quest for self-liberation." Brian Bond, *"A Week on the Concord and Merrimack Rivers:* T's Epic Venture" (Bowling Green State Univ., Ph.D., 1972), cites the influence of the epic and the pastoral on the book. Jonathan Bishop, "The Experience of the Sacred in T's *Week" (ELH,* 33, 1966, 66–91), explores T's attempts to "find the supernatural in the natural." Robert Sattelmeyer, Jr., "Away from Concord: The Travel Writings of HT" (Univ. of New Mexico, Ph.D., 1975), is an excellent discussion of *A Week* as travel literature (note also its appendix on the writing of *A Week).* Edwin Fussell, "T in His Time" *(RLV,* 39, 1976, 157–70), is a Marxist interpretation of the book. For the publishing history, see James P. Wood, "Mr. T Writes a Book" *New Colophon,* 1, 1948, 367–76), and Raymond Adams, "The Bibliographical History of T's *A Week on the Concord and Merrimack Rivers" (PBSA,* 43, 1949, 1–9). Albert Lownes, "Some Statistics about T's *Week" (TSB* 66), estimates distribution figures of the 1849 and 1862 editions. Christopher McKee, "T's First Visit to the White Mountains" *(Appalachia,* 31, 1956, 199–209), fills in the details of the mountain-climbing interlude in the book. For a modern retracing of T's journey, see Ray Mungo, "If Mr. T Calls, Tell Him I've Left the Country" *(Atlantic,* 225, 1970, 72–86).

*The Transmigration of the Seven Brahmans* (ed. Arthur Christy, New York, 1931; PE, *Translations).*

"Love" (PE, *Early Essays,* pp. 268–73). For a discussion of T's attitudes, see Joel Porte, "T on Love" *(University Rev.,* 31, 1964–65, 111–16, 191–94).

"Chastity and Sensuality" (PE, *Early Essays,* pp. 274–78).

"An Excursion to Canada" (PE, *Excursions).* Sidney Poger, "T as

Yankee in Canada" *(ATQ,* 14, 1972, 174–77), is a defense of the artistry of the essay, particularly its humor. Barrie Davies, "Sam Quixote in Lower Canada" *(HAB,* 20, 1969, 67–78), sees the essay as more consistent with T's other works than most critics have. Edmund Berry, "A Yankee in Canada" *(DR,* 23, 1943, 68–74), emphasizes T's chauvinism. Lawrence Willson, "T and the French in Canada" *(Rev. de L'Université,* 29, 1959, 281–97), discusses T's attitudes toward the French-Canadians therein. T's Canadian notebook is given in facsimile in Kenneth Cameron, *Transcendental Climate* (Hartford, 1963, I, pp. 244–309; II, pp. 310–411). This notebook is discussed in Lawrence Willson, "T's Canadian Notebook" *(HLQ,* 22, 1959, 179–200).

"Slavery in Massachusetts" (PE, *Reform Papers,* pp. 91–110). Robert C. Albrecht, "Conflict and Resolution: 'Slavery in Massachusetts' " *(ESQ,* 19, 1973, 179–88), is an excellent presentation of the historical background and analysis of the rhetorical effectiveness of the address. See also Wendell Glick, "T and Radical Abolitionism" (cited above).

*Walden* (PE). The most fully annotated edition is the *Variorum Walden,* edited by Walter Harding (New York, 1962). A particularly helpful edition is the *Annotated Walden,* edited by Philip Van Doren Stern (New York, 1970). See also Gordon Rohman, "An Annotated Edition of HDT's *Walden*" (Syracuse Univ., Ph.D., 1960), and Francis Allen, ed., *Walden* (Boston, 1910). A clue as to the corruption of many modern texts of *Walden* is provided in R. C. Reynolds and J. S. Sherwin, "Variant Punctuations in Two Editions of *Walden*" *(TSB* 74). For an evaluation of the textual accuracy of ten different college textbook editions, see J. R. McElrath, Jr., "Practical Editions: HDT's *Walden (Proof,* 4, 1975, 175–82). F. B. Sanborn's Bibliophile Society edition of *Walden* (Boston, 1909) is so corrupt as to be useless. See M. E. Cryder, "An Examination of the Bibliophile Edition of T's *Walden*" (Univ. of Chicago, M.A., 1920). J. Lyndon Shanley, *The Making of Walden* (Chicago, 1957), is an essential tool for anyone attempting to study the composition of the book, but equally important is Ronald Clapper, "The Development of *Walden:* A Genetic Text" (Univ. of California, Los Angeles, Ph.D., 1967). Thomas Woodson, "The Two Beginnings of *Walden:* A Distinction of Styles" *(ELH,* 35,

1968, 440–73), discusses some of T's revisions. For a comprehensive concordance of *Walden,* see R. C. Reynolds and J. S. Sherwin, *A Word Index to Walden* (Charlottesville, 1960; reprinted with corrections in *ESQ,* 57, 1969, Supplement).

By far the most thoughtful analysis of the book is Stanley Cavell, *The Senses of Walden* (New York, 1972), though it is not always an easy book to read. For a belletristic analysis that concerns itself with the book's form and style rather than with its ideas, see Charles Anderson, *The Magic Circle of Walden* (New York, 1968). There are three useful anthologies of criticism of *Walden:* Lauriat Lane, Jr., ed., *Approaches to Walden* (San Francisco, 1961); Joseph Moldenhauer, ed., *Studies in Walden* (Columbus, 1971); and Richard Ruland, ed., *Twentieth Century Interpretations of Walden* (Englewood Cliffs, 1968). *The Norton Critical Edition of Walden* (New York, 1966) includes not only annotations but a selection of critical essays. Joseph Moldenhauer, "The Rhetoric of *Walden"* (Columbia Univ., Ph.D., 1964), is a comprehensive study of the major rhetorical techniques. Its two appendixes, "A Checklist of Wordplays in *Walden"* (pp. 251–360) and "A Checklist of Commonplaces and Proverbs in *Walden,"* are particularly useful. The dissertation has been published in part as "Paradox in *Walden"* in Richard Ruland, ed., *Twentieth Century Interpretations of Walden* (Englewood Cliffs, 1968, pp. 73–84); and "The Rhetorical Function of Proverbs in *Walden" (JAF,* 80, 1967, 151–59). See also Donald Ross, Jr., "The Style of T's *Walden"* (Univ. of Michigan, Ph.D., 1967), and Howard Houston "Metaphors in *Walden"* (Claremont Graduate School, Ph.D., 1967). Donald Ross, Jr., "Verbal Wit and *Walden" (ATQ,* 11, 1971, 38–44), gives a long list of types of wordplay in *Walden.* Reginald Cook, "This Side of Walden" *(Eng. Leaflet,* 52, 1954, 1–12), is a useful analysis. Robert Kettler, "The Quest for Harmony" *(BSUF,* 15, 1974, 3–13), is an effective plea for seeing *Walden* whole and not simply as a nature book, as social criticism, or as a work of art. A very useful and well-illustrated little pamphlet for introducing the book is James Thorpe, *T's Walden* (Huntington Library, 1977). William Reger, "Beyond Metaphor" *(Criticism,* 12, 1970, 333–44), is a plea against overreading the symbolism of *Walden.* Michael West, "Scatology and Eschatology" *(PMLA,* 89, 1974, 1043–64), in analyzing its wordplay, is one of the most brilliant essays on *Walden*. Walter Harding, "Five Ways of Looking at *Walden*" *(MR,* 4, 1962, 149–62), discusses the varying appeals of the book. Lauriat Lane, Jr., "On the Organic Structure of *Walden*" *(CE,* 21, 1960, 195–202), and F. O. Matthiessen, *American Renaissance* (New York, 1941, pp. 137–46), both deal with the organic theory. For humor in the book, see Edward Galligan, "The Comedian at Walden Pond" *(SAQ,* 69, 1970, 20–37). For an analysis of *Walden* as pastoral, see Leo Marx, *The Machine in the Garden* (New York, 1964, pp. 242–65). For its imagery, see John Broderick, "Imagery in *Walden*" *(UTSE,* 33, 1954, 80–89), and Stanley Hyman, "HT in Our Time" *(Atlantic,* 178, 1946, 137–46). Eugene Walker, "Walden's Way Revealed" *(Man & Nature,* 1971, 11–20), is a fascinating study of the pond's geological eccentricities. Edward Deevey, "A Re-Examination of T's Walden" *(Quart. Rev. of Biology,* 17, 1942, 1–11), evaluates T's limnological studies in *Walden.* Roland Robbins, *Discovery at Walden* (Stoneham, Mass., 1947), tells of his excavation of the cabin site. Walter Harding, *A Centennial Check-List of the Editions of HDT's Walden* (Charlottesville, 1954), lists and describes 132 different editions. Annette Woodlief, *"Walden:* A Checklist of Literary Criticism through 1973" *(RALS,* 5, 1975, 15–58), is a comprehensive bibliography.

"A Plea for Captain John Brown" (PE, *Reform Papers,* pp. 111–38). "Martyrdom of John Brown," also known as "After the Death of John Brown" (PE, *Reform Papers,* pp. 139–44). "The Last Days of John Brown" (PE, *Reform Papers,* pp. 145–54). For discussions of the John Brown essays, see Wendell Glick, "T and Radical Abolitionism" (cited above). Truman Nelson, "T and the Paralysis of Individualism" *(Ramparts,* 1966, 16–26), argues that the Harpers Ferry incident made of T a "true revolutionary." Lauriat Lane, Jr., "T's Autumnal Archetypal Hero: Captain John Brown" *(Ariel,* 6, 1975, 41–49), suggests that T sees Brown's death in "ritual autumnal terms." In "T and His Audience: A Plea for Captain John Brown" *(AL,* 32, 1961, 393–402), Robert Albrecht shows how T worked over his sources to make a more effective speech. F. B. Sanborn, *Recollections of Seventy Years* (Boston, 1909), and James Redpath, *Echoes of Harper's Ferry* (Boston, 1860), add many details. For a facsimile of the broadside announcing the December 2, 1859, meeting, see *TSB* 54; and for the controversy concerning the planned eulogy for Brown, see Michael Meyer, "Discord in Concord on the Day of John Brown's Hanging" *(TSB* 146). In the spring of 1860 there was an attempt to kidnap Sanborn to force him to testify before a Senate committee on Concord's part in the John Brown affair. When he was freed by the state courts, he was honored by a testimonial in Concord, and there T spoke out again. Unfortunately, the text of that speech has disappeared, but fragments derived from a contemporary newspaper report are given in Walter Harding, *The Days of HT* (New York, 1965, pp. 424–25).

"The Succession of Forest Trees" (W, V, 184–204; PE, *Nature Essays).* For its significance in Thoreau's attitudes, see Leo Stoller, *After Walden* (Stanford, 1957). For its ecological significance, see Kathryn Whitford, "T and the Woodlots of Concord" *(NEQ,* 23, 1950, 291–306), and Edward Deevey, "A Re-Examination of T's *Walden"* (see above).

"Walking" (PE, *Excursions).* For T's interest in "the Wild," see John Burroughs, "T's Wildness" *(Literary Values,* Boston, 1902, 197–202); Howard Zahniser, "T and the Preservation of Wildness" *(TSB* 60); and Jonathan Fairbanks, "T: Speaker for Wildness" *(SAQ,* 70, 1971, 487–506).

"Autumnal Tints" (PE, *Excursions).* For a rewarding discussion, see Bernard Rosenthal, "T's Book of Leaves" *(ESQ,* 58, 1969, 7–11).

"Wild Apples" (PE, *Excursions).*

"Life Without Principle" (PE, *Reform Papers,* pp. 155–80). Oddly enough, there has never been a good analysis of this, one of T's most trenchant essays.

"Moonlight" (PE, *Nature Essays).* "Night and Moonlight" will be found in W, V, 323–36. Francis Allen edited *The Moon* (Boston, 1927). William L. Howarth's lengthy study of the manuscripts may be found in "Successor to *Walden?* T's 'Moonlight'—An Intended Course of Lectures" *(Proof,* 2, 1972, 89–115). See also his discussion in *Literary Manuscripts of HDT* (Columbus, 1974, pp. 335–54).

*The Maine Woods* (PE). There are many valuable footnotes in the Dudley Lunt edition (New York, 1950), which takes unwarranted liberties in rearranging the text. The best study of the book is still Fannie Hardy Eckstorm, "T's 'Maine Woods\" *(Atlantic,* 102,

1908, 245-50), but it should be tempered with Mary Sherwood, "Fanny Eckstorm's Bias" *(MR, 4, 1962, 139-47)*. See also Eckstorm, "Notes on T's 'Maine Woods' " *(TSB 51)*, and her *The Penobscot Man* (Bangor, 1924). Robert Cosbey, "T at Work: The Writing of 'Ktaadn' " *(Bull. N.Y. Pub. Lib., 65, 1961, 21-30)*, gives some valuable insights into T's methods of composition. Robert Sattelmeyer, Jr., "Away from Concord: The Travel Writings of HT" (Univ. of New Mexico, Ph.D., 1975), discusses the composition of all three of the essays and suggests that the "Allegash" section as it now stands may be unfinished, for it lacks the coda of the other two sections. For T's relationships with the Indians on these journeys, see Robert Sayre, *T and the American Indians* (Princeton, 1977), and also Philip Gura, "T's Maine Woods Indians: More Representative Men" *(AL, 49, 1977, 366-84)*. For a discussion of T's "traumatic experience" on the top of Katahdin, see Lewis Leary, "Beyond the Brink of Fear" *(Studies in the Lit. Imagination, 7, 1974, 67-76)*. John Worthington, "T's Route to Katahdin" *(Appalachia, 26, 1946, 3-14)*, clears up some geographical details of that trip. Some difficult to find but helpful pamphlets are Mary Sherwood, *Joseph Polis: T's Maine Guide* (Berwick, Ont., 1970), and Marion W. Smith, *T's West Branch Guides* (Millinocket, Maine, 1971) and her *T's Moosehead and Chesuncook Guides* (Millinocket, Maine, 1972).

*Cape Cod* (W, IV). For bibliographical data on editions of the book, see Kenneth Harber, "Preliminary Check-List of the Editions of *Cape Cod*" *(TSB 77)*. A particularly useful edition is that edited by Dudley Lunt (New York, 1951), for not only is it well annotated, but it is the only edition so far to append the *Journal* materials about the fourth journey. Alexander Adams, *T's Guide to Cape Cod* (New York, 1962), rearranges and abridges selections into a guided tour of the Cape. Herbert Gleason's remarkable early photographs for the text are collected in Thea Wheelwright, *T's Cape Cod* (Barre, 1971). The best discussion of the book is John McAleer, "T's Epic 'Cape Cod' " *(Thought, 43, 1968, 227-46)*. Suzanne Strivings, "T and His Sources: A Reading of *Cape Cod*" (Univ. of Texas, Ph.D., 1974), is valuable chiefly for its lengthy appendix (pp. 166-89) listing the sources for allusions and quotations in the book. See also "Preliminary Reading in Cape Cod

Background (1848-1850)," in Kenneth Cameron, *The Transcendentalists and Minerva* (Hartford, 1958, 378-88), and Emory Maiden, Jr., *"Cape Cod:* T's Handling of the Sublime and the Picturesque" (Univ. of Virginia, Ph.D., 1971).

*The Correspondence of HDT* (New York, 1958). The earliest edition of T's letters, that edited by Emerson, is *Letters to Various Persons* (Boston, 1865). More inclusive is F. B. Sanborn, ed., *Familiar Letters* (Boston, 1894). Sanborn's arbitrary editing is detailed in Walter Harding, "Franklin B. Sanborn and T's Letters" *(Boston Pub. Lib. Quart.,* 3, 1951, 288-93). Kenneth Cameron, *Companion to T's Correspondence* (Hartford, 1964), and his *Over T's Desk* (Hartford, 1965) both annotate the 1958 edition and add some uncollected letters. Walter Harding is presently working on a new comprehensive edition of the correspondence for PE.

*Collected Poems of HT* (Baltimore, 1964). Errors and omissions in earlier printings have been corrected in this 1964 edition. Sarah McEwen Miller, "A Concordance to the Collected Poems of HT" (Univ. of Toledo, M.A., 1966) is a little-known but very useful tool. Arthur Lewis Ford, Jr., *The Poetry of HDT* (Hartford, 1970), is the most comprehensive study. H. Grant Sampson, "Structure in the Poetry of T" *(Costerus,* 6, 1972, 137-54), asserts that most critics have overlooked the fact that T's poems are basically metaphysical. A very good analysis is Henry Wells, "An Evaluation of T's Poetry" *(AL,* 16, 1944, 99-109). See also Paul Williams, "The Concept of Inspiration in T's Poetry" *(PMLA,* 79, 1964, 466-72); Donovan L. Welch, "A Chronological Study of the Poetry of HDT" (Univ. of Nebraska, Ph.D., 1966). William Thomas, "T as His Own Editor" *(NEQ,* 15, 1942, 101-3), studies the genesis of one of the poems. Elizabeth Witherell is working on a new edition of the poems for PE.

*The First and Last Journeys of T,* edited by F. B. Sanborn (Boston, 1905). The Minnesota material in it has been superseded by Walter Harding, *T's Minnesota Journey: Two Documents (TSB* XVI), which also includes the texts of letters written by Horace Mann, Jr., who accompanied T on the trip. Further studies of the Minnesota material may be found in John Flanagan, "T in Minnesota" *(Minn. Hist.,* 16, 1935, 35-46); Robert Straker, "T's Journey to Minnesota" *(NEQ,* 14, 1941, 549-55); Evadene Swanson, "The Manuscript Journal of T's Last Journey" *(Minn. Hist.,* 20, 1939, 169–73); and Harriet Sweetland, "The Significance of T's Trip to the Upper Mississippi in 1861" *(TWA,* 51, 1962, 267–86).

*Journal* (J, I–XIV; PE, *Journal).* PE will eventually include a great deal of material not in J, such as the so-called Lost Journal of 1840–41, which is now given in Perry Miller, *Consciousness in Concord* (Boston, 1958). The pioneer work in restoring T's early *Journal* was done by Thomas Blanding. See his "The Text of T's Fragmentary Journals of the 1840's" (Marlboro College, Honors Thesis, 1970). The fragmentary Minnesota journal appears in Walter Harding, *T's Minnesota Journey (TSB* XVI). For the background of Ellery Channing's "Country Walking," see Rollo Silver, "Ellery Channing's Collaboration with Emerson" *(AL,* 7, 1935, 84–86), and Walter Harding, "Two F. B. Sanborn Letters" *(AL,* 25, 1953, 230–34). William L. Howarth, "Thoreau, the Journalist" (Univ. of Virginia, Ph.D., 1967), discusses the composition, content, and purpose of the *Journal* period by period.

There are numerous volumes of selections from the *Journal.* The two best general ones are Odell Shepard, ed., *The Heart of T's Journal* (Boston, 1927), and Carl Bode, ed., *Selected Journals of T* (New York, 1967). Francis Allen, ed., *Men of Concord* (Boston, 1936), concentrates on T's comments on his fellow townsmen. Laurence Stapleton, ed., *A Writer's Journal,* (New York, 1960) emphasizes T's comments on writing as an art. Helen Cruickshank, ed., *T on Birds* (New York, 1964), gathers together all his significant comments on birds.

*Huckleberries,* Leo Stoller, ed. (Iowa City, 1970; PE, *Nature Essays).*

"Reform and the Reformers" (PE, *Reform Papers,* pp. 181–97).

\*    \*    \*

William L. Howarth, *The Literary Manuscripts of HDT* (Columbus, 1974), catalogues and locates all of T's known literary manuscripts, including the notebooks, and describes the physical details of each.

Catalogues of the major collections of manuscripts include Viola

White, "Check List of the T Items in the Abernethy Library," in Reginald Cook, *The Concord Saunterer* (Middlebury, Vt., 1940), reprinted in White, *Check List: Abernethy Library of American Literature* (Middlebury, Vt., 1940); see also White, "Teacher's Avocation" *(TSB* 13); for the Henry W. and Albert A. Berg Collection in the New York Public Library, *TSB* 43; for the Concord Antiquarian Society, *TSB* 47; for Harvard University Library, *TSB* 43 and *TSB* 53; for Huntington Library, *TSB* 43; for the Pierpont Morgan Library in New York City, *TSB* 19; for the Alfred Hosmer Collection in the Concord Free Public Library, Herbert Hosmer, *The T Library of Alfred W. Hosmer* (Concord, Mass., 1949); See also Raymond Adams, "Fred Hosmer, the 'Lerned Clerk' " *(TSB* 36). Two large private collections, the Stephen H. Wakeman Collection and the William Harris Arnold Collection, were dispersed at public auctions in New York City in 1924. Their catalogues contain many important details. The private collection of Raymond Adams is listed in *The T Library of Raymond Adams* (Chapel Hill, 1936) and its *Supplement* (Chapel Hill, 1937). A small portion of the invaluable collection of Albert Lownes, of Providence, Rhode Island, now in Brown University Library, is listed in [Frank Walters's] *Catalogue of a Collection of Books by or Pertaining to HDT* (New York, n.d.). Arthur Christy, "A Fact-Book" *(Colophon,* XVI, 1934), gives a detailed description of one of the commonplace books. All the commonplace books are described in Anne Whaling, "Studies in T's Reading of English Poetry and Prose" (Yale Univ., Ph.D., 1946, appendix A). Kenneth Cameron has reproduced in facsimile a number of the T notebooks: *T's Literary Notebook in the Library of Congress* (Hartford, 1964); *T's Fact Book in the Widener Collection in the Harvard College Library* (Hartford, 1966, 2 vols.); and "T's Reading on Canada: M.S. M.A. 595 in the Pierpont Morgan Library, New York City," in *The Transcendental Climate* (Hartford, 1964, pp. 310–411). Richard Fleck, ed., *The Indians of Thoreau* (Albuquerque, 1974), gives a sampling of excerpts from the Indian notebooks. The best discussion of the Indian Notebooks is Robert Sayre, *T and the American Indian* (Princeton, 1977).

# 3.

## Thoreau's Sources

I

Thoreau was an inveterate reader and haunter of libraries. Despite his frequent protests that he preferred the outdoors to the scholar's cell, he was rarely without a book in hand. Yet he seldom if ever read for amusement. He avoided novels as a waste of time and paid little attention to contemporary belles lettres. But before he explored any new field, whether in science, history, philosophy, or the site of a new excursion, he prepared careful reading lists and read every book on the subject available to him.

Because he was not basically an original thinker—Canby (p. 151) says quite rightly, "His ideas are all borrowed; the originality is in the blending"—it is important to the student to know Thoreau's sources. The highly allusive nature of Thoreau's writings affirms his extensive reading. Fortunately, the record of his reading is nearly complete. We know what libraries he used, and most of them still have available the records of his book withdrawals. We know from his own catalogue the books he had in his own library. We know what texts were required reading for the courses he took

at Concord Academy and Harvard. And Thoreau kept voluminous commonplace books of his favorite quotations and made frequent notations on his reading in his *Journal.*

There is one major difficulty, however, a difficulty that holds
true for all of the American Transcendentalists: they were all
highly eclectic in their reading. They read widely but took from
their reading only those ideas that particularly appealed to them
and ignored the rest. In his *Journal* Thoreau once commented, "I do
not the least care where I get my ideas, or what suggests them" (J,
VIII, 135). He could, and often did, extract from a particular
source an idea quite at variance with the philosophy of its original
author. Nor was he beneath deliberately misquoting to better
make his point (Glick, "Thoreau's Use of His Sources" [*NEQ*, 44,
1971, 101-9]). He was fully aware of this lifelong tendency and felt
no need to apologize for it. A little more than two years before his
death Thoreau explained that:

> A man receives only what he is ready to receive, whether
> physically or intellectually or morally, as animals con-
> ceive at certain seasons their kind only. We hear and
> apprehend only what we already half know. If there is
> something which does not concern me, which is out of my
> line, which by experience or by genius my attention is not
> drawn to, however novel and remarkable it may be, if it
> is spoken, we hear it not, if it is written, we read it not, or
> if we read it, it does not detain us. Every man thus *tracks
> himself* through life, in all his hearing and reading and
> observation and travelling. His observations make a
> chain. The phenomenon or fact that cannot in any wise
> be linked with the rest which he has observed, he does not
> observe. (J, XIII, 77)

What Thoreau said of Oriental literature—"Like some other
preachers, I have added my texts . . . long after my discourse was
written" (J, II, 192)—is true of most of his other reading.

Although it is often extremely difficult to ascribe Thoreau's
ideas to specific sources, he did have certain fields of interest—
Oriental literature, the classics, English literature, American his-

tory, the American Indian, and travel literature—that have been explored by scholars in some detail.

II

Thoreau knew and appreciated many of the classics of Oriental literature. Woven into the natural ground cover of many of his works is a carpet of Oriental images, allusions, and affinities that serves to bind and unify his themes. In Oriental literature Thoreau found confirmation of his own views on the necessity and value of solitude and contemplation; he also found a repudiation of those Western standards that measure success in materialistic terms. In *A Week*, he declares that he was better acquainted with the Hindoo, Chinese, and Persian scriptures than those of the Hebrews (W, I, 72). Thoreau preferred some of the spiritual disciplines of the East to those of the West. In his August 10, 1849, letter to H. G. O. Blake, he writes that "rude and careless as I am, I would fain practice the yoga faithfully. . . . To some extent, and at rare intervals, even I am a yogi." And in *Walden* he adds, "I bathe my intellect in the stupendous and cosmogonal philosophy of the Bhagvat Geeta" so that "The pure Walden water is mingled with the sacred water of the Ganges" (PE, 298). It is clear that Thoreau felt at home with his immersion in Eastern literature.

Further evidence of his interest in Oriental literature may be found in the fact that when he edited portions of the "Ethnical Scriptures" for the *Dial*, he chose his selections from *The Laws of Menu* (January, 1843), the "Sayings of Confucius" (April, 1843), the "Chinese Four Books" (October, 1843), and "The Preaching of Buddha" (January, 1844). He translated *The Transmigration of the Seven Brahmans* from a French translation of the *Harivansa* of Langlois. When in 1855 Thomas Cholmondeley searched for an appropriate gift to send his friend Thoreau, he chose a collection of forty-four Oriental volumes.

Thoreau began his enthusiastic reading of Oriental literature while living at Emerson's in 1841 when he discovered a rich introduction to the Orient in Emerson's library, and after exhausting it he later turned to Harvard College Library for more books. According to Arthur Christy, "The common denominator of all that Thoreau took from the Hindus, Chinese and Persians was a mystical love for Nature. This reading, to be sure, was but a small portion of his wide literary interests ... but it was the most important of his reading in religious and philosophical literature" (*The Orient in American Transcendentalism,* p. 199). Thoreau was attracted more to Hindu than to Christian myth, "because Hinduism offers a pattern for a relationship with Nature which is reciprocal rather than exploitative. Its concept of time is circular and eternal rather than linear and finite, and its ethics is based on cultivation of one's being rather than fear of punishment and hope of reward" (Jeswine, "Henry David Thoreau: Apprentice to the Hindu Sages," p. 141).

The three most important Hindu influences upon Thoreau were *The Laws of Menu,* the *Bhagavad Gita,* and the *Sankhya Karika* (Jeswine, pp. 28–29 and passim). Thoreau's insistence upon the necessity for spiritual discipline is parallel to Hindu asceticism. "The Hindu Yogi wrapt in his contemplations is not a far cry from the picture Thoreau gives of himself, sitting in his sunny doorway lost in reverie, oblivious even of the songs of birds" (Christy, p. 221). As William Bysshe Stein and others have demonstrated, there are some patterns of yogic discipline in his work (especially in *A Week* and *Walden),* but one should not be oblivious of the fact that for Thoreau Oriental spirituality was equipped with a pragmatic Yankee handle on it, a fact sometimes overlooked by reductive readings of Thoreau's artistic and philosophical affinities. It is important to remember that the sacred water of the Ganges *mingled* with but did not inundate the pure water of Walden Pond. Nevertheless, a number of useful studies have been done that are filling out and qualifying Christy's early work. But a comprehensive, balanced study of the Oriental influence upon Thoreau remains to be published.

\*   \*   \*

Thoreau's training in the classics at Concord Academy and Harvard College was the beginning of a lifelong interest. His approach to the classics was not scholarly and thorough but selective. Ethel

Seybold notes that Thoreau was a classicist "only because and as far as his classicism furthered his search for reality" *(Thoreau: The Quest and the Classics,* p. 21). Thoreau was interested in classical myth primarily because he believed that it contained archetypal truths about man and the earth. For a writer who used the hyperbolic so much in his writings, myth was certainly not incompatible with truth. In *A Week* he writes that "To some extent mythology is only the most ancient history and biography. So far from being false or fabulous in the common sense, it contains only enduring and essential truth, the I and you, the here and there, the now and then, being omitted" (W, I, 75).

Thoreau's postcollege reading of the classics reveals, according to Seybold, a definite pattern that forms three general periods:

> The first was a literary period; he began by rereading authors which he had read in college and by making little explorations into fields suggested by that reading. Among the Greeks he read Homer and Orpheus, the Greek lyrists, especially Anacreon and Pindar; in drama, Aeschylus' *Prometheus Bound* and *Seven Against Thebes.* He investigated also Plutarch's *Lives* and *Morals,* Jamblichus' *Life of Pythagoras,* and Porphyry's *On Abstinence from Animal Food.* Among the Latin authors he read Vergil, Horace, Persius, and Ovid. In the second period, after Walden, in the early 1850's, he made the acquaintance of the agricultural writers, Cato, Varro, Columella, and Palladius, and confined himself to them with two exceptions, Sophocles' *Antigone* and a brief excursion into Lucretius. He did no new reading in Greek during this period. In the late 1850's he discovered the early naturalists: the Roman Pliny and among the Greeks, Aristotle, Theophrastus, and Aelian. His last reading was in Herodotus and Strabo. (pp. 15–16)

Seybold asserts that this reading in the classics provided Thoreau with "the source, the corroboration, or the extension of most of his favorite theories: of language, of government, of history and myth, of poetry and music, of the sameness of the universe" (p. 85).

As strong as Seybold is in her description of Thoreau's reading and what it meant to him, she tends to attribute too heavy a classical influence upon him, particularly in her attempt to interpret his life at Walden "as a conscious effort to realize the simplicity of Homeric life." She acknowledges that "It might also, of course, be interpreted as an attempt to realize the life of oriental contemplation or the primitive life of the North American Indian. However, the Greek pattern of life offered Thoreau the action which the oriental did not and the intellectuality which the Indian did not" (p. 51). Although this distinction is useful, it does not go far enough. It was not the Greek, the Oriental, or the Indian that was at the center of Thoreau's experience, but Thoreau himself confronting the facts of his own distinctly American romantic life for which he adapted the myths from many cultures to create his own unique myth. Sherman Paul succinctly summarizes this by pointing out that:

> [Thoreau] would have this advantage in creating his own myth, in reporting, as Whitman said, "all heroism from an American point of view"—that the reader would not need to turn to his library, but only to his experience, that by enacting the mythic process rather than appropriating a myth, what was native would also be universal. Perhaps the greatest value of the Walden experiment for Thoreau as a writer was this discovery, that Walden was as good as Greece, the Concord River as good as the Scamander, that by reducing his life he was also reducing his thought to essentials. "Carnac! Carnac!" he exclaimed at Walden, "this is Carnac for me...." (*The Shores of America*, p. 191)

For Thoreau it was the correctly perceived facts of the present, local moment that made relevant the classical myths, East or West. Thoreau was certainly influenced by the classics, but he resisted becoming a satellite of any source. Instead, his approach was eclectic, and that meant that it was *his* consciousness, *his* point of view that shaped his sources for his own purposes. Thoreau knew (like

Emerson's American Scholar) that if he planted himself deeply enough in his own instincts, the huge world would come around to him. And it did in his reading.

\* \* \*

Although Thoreau read French as readily as English and knew "German, Italian, and Spanish more or less" (Sanborn, *The Life of Henry David Thoreau*, p. 260), his reading in Continental literature was remarkably slight for someone who read so much. He apparently regarded much of European literature as irrelevant and, paradoxically, even provincial. There are no major influences upon Thoreau that can be directly attributed to his reading in Continental literature. Indeed, the record of that reading is quite meager.

While it is widely recognized that all the American Transcendentalists derived much of their inspiration from the German Transcendentalists, most of it came second hand through Coleridge and Carlyle. Thoreau learned to read German with the help of Orestes Brownson in the winter of 1835, but he apparently never really felt at home with the language. He read Goethe intensively just after graduating from college and included a tribute to him in *A Week* (W, I, 347–53), a tribute that is qualified by Thoreau's criticism of Goethe for being too consciously artistic rather than a "Man of Genius" who relies on his "unconscious" for inspiration.

Although Norman Foerster ("The Intellectual Heritage of Thoreau," p. 197) says that "It is perfectly obvious that no French writers meant much to Thoreau," many have thought him a follower of Rousseau. There is, however, no evidence that he ever read Rousseau directly; he was acquainted with his ideas only through secondary sources, and he was even further removed by temperament:

> The tormenting desire of European, especially Continental romanticism—the sighs, the aching void, the meltings, the sweet abandon, the boundless longing and utter weariness were more remote from his experience than the moral integrity of the Puritans and the serene reason of

the Greeks. . . . It is entirely certain that when Thoreau speaks, in the romantic vein, of following his genius, or instincts, he does not unwittingly urge, as romanticism too often does, obedience to the instincts of his temperament, but the very opposite—the subjection of these instincts to the instincts of a higher, and peculiarly human, self. (Foerster, *Nature in American Literature,* pp. 128–29)

According to Sanborn, Thoreau's favorite Italian author was Tasso, but that he was also familiar with Dante both in the original and in translation has been indicated by J. Chesley Matthews. That he was also somewhat interested in an almost forgotten Italian contemporary, Silvio Pellico, has been pointed out by John C. Broderick.

Thoreau's interest in Scandinavian literature was threefold. He read widely in the writings of the scientists, Linnaeus, Kalm, and to a lesser extent, Biberg and Fries. He was familiar with Swedenborg, probably through Emerson, though he wrote B. B. Wiley (December 12, 1856), "I cannot say that Swedenborg has been directly and practically valuable to me." And finally, he read extensively in Norse mythology and the records of Norse exploration in North America: an English version of *Heimskringla,* the *Prose Edda,* Rafn's *Antiquitates Americanoe,* and Samuel Laing's *Sagas of the Norse Kings.* Of the literature of the other Continental peoples Thoreau apparently knew little.

\* \* \*

That the early English writers held a particular fascination for Thoreau has long been accepted as an axiom by scholars. His friends Channing and Sanborn frequently attested to it. There was a legend that he had read the entire set of Chalmers's *English Poets* (twenty-one large volumes) before he entered college and later a second and possibly a third time. Frequent mention was made of the influence of the seventeenth-century writers, particularly Browne and Donne, upon his style.

Anne Whaling ("Studies in Thoreau's Reading"), however, has made the only extended study of Thoreau's interest in the early English writers, and she has come to a different conclusion. She was able to find no conclusive evidence that Thoreau displayed any extensive interest in these authors before the last two months of his college career and theorizes that the reading he did then was probably a classroom assignment (p. 47). She does agree that he read fairly thoroughly in these authors in the six years after he graduated from college, entering many extracts in his commonplace books. But "after November, 1843, there is no clear evidence . . . of any sustained reading of early English writers except in the special fields of natural history and exploration" (pp. 127–28). "He did not, on the evidence available, have any deep general interest, historical or critical, in the seventeenth century. He had no precocious interest in its poetry or prose, nor do the extracts made in college and immediately after reflect anything that could be called a 'strong fascination.' Even his interest in the older English poetry and prose, as they were defined in his day, was limited" (p. 170). The many quotations from the period that flavor his published writings, particularly *A Week,* were virtually all taken from the extracts he had made in his commonplace books. The evidences of stylistic influence that have been frequently pointed out are so tenuous and generalized as to have no real significance. However, Whaling does acknowledge that "even though his acquaintance with the older English poetry and prose was somewhat less extensive than tradition has implied . . . the reading remains a considerable achievement and a significant factor in the modest excellence of Thoreau's work" (p. 193).

Of the earlier English writers, he was most attracted to the major figures—Chaucer, Shakespeare, and Milton. There are extended tributes to Chaucer in *A Week* (W, I, 391–400), fairly frequent references to his works in his *Journal,* and a misquotation of him in *Walden* (PE, 212). Thoreau "picked up the reverent manner toward Shakespeare which was in the air. . . . But Thoreau's actual feeling about Shakespeare seems not to have been very warm and intimate" (Dunn, *Shakespeare in America,* p. 260). There are frequent allusions to, and quotations from, the plays that indicate a familiarity with the Shakespeare canon, but there is little of the adulation of the bard that one finds in Emerson's works, for example. For Milton, however, Thoreau held an "exaggerated reverence" (Whaling, p. 41). He wrote a "volunteer essay" on "L'Allegro" and "Il Penseroso" in college and quoted from *Paradise Lost* and *Lycidas* so extensively throughout his writings that one suspects he must have committed large portions of Milton to memory.

Of the lesser writers, Sir Walter Raleigh stood high in Thoreau's esteem. He delivered an essay on Raleigh before the Concord Lyceum on February 8, 1843, and incorporated portions of this essay in *A Week* (W, I, 106 ff.). Though Thoreau admired Raleigh's style, he was far more interested in the man. Among other early English writers that have been linked to Thoreau are Francis Quarles, Sir Thomas Browne, Izaak Walton, Bishop Joseph Hall, George Herbert, John Smith, Sir Francis Bacon, and Daniel Defoe.

And finally, perhaps more than any other English work, the King James Bible exerted a profound influence on Thoreau's style. Althought he often belittled his knowledge of the Scriptures and declared he was more familiar with the Oriental sacred writings, his familiarity with the King James Bible is obvious. There are "over five hundred references of allusions to, or extracts from the Scriptures" in Thoreau's writings (John R. Burns, "Thoreau's Use of the Bible," p. 3). His use of biblical allusions, according to Burns, made his style more effective because it provided his writing with the kind of authority that could both convince and move his readers.

Thoreau had surprisingly little interest in the later English literature. As Norman Foerster has said, "In the entire long procession from Dryden to Matthew Arnold, Thoreau had but a handful of friends" ("Intellectual Heritage of Thoreau," p. 212). His lack of interest in eighteenth-century English literature is outstanding. A notable exception is Ossian. Thoreau read the Ossianic poems while on Staten Island; delivered a lecture on the "Ancient Poets," particularly Ossian, on his return to Concord in November, 1843; and included fifteen quotations from Ossian in *A Week*. But since he thought the Ossianic poems genuine, his interest in them could hardly be considered a demonstration of an affinity for eighteenth-century literature.

One other eighteenth-century English author did arouse Thoreau's interest. That was the Reverend William Gilpin, the leader of the vogue for the "picturesque." Thoreau not only read most of his available works and recommended them highly to his friend Daniel Ricketson, but he discussed Gilpin at greater length in his *Journal* than he did any other noncontemporary figure. Thoreau's continued interest in the picturesque landscape can be traced in large part to his reading of Gilpin, although, as William Templeman points out, he was often disappointed that Gilpin failed to display a moral as well as an aesthetic interest in nature.

When we turn to the English romanticists, we find surprisingly little explicit comment in Thoreau's writings. He owned the works of Shelley, Keats, and Byron, but almost never mentioned them in his writings. It is obvious that he read widely in Wordsworth, for, though again he does not quote him frequently, his works contain many an allusion to, or echo of, Wordsworth, particularly the ode on the "Intimations of Immortality." "Thoreau saw nature as he did because of his own inherent emotional make-up, but ... he found a kindred and stimulating spirit in Wordsworth" (James Southworth, "Reply to W. D. Templeman," *PMLA*, 49, 1934, 974).

Coleridge was of interest to Thoreau not as a poet but as the interpreter and exponent of the German Transcendentalists. James Marsh's American edition of Coleridge's *Aids to Reflection* was one of the bibles of the American Transcendentalists, and Thoreau read it with avidity. Carlyle served much the same purpose for Thoreau. Thoreau's essay "Thomas Carlyle and His Works" is one of his few explicit attempts at literary criticism. "For Carlyle's themes, Thoreau cared little enough, for his ideas little more, at least in the form which Carlyle gave them; but for his style he cared a great deal" (Foerster, "Intellectual Heritage of Thoreau," p. 200).

There is occasional reference to Tennyson in Thoreau's works, a rather surprising interest in De Quincey and Felicia Hemans, and, in the late 1850s, some interest in Ruskin. Dickens and Scott are mentioned halfheartedly. And there, for all practical purposes, Thoreau's interest in later English literature ends.

*    *    *

Thoreau's interest in American literature was primarily historical. He read avidly everything he could lay his hands on concerning early America: he studied the records of the early Norse
explorations; he continued with the writings of the French and
English explorers; he searched the documents of the first settlers—
and here he was fortunate in that the various state historical societies and commissions of Massachusetts, New York, and New
Hampshire in particular were reprinting many of the rarer pieces
just when his interest in the field was at its height. And he read
thoroughly in the local histories, not only of Concord and eastern
Massachusetts and the areas he visited on his excursions (although
he was particularly conscientious about reading these), but any
local histories he could find. "If it should prove at all possible—and
he [Thoreau] saw no reason why it should not, apparently—he
wished to know every place as he knew Concord: completely, both
as it was in the present and as it had been in the past" (Lawrence
Willson, "The Influence of Early North American History," p.
106). "No man in his time, or perchance in any other, was so
thoroughly informed on purely local history as he" (p. 115).

"Josselyn [*Account of Two Voyages to New England*] should head the
list of Thoreau's authorities on early America, because he apparently read him first and certainly refers to him most often" (p.
102). Edward Johnson's *History of New England . . . or Wonder-Work-
ing Providences* was another favorite. The many volumes of Jesuit
Relations Thoreau had to read in the French were often turned to.
But it would be idle to attempt to list all the volumes in the field
with which he was familiar. He himself has cited most of them in
his various "excursions." The importance of these writings to Thoreau is especially emphasized by Philip F. Gura, who argues that
Thoreau found them to be closer to nature, to facts, and to life
than most other works he read ("Thoreau and John Josselyn").

Gura's argument seems quite reasonable, given that Thoreau
read relatively little in the American literature contemporary to
him. His disdain for fiction kept him away from Cooper, although
there are indications that he read some of Irving and at least Melville's *Typee*. There are numerous allusions to Hawthorne's tales in
his *Journal*. In poetry, only Whitman interested him, though he
found some of Whitman's sensuality disagreeable. Thoreau read

primarily the early essays and poetry of Emerson. It was Emerson the man, not the author, who attracted him. In sum, what is significant about Thoreau's relationship to the American literature written during his lifetime is that he ignored most of it.

\* \* \*

A field of intense interest to Thoreau was the lore of the American Indian. Although he had been interested in the Indian from childhood and early started collecting Indian relics on his walks through the countryside, it was not until 1848 that he began an intensive reading on the subject. But in the last fourteen years of his life, he read at least two hundred works on the subject, and he filled twelve manuscript notebooks, containing about three thousand pages, with more than half a million words, mainly extracts from books, pamphlets, and magazine articles on the American Indian. Beginning with F. B. Sanborn, it has been widely assumed that he intended to write a book on the Indian (Thoreau had even worked out a tentative table of contents) and that illness forced him to abandon the project. Robert F. Sayre, however, has questioned this assumption in *Thoreau and the American Indians* (pp. 101–23) and suggests that he used his Indian notebooks as a source for his other writings.

Sayre's study demonstrates that Thoreau was strongly influenced by a "savagist" view of the Indians, "the nineteenth-century white man's idea of Indian life" as both ideal and primitive (p. 3). Thoreau's Indian notebooks which he filled with information and quotations from travelers, missionaries, and ethnographers, gradually provided Thoreau with a clearer understanding of the Indian, a view that was informed less by stereotyped myths and more by the reality of their condition. Working carefully, "Thoreau took from the literature of savagism a composite picture of Indian life in North America which disproves savagism" (p. 127). Sayre uses the extracts from Thoreau's own reading to show how this was achieved.

Thoreau drew upon many sources for his reading, but some of the more important ones were the various Jesuit Relations, the writings of Henry Rowe Schoolcraft, George Henry Loskiel, and

John G. E. Heckewelder. He was interested in virtually anything
pertaining to the Indian, whether from New England, the West, or
even the Arctic regions. The heterogeneous mass of materials Thoreau gathered, though largely unorganized by him, are revealing in
Sayre's hands.

*   *   *

One of the many paradoxes about Thoreau, according to John
Aldrich Christie in *Thoreau as World Traveler,* is that he is "a man
who on the one hand reiterates his disdain for travel and on the
other peppers his writings with its products; a writer who urges his
readers to concentrate upon a knowledge of their own local plot of
ground at the same time that he makes sure in his writing that
their acquaintance with the world be nothing less than global; the
seemingly contented provincial who is all the while devouring the
accounts of other men's furthest travels" (p. 48). "In his published
writings (including the *Journal*) Thoreau refers directly to his reading in at least eighty-three different travel works" (p. 42), and "we
are able to identify, in many cases to the very edition, a minimum
of one hundred and seventy-two separate travel accounts read by
Thoreau" (p. 44). In his writings he is at home in distant places,
mentioning some five hundred foreign locales and more than one
hundred American (pp. 277–78 n.1).

Thoreau was particularly interested in books about Canada
(many of them read in preparation for the writing of *A Yankee in
Canada*); American exploration (including many of the government
reports on various western expeditions; sea voyages (such as those
of Darwin and Cook); South America, Africa, Asia (often in con-
junction with his Oriental studies); and the Arctic regions (pp. 95–
198). Thoreau read new travel books as well as old ones, and this
reading—this movement through both space and time—helped to
create the "excursions of the imagination" (J, III, 5) in his writings
that make it impossible to describe as provincial this man who
rarely traveled far from home.

Christie argues that "The concept of travel became the single
most reiterated and conspicuous symbol in all of Thoreau's writ-

ings" (p. 265). "Placed in the context of his philosophy of life, all travel was but means to an end, in Thoreau's case only one means to the particular end which he pursued: the discovery of the nature of transcendent reality" (p. 84). Thoreau's many references to his travel reading suggest his efforts to provide a universal dimension to his works, "to make local objects suggest their global counterparts" (p. 238). Although Christie may overstate his point that the concept of travel, exploration, and discovery became the most frequent symbol in all of Thoreau's writings, his discussion of how it is manifested in the writings is valuable.

*     *     *

Thoreau's reading was prodigious, and it has, therefore, been impossible in these few pages to do any more than roughly indicate some of Thoreau's areas of interest and to attempt to explain what attracted him to these fields and what he derived from them. It is no more possible to explain Thoreau by what he read or did not read than it is to account for *Moby Dick* by quoting extracts of the sort that inform us that "The whale is a mammiferous animal without hind feet." But to point this out is not the same as abandoning the subject. For there is still much to be done, as Thoreau's own reading lists generously suggest; and this passage from the "Reading" chapter of *Walden* should give impetus to a good many more source studies: "There are probably words addressed to our condition exactly, which, if we could really hear and understand, would be more salutary than the morning or the spring to our lives, and possibly put a new aspect on the face of things for us. How many a man has dated a new era in his life from the reading of a book" (PE, 107).

## III

When we turn to the influence of Thoreau's educational experience, we find we know so little about his early schooling that it is useless to attempt to draw any significant conclusions. We can guess that his primary education was similar to that of most of his contemporaries in New England schools and that it apparently provided him with an adequate background in the three R's.

About his secondary education, Thoreau himself wrote, "I was fitted, or rather made unfit, for college, at Concord Academy & elsewhere, mainly by myself, with the countenance of Phineas Allen, Preceptor" *(Correspondence,* p. 186). Fortunately, many of Allen's records for the Concord Academy are extant. They reveal that Thoreau received, despite his comment, a better-than-average training in the classics, mathematics, and languages in preparation for his matriculation at Harvard and that he also received noteworthy training in composition and public speaking.

Thoreau's Harvard education emphasized the classics and was more designed to produce a minister than a self-appointed inspector of snowstorms. In spite of the memorizing that was required by the conservative curriculum, Thoreau did manage to inspect areas of knowledge that were useful to him. Indeed, Christian P. Gruber points out that many of the most typical Thoreauvian ideas (most notably those on "the pleasure of solitary or semi-solitary communion with nature") are common to the college themes and articles contributed to the undergraduate magazine *Harvardiana* by Thoreau's classmates ("The Education of Henry Thoreau," p. 49). More significantly, Joseph J. Kwiat has argued that Thoreau became familiar with Scottish Common Sense philosophy by the end of his junior year, a familiarity that Kwiat describes as a "major influence" pointing away from Lockean empiricism toward a Transcendental faith in intuition ("Thoreau's Philosophical Apprenticeship"). Kwiat's argument has been qualified, however, by Joel Porte *(Emerson and Thoreau),* who points out that Locke had some lasting influences on Thoreau.

Although Thoreau's science courses at Harvard were, of course, primitive by modern standards, they did "manage to insinuate a good bit of science and scientific method into Thoreau's consciousness" (Gruber, p. 164). They also provided him with the kind of technical knowledge that helped him deal with his practical affairs, such as surveying. In addition, much of the information he picked up from the Department of Mathematics and Natural Philosophy provided him with a great number of concepts and a large storehouse of tropes for his future literary use (pp. 167–69). These branches of education at Harvard were very much connected to the taproot of Thoreau's identity.

\*     \*     \*

There is more to the making of Thoreau than his books and his formal education, however. He had no further formal schooling after 1837, and even though he was an inveterate reader throughout his life, he found many other sources for ideas and attitudes. There has been comparatively little attempt to place Thoreau against the background of his times, and yet we must do so if we would attempt to understand what made him what he was.

Thoreau's family life is suggestive of what he was to become. Thoreau's father was as little out of the ordinary as most of the rest of his ancestors, although his knowledge of local history (J, XI, 437) undoubtedly whetted Thoreau's interest in early Americana. His father's long series of business failures during Thoreau's youth must have had a profound influence on Thoreau's outlook toward society. Would Thoreau have been so critical of the economic structure, for example, if he had not been raised in an atmosphere of financial insecurity? In addition, Thoreau's mother was a strong-minded woman who was actively concerned with abolitionist issues and social work, as well as having an abiding interest in natural history. His relationship to his brother John has been widely discussed, and though there are disagreements concerning the nature of their relationship, nearly every biographer of Thoieau has agreed that it was an important one for him.

Foremost of the local influences outside his family was, of course, Emerson. For many years it was the fashion to deride Thoreau as an imitator of Emerson. James Russell Lowell charged that Thoreau's works were but "strawberries from his [Emerson's] own garden." Many of their contemporaries accused Thoreau of imitating Emerson's voice and mannerisms, and some even went so far as to accuse him of imitating Emerson's nose. Their handwriting was so much alike that it is often difficult to distinguish between the manuscripts of the two. But both men quite understandably resented these charges of imitation, and Emerson in particular frequently spoke out against them. In his *Journal* for June 24, 1863, Emerson points out most distinctly the difference between the two: "In reading him [Thoreau], I find the same thought, the same spirit that is in me, but he takes a step beyond, and illustrates by excellent images that which I should have conveyed in a sleepy generality." In other words, in their prose Emerson typically tends toward the abstract, Thoreau toward the concrete; Emerson toward the ideal, Thoreau toward the practical.

Yet it must be remembered that Emerson's influence was exerted primarily through his personal association rather than through his books. *Nature* was a major influence, and certainly Emerson's early essays played an important part in Thoreau's life; but by 1851 Thoreau was commenting in his *Journals* (III, 134) that he rarely looked at Emerson's books. It was through their daily association in the streets and woods of Concord and through Thoreau's two lengthy residences in Emerson's house that Emerson exerted his chief influence. Nor was the influence one-sided. For example, it was Thoreau who provided Emerson with his knowledge of the world of nature around him.

Thoreau was the self-reliant "Man Thinking" that Emerson called for in essays such as "The American Scholar" and "Self-Reliance," but Emerson occasionally winced at this physical, concrete, and particularized version of his ideas. Emerson's own reticent approach to experience inhibited his response to Thoreau. When Thoreau was jailed for his civil disobedience, Emerson "thought it mean and skulking, and in bad taste" (Alcott, *Journals,* p. 183). In later years Emerson thought more highly of Thoreau's "escapade." When the Fugitive Slave Law was passed, Emerson wrote in his *Journals* that he would attempt everything he could do "in opposition to the execution of the law." But it was Thoreau who delivered a lecture on "Slavery in Massachusetts." In 1859, when word was received of John Brown's raid against Harpers Ferry, it was Thoreau, not Emerson, who called a meeting in Concord to defend Brown. Emerson did not come to Brown's defense until Thoreau had paved the way. "In the sage of Concord Thoreau soon began to suspect that there was too much of the merely genteel, too little of the genuine wildness which he valued so much in himself and which he cultivated by direct association with physical nature" (Krutch, p. 49).

It was through personal contact with Emerson and through *Nature* that Thoreau first learned of the Transcendentalist philosophy and the people associated with it. The first volume of Thoreau's published *Journal* (1837) is filled with echoes of Transcendental idealism. Like the Transcendentalists, he wanted to "penetrate the surface of things"; he wanted to come to spiritual truth instinctively. Unlike his contemporaries (except for Whitman), Thoreau found that spiritual truth in experience detailed with facts rather than abstractions. Thoreau is very nearly Lockean in his emphasis on the use of the senses in his approach to nature, but he is decidedly Transcendental in what he expects to perceive. In *Walden* he explains his means and ends: "Men esteem truth remote, in the outskirts of the system, behind the farthest star, before Adam and after the last man. In eternity there is indeed something true and sublime. But all these times and places and occasions are now and here. God himself culminates in the present moment, and will never be more divine in the lapse of all the ages. And we are enabled to apprehend at all what is sublime and noble only by the perpetual instilling and drenching of the reality which surrounds us" (PE, 96–97). Thoreau discovered his own image mirrored in the pond more than he did in Emerson.

In his junior year at Harvard, Thoreau interrupted his studies with an interlude of schoolteaching at Canton, Massachusetts, under the direction of Orestes Brownson. It is Gruber's contention that since "Thoreau's flight from orthodoxy was complete before Emerson's personal influence became strong" (p. 186), and since "various of Thoreau's college essays of his senior year contain ideas so similar to Brownson's that one can only conclude that he was making use of what his new friend and mentor had taught him" (p. 192), "the impact of Brownson was in quickening Thoreau's reaction to orthodox views of Christianity and to society as presently constituted, and in strengthening his reliance upon his own faculties and perceptions" (Gruber, p. 198). "There is no question that [Orestes Brownson] opened Thoreau's eyes to the intellectual tumult of the age as they had never been opened before" (Glick, "Thoreau and Radical Abolitionism," p. 14).

New England in the 1830s and 1840s was a hotbed of reform. As Emerson wrote to Carlyle: "We are all a little wild here with numberless projects of social reform. Not a reading man but has a draft of a new Community in his waistcoat pocket" (letter of October 30, 1840). Talk of Fourierism, vegetarianism, the water cure, phrenology, and mesmerism filled the air. But Thoreau found few reformers to his liking. He was more interested in self-reformation than in social reformation.

A notable exception was the abolitionist movement. As Wendell Glick has pointed out, Concord sponsored one of the most active antislavery societies in the country. Seven members of Thoreau's household were dues-paying members. The periodicals of the movement were subscribed to by members of his family. Leading abolitionists dined at his mother's table whenever they visited town. He numbered among his intimate friends such antislavery men as Alcott, Ricketson, and Parker Pillsbury, and he met at one time or another virtually all the leaders from Garrison down. The Concord Lyceum, by the mid-1840s, was open frequently to antislavery lecturers. "Thoreau never joined the Abolitionist organizations. So deeply ingrained was his feeling that organizations were the breeders of all 'unnatural' restraints upon human liberty that he could not trust even an organization with aims which were almost exactly like his own" (Glick, p. 155). However, he did not remain uninfluenced. Abolitionism from 1835 to 1855, under the leadership of William Lloyd Garrison, gradually evolved its philosophy of action from concentration on individual reform to attacks on the institutions of church and government, which abolitionists felt were retarding reform, and finally to active social reform. And Glick has found a similar evolution in Thoreau's social thought. "Almost invariably the radical positions which Garrison took up before 1855 became those of Thoreau a few years later" (Glick, p. 23). Thoreau applied his Transcendental perceptions to politics as well as to nature.

Less tangible but almost as important as Transcendentalism was the impact of New England Puritanism upon Thoreau. Though Transcendentalism was a clear break from any doctrinal Christianity, it maintained a religious tone. Alexander Kern shows that Thoreau "can be seen as a significant if unorthodox part and hence product of the American Protestant tradition" ("Church, Scripture, Nature and Ethics in Henry Thoreau's Religious Thought," p. 79). Thoreau inherited from the Puritans their sense of high purpose and determination, their suspicion of worldly things, and their insistence that discipline serve as a check on passion. Thoreau also shared the Puritan tendency to read nature for spiritual meanings as well as the religious tone that pervades their writings. And finally, that sense of guilt and sin that is woven throughout the fabric of Thoreau's writings sounds at times like echoes from a Puritan journal.

\*    \*    \*

The influences upon Thoreau are many and complex. What makes them so difficult to describe is the fact that he filtered them all through his own consciousness as he rejected, selected, and modified them so that they became fit for his own use. Consequently, there are a number of sources that may be cited that influenced Thoreau, but it is not so simple to describe the extent of the influence without going through a process similar to Thoreau's own rejection, selection, and modification. One thing is clear, however: living in Concord—both the town and the personal concord he created by blending his various sources—was as central to him as his own individuality. He had, after all, "been born into the most estimable place in all the world, and in the very nick of time, too" (J, IX, 160).

### Sources for Chapter Three

A number of lists of T's borrowings from libraries have been published by Kenneth W. Cameron. These include "Books T Borrowed from Harvard College Library," in *Emerson the Essayist* (Raleigh, 1945, pp. 191–208); "T Discovers Emerson: A College Reading Record" *(Bull. N.Y. Pub. Lib.,* 57, 1953, 319–34), listing the books he borrowed from the Institute, an undergraduate club at Harvard; and "Emerson, T and the Society of Natural History" *(AL,* 24, 1952, 21–30), listing the books he borrowed from that Boston society. Cameron, *The Transcendentalists and Minerva* (Hartford, 1958, 3 vols.), reprints the Institute list (pp. 81–89) and adds "T's Notes on Harvard Reading" (pp. 130–358), which includes facsimile reproductions of many of T's reading lists and notes with helpful annotations and identifications by Cameron. Also included are "Ungathered T Reading Lists" (pp. 359–88), which contains among others his Cape Cod, surveying, and Oriental reading lists; "The Concord Social Library in 1836",(pp. 496–506), the catalogue of a library T probably used; "The Concord Town Library in 1852" (pp. 818–27), the catalogue of another library T likely used; and "T's Index at Harvard College" (pp. 871–82), some more reading notes. Cameron lists "Books T Desired to Purchase in 1859" *(ESQ,* 23, 1961, 16) and includes in *Transcendental Climate* (Hartford, 1963, 3 vols.) "Books T Read Concerning Concord" (III, 1012–21). Cameron's *T's Literary Notebooks in the Library of Congress* (Hartford, 1964) is a facsimile of T's extracts from Oriental, English, and other writers. See also Cameron's *Transcendental Apprenticeship: Notes on Young HT's Reading: A Contexture with a Researcher's Index* (Hartford, 1976). Walter Harding, *T's Library: A Catalog* (Charlottesville, 1957), lists and describes the books in T's library; in addition, see Harding, *Emerson's Library* (Charlottesville, 1967), which lists many books T read.

T's imprecise use of quoted materials in his writings is considered surprising by Wendell Glick, "T's Use of His Sources" *(NEQ,* 44, 1971, 101–9), but Douglas A. Noverr, "A Note on Wendell Glick's 'T's Use of His Sources' " *(NEQ,* 44, 1971, 475–77), points out that T was following the casual conventions of his day in his disregard for quoting accurately. Carl F. Hovde, "Literary Materials in T's *A Week" (PMLA,* 80, 1965, 76–83), had earlier concluded that T often used quotations out of context for his own purposes. John L. Magnus, Jr., "T's Poetic Cosmos and Its Relation to Tradition: A Study of His Reading and His Writings, 1837–54" (Johns Hopkins Univ., Ph.D., 1965), concurs and attempts to show how T's diverse reading is unified by T's myth of rebirth in his own works. Dennis N. Ribbens, "The Reading Interest of T, Hawthorne, and Lanier" (Univ. of Wisconsin, 1969), sees T, after 1850, taking an increased interest in readings based on particular facts rather than abstractions.

The best brief interpretive study of T's reading remains Norman Foerster, "The Intellectual Heritage of T" *(Texas Rev.,* 2, 1917, 192–212), which is reprinted in *Twentieth Century Interpretations,* ed.

Richard Ruland (Englewood Cliffs, 1968, pp. 34–49). Nearly all the major biographies and critical studies have also devoted space to the subject. There is, however, no comprehensive and definitive study of T's sources, although Robert Sattelmeyer is now engaged in such a project entitled *T's Reading*.

The pioneer study of the Oriental influence on T is Arthur Christy, *The Orient in American Transcendentalism* (New York, 1932). Sreekrishna Sarma, "A Short Study of the Oriental Influence upon HDT with Special Reference to His *Walden*" (*JA*, 1, 1956, 76–92), points out some errors in Christy's treatment of yoga; see also S. D. Strachner, "T's Orientalism: A Preliminary Reconsideration" (*TJQ*, 6, 1974, 14–17), which, in addition to offering some corrections of Christy's work, discusses why T scholars have tended only to affirm T's interest in Oriental literature rather than explore it in his writings. Christy's appendix of Oriental books available to T is valuable, as is William Bysshe Stein, "A Bibliography of Hindu and Buddhist Literature Available to T through 1854" (*ESQ*, 47, 1967, 52–56). Christy also provides a brief summary of the Oriental influence in his introduction to *Transmigration of the Seven Brahmans* (New York, 1932). Three other useful introductions to Oriental works T used are published by Scholars' Facsimiles and Reprints (Gainesville, Fla.): *The Bhagvat-Geeta*, a reprint of the Charles Wilkins translation, with an introduction by George Hendrick (1959); *Two Brahman Sources of Emerson and T*, a reprint of Rajah Rammohun Roy's *Translation of Several Principal Books, Passages, and Texts of the Veds* and William Ward's *A View of the History, Literature and Mythology of the Hindoos*, with an introduction by W. B. Stein (1967); and *The Chinese Classical Work Commonly Called the Four Books*, a reprint of the David Collie translation, with an introduction by W. B. Stein (1970). Miriam A. Jeswine, "HDT: Apprentice to the Hindu Sages" (Univ. of Oregon, Ph.D., 1971), is the lengthiest study of the Oriental influence on T. Included in her work is a chapter on the Hindu books T read and his notes and extracts for them (pp. 28–77). For a discussion of the Oriental volumes T was given, see Mohan Lal Sharma, "Cholmondeley's Gift for T: An Indian Pearl to the United States" (*Jour. of Ohio Folklore Soc.*, 3, 1968, 61–89). Works that discuss affinities more than direct influences on T are Kamala Bhatia, *The Mysticism of T and Its Affinity with Indian Thought* (New Delhi, 1966); David T. Y. Chen, "T and Taoism," in C. D. Narasimhaiah, ed., *Asian Response to American Literature* (New York, 1972, pp. 406–16); and Kichung Kim, "On Chuang Tzu and T" *(LE&W,* 17, 1973, 275–81). For the importance of *The Laws of Menu* to T see Sherman Paul, *The Shores of America* (Urbana, 1958, pp. 69–75). Lyman V. Cady discusses "T's Quotations from the Confucian Books in *Walden"* (*AL,* 33, 1961, 20–32) and finds that T used them in a non-Confucian, individualistic way. Roger C. Mueller explains "T's Selections from *Chinese Four Books* for the *Dial"* *(TJQ,* 4, 1972, 1–8); Mueller provides other valuable background information in "The Orient in American Transcendental Periodicals (1835–1886)" (Univ. of Minnesota, Ph.D., 1968). David G. Hoch, "Annals and Perennials: A Study of Cosmogonic Imagery in T" (Kent State Univ., Ph.D., 1969), examines T's use of imagery from Oriental cosmogonies and its relation to his art. Studies of the Oriental influence on T's works are mostly limited to *A Week* and *Walden.* William Bysshe Stein has written a detailed study of *A Week;* his "T's *A Week* and Om Cosmography" *(ATQ,* 11, 1971, 15–37) traces the soul's absorption into *Brahman;* see also by Stein, "T's First Book: A Spoor of Yoga" *(ESQ,* 41, 1965, 4–15). The yogic elements in *Walden* and its parallels to the *Bhagavad Gita* have been described in a number of articles; see four by Stein: "T's *Walden* and the *Bhagavad Gita"* *(Topic,* 3, 1963, 38–55) is an overview of parallels, while the following three articles examine in detail the first three chapters of *Walden*— "The Yoga of *Walden:* Chapter I (Economy)" *(LE&W,* 13, 1969, 1–26); "The Hindu Matrix of *Walden:* The King's Son" *(CL,* 22, 1970, 303–19); and "The Yoga of Reading in *Walden"* *(TSLL,* 13, 1971, 485–95). Other studies of *Walden* and Hindu devotional arts are Frank MacShane, *"Walden* and Yoga" *(NEQ,* 37, 1964, 322–42); David G. Hoch, *"Walden:* Yoga and Creation," in R. J. De-Mott and S. E. Marovitz, eds., *Artful Thunder* (Kent, Ohio, 1975, pp. 85–102); and Michael Gates, *"Walden:* Yantra above Yantras" *(ESQ,* 22, 1976, 14–23). Beginning students may find useful as general background Nathaniel Kaplan and Thomas Katsaros, *The Origins of American Transcendentalism in Philosophy and Mysticism* (New Haven, 1975), which provides brief overviews of the many influences upon Transcendental thought.

The most complete study of T's classicism is Ethel Seybold, *T: The Quest and the Classics* (New Haven, 1951). Most valuable is its appendix identifying the particular editions T used and indexing his references to classical authors. Hubert Hoeltje, "T and the Concord Academy" *(NEQ,* 21, 1948, 103–9), describes in detail his classical training in Concord Academy; in addition, see Cameron, "Young T and the Classics: A Review" *(ATQ,* 35, 1977, 1–128), for information on T's reading in the classics at Concord Academy, the curriculum, and a reproduction of some of the classical texts T used there. Cameron also comments on "T's Early Compositions in the Ancient Languages" *(ESQ,* 8, 1957, 20–29). T's use of myth is central to Sherman Paul's *The Shores of America* (Urbana, 1958, pp. 293–353 and passim), which describes his stay at Walden as "a fable of the renewal of life." Louise C. Kertesz, "A Study of T as Myth Theorist and Myth Maker" (Univ. of Illinois, Ph.D., 1970, pp. 7–61) traces the eighteenth and early-nineteenth-century sources of T's theory and myth. Reginald Cook, "Ancient Rites at Walden" *(ESQ,* 39, 1965, 52–56), discusses some Greek mythic echoes. There are two studies that draw upon T's reading of Greek pastorals: in a provocative and lengthy discussion, John Seelye, "Some Green Thoughts on a Green Theme" *(TriQ,* 23/24, 1972, 576–638), traces T's use of two antithetical pastoral traditions, the "reactionary" and the "revolutionary," and their political implications for T's thought. Another study related to T's reading in pastoral literature is Gordon E. Slethaug, "T's Use of the Pastoral and Fable Traditions" (Univ. of Nebraska, Ph.D., 1968).

For T's acquaintance with German literature, see Stanley M. Vogel, *German Literary Influences on the American Transcendentalists* (New Haven, 1955); and for a study that finds likenesses between German romanticism and T but minimizes any direct influence, see Paul Elmer More, "T's Journal," in *Selected Shelburne Essays* (New York, 1935; reprinted frequently as "T and German Romanticism"). For T's interest in Goethe see Anton Huffert, "T as a Teacher, Lecturer, and Educational Thinker" (New York Univ., Ph.D., 1951, pp. 176–200); see also the index in James McIntosh, *T as Romantic Naturalist* (Ithaca, 1974). Grant Loomis points out similarities but no direct source in "T and Zimmerman" *(NEQ,* 10, 1937, 789–92). T's affinities with Rousseau are discussed in M. J.

Temmer, "Rousseau and T" *(YFS,* 28, 1962, 112–21), and L. Gary
Lambert, "Rousseau and T: Their Concept of Nature" (Rice
Univ., Ph.D., 1969); neither, however, makes a claim that T read
Rousseau. K. W. Cameron, "T's Notes from Dubuat's *Principles"
(ESQ,* 22, 1961, 68–76), publishes some notes T took and translated from the French; J. Chesley Matthews examines "T's Reading in Dante" *(Italica,* 27, 1950, 77–81); and John C. Broderick
discusses Pellico in "T and *My Prisons" (Boston Pub. Lib. Quart.,* 7,
1955, 48–50). For "Scandinavian Influences in the Writings of T,"
see Adolph B. Benson *(SS,* 16, 1941, 201–11, 241–56). Though not
a source study, Brian R. Harding's "Swedenborgian Spirit and
Thoreauvian Sense: Another Look at Correspondence" *(JAmS,* 8,
1974, 66–79), argues that correspondential vision was important to
T.

The major work on T's interest in the early English writers is
Anne Whaling, "Studies in T's Reading of English Poetry and
Prose, 1340–1660" (Yale Univ., Ph.D., 1946). Caroline Spurgeon,
*Five Hundred Years of Chaucer Criticism and Allusion* (Cambridge, En-
gland, 1925), cites some, but not all, of T's major references to
Chaucer. Esther Cloudman Dunn, *Shakespeare in America* (New
York, 1939, pp. 260–63), discusses T's interest in Shakespeare. No
separate study of T and Milton has been published, but there is
Buford Jones, "A Thoreauvian Wordplay and *Paradise Lost" (ESQ,*
47, 1967, 65–66). For Quarles see Ernest Leisy, "Francis Quarles
and HDT" *(MLN,* 60, 1945, 335–36). T and Browne are discussed
in F. O. Matthiessen, *American Renaissance* (New York, 1941, pp.
110–30). See also for Raleigh and Browne the index to Paul's *The
Shores of America.* Thomas Blanding, "Walton and *Walden" (TSB*
107), finds an echo in "Brute Neighbors" from the *Compleat Angler.*
Walter Gierasch, "Bishop Hall and T," is in *TSB* 31, 1950. Darlene
Unrue, "John Smith and T: A-Fishing in the Same Stream" *TJQ,*
8, 1976, 3–9), finds similarities between *Walden* and *A Description of
New England.* Affinities with T are also found in George W. Smith,
Jr., "T and Bacon: The Idols of the Theatre" *(ATQ,* 11, 1971, 6–
13), and in W. H. Bonner and M. A. Budge, "T and Robinson
Crusoe, An Overview" *(TJQ,* 5, 1973, 16–18). For evidence of T's
interest in the metaphysical poets, see Carl Bode, *Collected Poems of
HT,* Enlarged Edition (Baltimore, 1964; "Textual Notes," passim).

Raymond Himelick, "T and Samuel Daniel" *(AL,* 24, 1952, 177–85), is a study of how T wrenched quotations from the Elizabethan poet to serve his own purposes. The most complete study of T's biblical allusions is John R. Burns, "T's Use of the Bible" (Univ. of Notre Dame, Ph.D., 1966); especially helpful are the three extensive compilations Burns provides that list the locations of T's biblical allusions and references, the biblical texts he used, and passages from his works based on Scripture (pp. 82–226). For a more focused study, see Larry R. Long, "The Bible and the Composition of *Walden,"* in Joel Myerson, ed., *Studies in the American Renaissance* (Boston, 1979, pp. 309–53). For T's interest in Ossian, see Ernest Leisy, "T and Ossian" *(NEQ,* 18, 1945, 96–98). For his reading of Gilpin, see William Templeman, "T, Moralist of the Picturesque" *(PMLA,* 47, 1932, 864–89), but note also James Southworth, "Reply" *(PMLA,* 49, 1934, 971–74), and Gordon V. Boudreau, "HDT, William Gilpin, and the Metaphysical Ground of the Picturesque" *(AL,* 45, 1973, 357–69). The fullest exploration of the similarities and differences between T and Wordsworth is Laraine R. Fergenson, "Wordsworth and T: A Study of the Relationship between Man and Nature" (Columbia Univ., Ph.D., 1971); part of this appears as "Was T Re-reading Wordsworth in 1851?" *(TJQ,* 5, 1973, 20–23); see also the index in James McIntosh, *T as Romantic Naturalist* (Ithaca, 1974). With the exception of Fergenson's study of T and Wordsworth, there have been no extended studies of T's interest in nineteenth-century English literary figures.

The fullest study of T's interest in early American literature is Lawrence Willson, "The Influence of Early North American History and Legend on the Writings of HDT" (Yale Univ., Ph.D., 1949). Philip F. Gura, "T and John Josselyn" *NEQ,* 48, 1975, 505–18), presents a convincing and suggestive argument for the need to reassess the significance on T's reading in American exploration and travel narratives. Eugene Green, "Reading Local History: Shattuck's *History,* Emerson's *Discourse,* and T's *Walden"* (*NEQ,* 50, 1977, 303–14), examines T's attitude toward the writing of local history. For T's interest in local history as it was manifested in folklore, see Lonnie L. Willis, "Folklore in the Published Writings of HDT" (Univ. of Colorado, Ph.D., 1966); this includes a useful compendium index of folklore in T's writings (pp. 74–374). A more analytic study of T's use of folklore is Richard F. Fleck, "HDT's Interest in Myth, Fable and Legend" (Univ. of New Mexico, Ph.D., 1970).

The major work on T's reading harvested in the Indian notebooks is Robert F. Sayre, *T and the American Indians* (Princeton, 1977). Albert Keiser also discusses them in "T's Manuscripts on the Indians" *(JEGP,* 27, 1928, 183–99); and he evaluates T's attitude toward the Indian in "T—Friend of the Native," in *The Indian in American Literature* (New York, 1933, pp. 209–32). Lawrence Willson discusses T's reading of the Jesuit Relations in "T and Roman Catholicism" *(CHR,* 42, 1956, 157–72). Willson discusses T's reading in Indian literature in his dissertation (pp. 211–91); Fleck's dissertation also includes information on Indians; and Willis provides a list of references to Indians in T's published works (pp. 149–62); all three are cited above. See also Reginald Cook, "An Indian Memory," in *Passage to Walden* (Boston, 1949, pp. 80–98), and Jason A. Russell, "T: The Interpreter of the Real Indian" *(QQ,* 35, 1927, 37–48). Richard Fleck finds "Evidence for T's 'Indian' Notebooks as Being a Source for His Journal" *(TJQ,* 1, 1969, 17–19), and he reprints some of T's extracts in *The Indians of T: Selections from the Indian Notebooks* (Albuquerque, 1974); Edwin S. Fussell, "The Red Face of Man," in *T: A Collection of Critical Essays,* ed. Sherman Paul (Englewood Cliffs, 1962, pp. 142–60), speculates on the sort of Indian book T would have created had he written it. T's interest in John Dunn Hunter is discussed in Richard Drinnon, *White Savage* (New York, 1972, pp. 246–55).

The authoritative study of T's reading and use of travel literature is John Aldrich Christie, *T as World Traveler* (New York, 1965); Christie includes illustrations and a useful bibliography of books describing travels outside New England read by T (pp. 312–33). An interesting collection of maps and illustrations that sheds light on T's fascination with travel is Robert F. Stowell, *A T Gazetteer,* William L. Howarth, ed. (Princeton, 1970).

Hubert Hoeltje, "T and the Concord Academy" *(NEQ,* 21, 1948, 103–9), presents the records of Phineas Allen's teaching. The most extensive study of the influence of T's Harvard education is Christian Gruber, "The Education of HT, Harvard 1833–37" (Princeton Univ., Ph.D., 1953). Joseph Kwiat discusses Scottish philosophy in "T's Philosophical Apprenticeship" *(NEQ,* 18, 1945, 51–69); see also Edgeley Todd, "Philosophical Ideas at Harvard College, 1817–1837" *(NEQ,* 16, 1943, 63–90). Annette M. Woodlief, "The Influence of Theories of Rhetoric on T" *(TJQ,* 7, 1975, 13–22), discusses Richard Whately's *The Elements of Rhetoric,* which T studied at Harvard. Whately's influence is discussed along with George Campbell's in Richard H. Dillman, "T's Psychological Rhetoric" (Univ. of Oregon, Ph.D., 1978), a part of which appears as "The Psychological Rhetoric of *Walden" (ESQ,* 25, 1979, 79–91). And for a variety of materials on curriculum and textbooks, see Cameron, *T's Harvard Years* (Hartford, 1965).

Richard Lebeaux, *Young Man T* (Amherst, 1977), examines T's life before Walden and provides an Eriksonian analysis of the influence upon T's family life and his Concord background. All the major biographies include discussions of T's family and town life.

For the relationship of T and Emerson, see the Sources for Chapter One; see also Charles Berryman, "The Artist-Prophet: Emerson and T" *(ESQ,* 43, 1966, 81–86), for a discussion of T as an embodiment of Emerson's idea of the poet; Edward J. Rose, "The American Scholar Incarnate" *(ESQ,* 19, 1973, 170–78), for Emerson's man of nature, books, and action; and Leonard Neufeldt, "The Severity of the Ideal: Emerson's 'T' " *(ESQ,* 58, 1970, 77–84), for a description of the major differences between them expressed in Emerson's eulogy for T.

There is no definitive study of American Transcendentalism, but there are several useful overviews: Alexander Kern, "The Rise of Transcendentalism," in Harry Hayden Clark, ed., *Transitions in American Literary History* (Durham, 1954, pp. 247–314); Paul F. Boller, Jr., *American Transcendentalism, 1830–1860* (New York, 1974); and Donald N. Koster, *Transcendentalism in America* (Boston, 1975). Perry Miller, *The Transcendentalists* (Cambridge, 1950) and *American Transcendentalists* (New York, 1957), collect some of the major documents of the movement. A useful overview of American life contemporary to T is Russel B. Nye, *Society and Culture in America, 1830–1860* (New York, 1974). See also for a wider overview: Perry Miller, "T in the Context of International Romanticism" *(NEQ,* 34, 1961, 147–59). For T's visit with Brownson, see Cameron, "T and Orestes Brownson" *(ESQ,* 51, 1968, 53–73); and for his relationship to members of the Transcendental Club, see Ronald E. Tranquilla, "HDT and the New England Transcendentalists" (Univ. of Pittsburgh, Ph.D., 1973). Wendell Glick, "T and Radical Abolitionism" (Northwestern Univ., Ph.D., 1950), describes in detail the effect of Garrison and his followers on T.

Alexander C. Kern, "Church, Scripture, Nature and Ethics in HT's Religious Thought," in Robert Falk, ed., *Literature and Ideas in America* (Athens, Ohio, 1975, pp. 79–95), links T to a tradition of American Protestantism. Wesley T. Mott discusses "Emerson and T as Heirs to the Tradition of New England Puritanism" (Boston Univ., Ph.D., 1975). The Puritan tradition is related to T's art in Errol M. McGuire, "The Art of Growing Pure: Nature and Grace in HDT" (Univ. of Chicago, Ph.D., 1978). For a study that argues that T's writing was influenced by two Puritan genres, the sermon and the "excursion" (e.g., *Pilgrim's Progress*), see Sidney B. Poger, "T: Two Modes of Discourse" (Columbia Univ., Ph.D., 1965). Mason Lowance traces a line of development in "From Edwards to Emerson to T: A Revaluation" *(ATQ,* 18, 1973, 3–12). William D. Drake, "The Depth of Walden: T's Symbolism of the Divine in Nature" (Univ. of Arizona, Ph.D., 1967, pp. 1–65), relates the late Puritans, the Mathers and Edwards, to T's Transcendental symbolism. Egbert S. Oliver, "T and the Puritan Tradition" *(ESQ,* 44, 1966, 79–85), argues that T was prompted by the spirit of the seventeenth-century English Puritans when he defended John Brown. T's response to the Pilgrims is described by Lawrence Willson, "Another View of the Pilgrims" *(NEQ,* 34, 1961, 160–77). And for a study that finds parallels with T and an earlier religious tradition, see Gordon V. Boudreau, " 'Remember Thy Creator': T and St. Augustine" *(ESQ,* 19, 1973, 149–60).

Annotated editions and source studies of individual works are listed in the Sources for Chapter Two. The index should also be consulted for additional source studies in other chapters.

# 4.

# Thoreau's Ideas

Because Thoreau, like Emerson and Whitman, refused to be intimidated by "foolish" consistencies, he did not worry about inconsistencies in his life or writings. Thoreau did not consider it "a ground for complaint if a man's writings admit of more than one interpretation" (*Walden*, PE, 325). It is, therefore, important to recognize that a brief summary of Thoreau's ideas is necessarily somewhat reductive and selective. He never claimed to be a systematic philosopher, and he made no attempt to resolve the many competing ideas and attitudes he recorded during his lifetime. Like most of the other Transcendentalists, he was essentially eclectic, and as his reading indicates, he was fully capable of adapting ideas from various sources that seemed to be mutually exclusive. In addition, like most other people, he sometimes changed his mind as he grew older or as issues evolved. Moreover, his use of hyperbole makes it all too easy (and tempting) to drive him into an ideological corner that might exaggerate and isolate a particular idea from the rest of his thought. Thoreau's own comments on his use of hyperbole suggest the nature of the problem: "He who cannot exaggerate is not qualified to utter truth. No truth we think was ever expressed but with this sort of emphasis, so that for the time there seemed to be no other" ("Thomas Carlyle and His Works," PE, 265). It is necessary to be aware that the "truth" of a moment in his writings may not reflect the full range of Thoreau's ideas on a given subject.

Unfortunately, there have been students of Thoreau who have not taken into account the fact that Thoreau did not formulate and unify his thinking. Approaching his writings with a preconceived notion that there was a unity to his ideas, they have attempted to impose a consistency where little or no consistency existed. They have accepted those ideas of his that fitted their own particular orthodoxy and silently rejected the rest. Thus, they have been able to "prove," for example, that Thoreau was an individualist or collectivist, an activist or recluse, a pacifist or militarist, a pessimist or optimist. This binary sensibility does not do justice to Thoreau's complexity or to his ambivalence. Many of the questions and issues to which he addressed himself throughout his life remained constant, but some of his answers were only provisional, even though "for the time there seemed to be no other." To acknowledge the competing nature of some of Thoreau's thought is not to argue, however, that it is impossible to provide an outline of many of his ideas, but we should be wary of how simple it is to inadvertently flatten the landscape of his thinking.

*    *    *

Although there is no single ideology or set of ideas that completely characterizes Thoreau's thought, the one that comes closest is Transcendentalism—and that because it is itself so amorphous and subject to qualifications, depending upon which Transcendentalists one is describing. The Transcendentalists developed no rigid orthodoxies or doctrines; they, no more than Thoreau, created carefully constructed systems, but they did in general affirm certain principles. Alexander Kern ("The Rise of Transcendentalism, 1815–1860") lists the most important concepts adopted by the Transcendentalists:

(1) an intuitive idealism which accepted ideas as ulti-
mates; (2) a view of the imagination or intuition (in their
language Reason) giving a direct apprehension of reality
which the logical faculties (the Understanding) could not
furnish; (3) the concept of an organic universe in which
Nature, suffused by an immanent God, corresponded
with spirit in such a way that the connections and indeed
the whole could be grasped by contemplation and intuition; (4) a living religion in which miracles seem natural;
(5) the divinity of man, who consequently did not need
salvation; (6) a concept of Genius which could produce
works of art by recording its intuitions through the use of
nature symbols; (7) a freedom and spontaneity in art to
permit the creation of works liberated from the artifi-
cialities produced by talent or mechanical rules alone; (8)
an individual moral insight which should supersede the
dollar as the standard of conduct; (9) self-improvement
as the primary avenue of social improvement; (10) individualism, i.e., reliance on God, rather than conformity
to the will of a political or social majority; (11) an optimism about the potentialities of individual lives and the
universe. (pp. 250–51)

If we are willing to grant Thoreau the broad margin he always
demanded, it is accurate to say that he subscribed to these Transcendental concepts.

Thoreau went to the woods to solve some of the practical problems of life and to be instructed by nature. Although he would
have been the first to admit (as he does in his parable of the hound,
bay horse, and turtle-dove in *Walden*) that the perfect life was an
unattainable ideal, he was convinced at an early age of the direction in which to aim. It was "the perfect correspondence of Nature
to man, so that he is at home with her" (J, X, 127). "I love to see
anything that implies a simpler mode of life and a greater nearness
to the earth" (J, XIV, 88). "In society you will not find health, but
in nature. You must converse much with the field and woods, if
you would imbibe such health into your mind and spirit as you

124    *The New Thoreau Handbook*

covet for your body. . . . Without that our feet at least stood in the
midst of nature, all our faces would be pale and livid" ( J, I, 306). It
was for this that he wished to live a life apart from the bustling
nineteenth century. It was for this reason he disliked cities. They
denied man his opportunity of communing with nature. It was for
this also that he condemned the businessmen and upstanding citizens of his community. They were too busy to commune with
nature. The world was too much with them, or rather, they were
too much with the world.

He saw a close association with nature as a means toward a
fuller life. It was a purgative, a panacea for the ills of civilization:
"I have come to this hill to see the sun go down, to recover sanity
and put myself again in relation with Nature" ( J, VI, 329). "Nature, the earth herself, is the only panacea. They bury poisoned
sheep up to the necks in earth to take the poison out of them" ( J,
XII, 350). "It is important, then, that we should air our lives from
time to time by removals, and excursions into the fields and
woods,—starve our vices" ( J, XII, 343).

By starving his vices, he fed his soul. But his response to nature
was more than simply a kind of athletic, individual morality; he
looked to it for larger reasons as well. Thoreau closely observed
nature, not only for its detailed facts, but also for its potential
meanings. The ultimate spiritual truths he sought went beyond the
data he derived from his senses: "My genius makes distinctions
which my understanding cannot and which my senses do not report" ( J, II, 337). As much as he was responsive to the most minute
details and colors and textures of nature, as much as he studied the
subtle changes of the seasons, his purposes were, finally, aimed at
revealing spiritual laws more than natural laws, metaphysics more
than physics. With this Transcendental mode of perception, Thoreau beheld rather than inspected his world: "Time [and nature
itself] is but the stream I go a-fishing in. I drink at it; but while I
drink I see the sandy bottom and detect how shallow it is. Its thin
current slides away, but eternity remains. I would drink deeper;
fish in the sky, whose bottom is pebbly with stars" *(Walden*, PE,
98). This remarkable passage—a poetic blend of nature and transcendence—confirms Thoreau's claim that "My profession is to be

always on the alert to find God in nature, to know his lurking-places, to attend all the oratorios, the operas, in nature" (J, II, 472). His seemingly casual saunterings through the woods of Concord were, in fact, an intense search for the spiritual truths he believed to be latent there.

Thoreau's early *Journals*, up to approximately 1850, contain many avowals characteristic of Transcendental thought, but as he grew older he recorded numerous moments when he felt that he was becoming bogged down in facts that yielded no transcendent values to him. In the early 1850s he laments this change: "I fear that the character of my knowledge is from year to year becoming more distinct and scientific; that, in exchange for views as wide as heaven's scope, I am being narrowed down to the field of the microscope. I see details, not wholes nor the shadow of the whole. I count some parts and say, 'I know' " (J, II, 406). Critics have noted this change, and some have argued that the *Journals* from 1850 to 1861, which are filled with pages of physical measurements of nature, "record the desperation of the spiritual seeker who has lost his communion" (Sherman Paul, *The Shores of America*, p. 256). Although Thoreau certainly worried that he had not fully achieved the high expectations he had as a youth and he lamented that he felt "dissipated by so many observations" (J, V, 45), the increased numbers of lists that appear in the final decade of the *Journals* are not convincing evidence that in those later years he abandoned his earlier Transcendentalism for a purely scientific observation. Thoreau's observations do become more detailed and exact in his *Journals*, especially after 1856, but as William L. Howarth has pointed out, the differences between the earlier and later *Journals* are "mostly a matter of degree, not essence," because "surviving manuscripts indicate that in previous years he kept purely factual observations out of the daily record" ("Thoreau, the Journalist," p. 171). The change takes place primarily in the *Journal*, not in Thoreau's perceptions; Howarth argues that:

The spirit behind Thoreau's last studies was ... Transcendental as ever; commentators have missed this point

> because they object to his methods. In introducing charts
> and tables to the *Journal* he altered only his strategy of
> recording, not his major goals. He continued to assume
> that intuition was the source of all scientific discovery
> (14:267); but he also knew that only physical evidence
> can confirm intuitions. (p. 227)

His Transcendental point of view was tempered, but it was never abandoned.

Thoreau's experience climbing Mount Ktaadn in 1846 has also been used as evidence to argue a change in his Transcendental view of nature. The bewildered account Thoreau provides in part of *Maine Woods* is in stark contrast to his typically benign presentation of nature in his other writings. Above the timberline, Thoreau describes the desolation he sees as "savage and awful"; nature is here "vast, terrific," not the "Mother Earth that we have heard of," but rather "the home . . . of Necessity and Fate" (p. 70). Many critics have discussed this powerful passage and have argued that Thoreau's disoriented response marks a permanent change in his view of nature. Leo Stoller, for example, asserts that "The universe pantheistically informed with a benign godhead had suddenly dissociated into its parts. For the rest of his life he was to strive in vain to reunite them" (*After Walden*, p. 47). Jonathan Fairbanks has argued, however, that this exaggerates Thoreau's response to Ktaadn; although Thoreau was deeply moved by the experience when it occurred, it did not divide his view of nature for the remainder of his life: indeed, "though perhaps Thoreau should have been more deeply affected by Katahdin, he was not," because he was a "fluctuating thinker" rather than an evolving one ("Thoreau: Speaker for Wildness," pp. 498–99). James McIntosh develops this idea further: "The *Week* and *Walden*, both thoroughly romantic in conception, were both completed and published after the writing of 'Ktaadn,' *Walden* seven years after. It is a seldom noted fact that Thoreau was working on 'Ktaadn,' the *Week*, and the first version of *Walden* all during his stay at the pond." McIntosh concludes then that "Thoreau was not committed in this period to one view of nature, but was capable of consciously entertaining different and even opposing views" (*Thoreau as Romantic Naturalist*, pp. 210–11). There were no sharks in Walden pond.

\* \* \*

Related to Thoreau's responses to nature are his writings on natural history and his attitudes toward science. Although he studied nature closely with a scientific eye and recorded his findings with patient discipline, he was suspicious of those who were "mere accumulators of facts" about nature (J, I, 18). "The scientific differs from the poetic or lively description somewhat as the photographs, which we so weary of viewing, from painting and sketches, though this comparison is too favorable to science" (J, XIV, 117). Thoreau goes on to say in this same passage, written in 1860 when he continued to amass details of the natural environment around Concord, that "All science is only a makeshift, a means to an end which is never attained. After all, the truest description, and that by which another living man can most readily recognize a flower, is the unmeasured and eloquent one which the sight of it inspires. No scientific description will supply the want of this, though you should count and measure and analyze every atom that seems to compose it." Ultimately, Thoreau was more interested in his perception of nature, "its relation to man," than he was in a "mechanically daguerreotyped" record of nature (J, XIV, 118). Nevertheless, he had a deep respect for, and abiding interest in, natural facts—more so than any of the other Transcendentalists—because those facts were the means by which he might behold larger truths about the spiritual landscape within himself.

Thoreau's negative assessments of the science contemporary to him were partly the result of the emphasis then placed upon classifying species. Krutch has pointed out that "The only official science of which he had any knowledge was of the sort least likely to stimulate philosophical thought. . . . He was living toward the end of the heyday of the anatomist and the taxonomist, when natural history did not mean primarily either the study of habits and life histories . . . or, still less, those attempts to understand man as part of nature" (pp. 181–82). Thoreau was never enthusiastic about murdering to dissect; "this is not the means of acquiring true knowledge" (J, VI, 311). "This haste to kill a bird or a quadruped and make a skeleton of it . . . reminds me of the fable of the man who killed the hen that laid the golden eggs, and so got no more gold. It is a perfectly parallel case" (J, XIV, 109). Rather than hold a bird in his hand, Thoreau would "rather hold it in my affections" (J, VI, 253).

The accuracy and value of Thoreau's own scientific observations have often been questioned owing to his preference for subjectivity over objectivity. Even Bradford Torrey, the editor of the 1906 edition of the *Journal,* thought that he "leaves the present-day reader wondering how so eager a scholar could have spent so many years in learning comparatively so little" (J, I, xliii). Thoreau himself realized that few would understand his aims. When he was invited to join the [American] Association for the Advancement of Science, he noted in his *Journal* that he was declining the invitation because, "The fact is I am a mystic, a transcendentalist, and a natural philosopher to boot. . . . I should have told them at once that I was a transcendentalist. That would have been the shortest way of telling them that they would not understand my explanations. . . . If it had been the secretary of an association of which Plato or Aristotle was the president, I should not have hesitated to describe my studies at once and particularly" (J, V, 4–5).

Thoreau's errors of observation in natural history are not difficult to understand. In the first place, he lacked adequate scientific equipment. He owned no bird glasses at all until 1854, and then he acquired a telescope rather than the far more efficient binoculars. He used his hat as a botany box. And apparently he had to borrow a microscope when he wanted to use one. But he deliberately did without scientific instruments, frequently because he believed they gave a distorted picture of nature. Then too there were few adequate reference books available in his time. Most of the natural history books in his library were British, simply because there were no comparable American counterparts, although he did own Gray's botany, Wilson's ornithology, Harlan's and Audubon's fauna, and Jaeger's entomology, among others. What is even more important was that American science was still in its most elementary stages.

It is likely that Thoreau would have had fewer complaints about the narrowness of the scientific view if he could have read some of our twentieth-century ecological studies. And it is worth noting that some twentieth-century scientists have come to appreciate the values of his broad approach, which, though not sophisticated by contemporary standards, was sensitive to the complex relationships of a total environment. Indeed, the first supplement to the *Oxford English Dictionary* (1972) cites a letter by Thoreau (January 1, 1858) as the earliest known use of the word "ecology"; this listing is, however, mistaken. Further editorial work on the *Correspondence* has demonstrated that the word Thoreau wrote was "geology," not "ecology." The poetic truth nevertheless remains, because although Thoreau did not coin the word, he certainly helped to give it currency by recording for future readers his own sensitive responses to nature.

More specifically, however, Thoreau has been credited with making contributions to several scientific fields. His work on the theory of the succession of forest trees, conducted independently of other botanists of his day, remains a standard treatise on the subject. In addition, his valuable detailed *Journal* accounts of the flora and fauna in and around the Concord area have been recognized as important resources for studies of American natural history. Thoreau's observations have also been useful to limnologists, phenologists, meteorologists, and other natural scientists who have found that the field notes of this self-appointed inspector of snowstorms are often worth citing in their own studies. He never underestimated the value of a fact:

> Amateur though he may have remained in any single field, and protester throughout his life that science's perspective was untrustworthy, yet Thoreau's microscope, spyglass, charts, weather tables, presses, and collections, his geological surveys, and "Zoological Notes," his perusal of the reports of the Smithsonian Institution, of the Boston Society of Natural History, and of the Mas-

sachusetts Agricultural Society, his reading of Audubon, Wilson, Macgillivray, Bechstein, Lyell, and Nuttal, of Loudon, Gray, Harlan, and Lovell, of Fitch, Harris, Kirby, and Spence, of Agassiz and Gould, Abbott, Sowerby, and Chambers, his own field notes and his essays, all attest to the respect and interest which he showed for the natural scientist's acute eye and practiced induction. (Christie, p. 79)

Like his responses to science, Thoreau's attitudes toward religion were mixed. He found many religious practices and beliefs to be manifestations of bad faith. Just as he found the scientific perspective of his day inadequate, so too did he find sectarian creeds incompatible with his faith in the spirit he found latent in the world: "We are wont foolishly to think that the creed which a man professes is more significant than the fact he is" (J, IX, 144). Thoreau emphasized the interior, spiritual dimensions of religion rather than outward forms. "What is religion? That which is never spoken" (J, XI, 113). Unlike many of his contemporaries, Thoreau could never take seriously theological issues; he found any creed's catechism an occasion to head for the door even if such behavior was considered to be the latest form of infidelity. "What is called [sectarian] faith is an immense prejudice" (J, XI, 326); it was, therefore, unnecessary for him to "consult the D.D.'s and all the letters of the alphabet before printing a sentence" (J, XI, 325). As he points out in "Life Without Principle," Thoreau preferred "chickadee-dees" (PE, 167).

Although he numbered many clergymen among his friends, he disliked ministers in general, complaining that they were men who could not butter their own bread and yet who combined with a thousand like them to "make dipped toast for all eternity" (J, IX, 284). When one clergyman told Thoreau that he was going to dive into his inmost depths, Thoreau replied, "I trust you will not strike your head against the bottom" (J, V, 265). He complained: "The church! it is eminently the timid institution, and the heads and pillars of it are constitutionally and by principle the greatest cowards in the community" (J, XI, 325). He wished that "ministers were a little more *dangerous*" (J, XII, 407) rather than engendering

moral complacency in their congregations. Thoreau found especially abhorrent the churches' opposition to abolitionism, a position he vehemently denounced in his various antislavery papers. In
spite of this, Unitarians frequently claim him as one of their own
on the basis of the fact that he was baptized by a Unitarian minister and buried from a Unitarian church. But Thoreau specifically renounced membership in the Unitarian church. When he
was invited to deliver a lecture in the basement of an orthodox
(i.e., Trinitarian) church, he "trusted he helped to undermine it"
(J, IX, 188).

It would be a mistake, however, to think that Thoreau was irre-
ligious. The many studies that have been written that associate
him with one religious practice or another of the East or West
provide ample evidence of his deep religious attitudes toward life.
As he said on his deathbed, he had no quarrel with God. Though
he did not consider himself a member of any particular organized
religion, he certainly organized his thoughts around religious principles. What attracted him to some of the world's major religions
were their universal and ethical values, not their parochial pecu-
liarities. He insisted that he did "not prefer one religion or philosophy to another. I have no sympathy with the bigotry and
ignorance which make transient and partial and puerile distinctions between one man's faith or form of faith and another's,—as
Christian and heathen. I pray to be delivered from narrowness,
partiality, exaggeration, bigotry. To the philosopher all sects, all
nations, are alike. I like Brahma, Hari, Buddha, the Great Spirit,
as well as God" (J, II, 4). The word "like" is an interesting choice
in this context. Where is "worship"? For the orthodox it must seem
an irreverent choice, but for the thinker who transcends sectarian
boundaries in the interests of experiencing "God" (or whatever
other convenient term that might be used to suggest spiritual self-
realization), the word "like" accurately evokes the sense of confidence that informs Thoreau's blending of the Eastern and Western
religious thought available to him, a blending that would serve
"his desire to commune with the spirit of the universe" (J, II, 150).
His religious attitudes were not to be confined by any catechisms
or primers, as his following rendition of the *New England Primer*
makes clear; the first two lines are from the *Primer*'s illustration of

the first letter of the alphabet; the final two lines are Thoreau's:

> In Adam's fall
> We sinned all.
> In the new Adam's rise
> We shall all reach the skies. (J, II, 153)

Thoreau's method of reaching the skies has been called mystical—he described himself this way ("I am a mystic") to the Association for the Advancement of Science—but it is important to keep in mind that Thoreau said this in the same breath that he described himself as "a transcendentalist, and a natural philosopher to boot," which was his way of letting the scientists know that they would not understand his basic concerns. His mysticism is best understood as an element of his Transcendentalism rather than as a separate, highly disciplined mode of attaining spiritual fulfillment that firmly fixes Thoreau in a particular mystical tradition. Like other Transcendentalists, Thoreau did, however find mysticism appealing. "The mystical consciousness, a nonempirical and nonrational mode of apprehending reality, was bound to interest Transcendentalists who were eager to pierce to the heart of things by means of intuitive Reason. The central aim of the mystical experience [was] an immediate grasp of the undifferentiated unity of the universe as a whole" (Paul F. Boller, *American Transcendentalism, 1830–1860*, p. 81). Whatever could contribute to Thoreau's apprehension of ultimate reality, he made his own. "The highest law," the law that went beyond sectarian orthodoxies, dogmas, and traditions, "gives a thing to him who can use it" (J, VIII, 19).

*    *    *

Thoreau's responses to the social and political issues of his day were informed by that fact that he "commonly attend[ed] more to nature than to man" ("The Last Days of John Brown," PE, 145). Ordinarily, he preferred to turn his back on the world of politics because he placed his faith in the efficacy of individual reform rather than collective or social reform. "Man and his affairs,—

Church and State and school, trade and commerce and agriculture,—Politics—for that is the word for them all here to-day," occupied "but a narrow field" in Thoreau's landscape (J, II, 53). Yet it was a persistent and significant area of his life. Occasionally, his walks in nature were spoiled by that "narrow field": "Who can be serene in a country where both the rulers and the ruled are without principle?" ("Slavery in Massachusetts," PE, 108). His own Transcendental principles demanded that he put his trust in self-reform, since only individuals, not society, were capable of genuine reform. Thoreau believed that reform must come from within and could not be imposed by any outside force. "Alas! this is the crying sin of the age, this want of faith in the prevalence of a man. Nothing can be effected but by one man." He insisted that "We must first succeed alone that we may enjoy our success together" ("Paradise [To Be] Regained," PE, 42).

Thoreau was as suspicious of reformers as a class as he was of clergymen. He despised the "slimy benignity" of reformers who "rubbed you continually with the greasy cheeks of their kindness" and "lay their sweaty hand on your shoulder, or your knee, to magnetize you" (J, V, 264–65). Thoreau wanted to be spared the misdirected good intentions of those who set about to reform the world instead of themselves. He would rather, as he put it in *Walden*, "suffer evil the natural way" (PE, 74). Although Thoreau questioned the motives of reformers and wondered if they were more interested in forwarding their careers than their causes, he was equally critical of conservatives who believed it their duty to preserve the existing public laws and institutions. Thoreau's satirical wit was nonpartisan: "The heads of conservatives have a puny and deficient look, a certain callowness and concavity.... We wonder to see such a head wear a whole hat" ("Reform and the Reformers," PE, 182).

Far more than the individual reformers, he mistrusted the reform societies. No matter what their purpose, societies tended to institutionalize themselves and become conservative. They destroyed rather than developed the strength of the individual:

Speaking of Fourier communities with Bellew, I said that I suspected any enterprise in which two were en-

> gaged together. "But," said he, "it is difficult to make a stick stand unless you slant two or more against it." Oh, no," answered I, "you may split its lower end to two or three, or drive it single into the ground, which is the best way; but most men, when they start on a new enterprise, not only figuratively, but really, *pull up stakes.* When the sticks prop one another, none, or only one, stands erect."
> (J, VII, 500)

Given this point of view, Thoreau would have nothing to do with Brook Farm, Fruitlands, or other communal societies of his time, and he felt the same way about the Democratic and Republican or any other parties.

Of all the reform movements contemporary to him, the one that most challenged his basic principles of individual reform was the abolitionist movement. It is hardly surprising that Thoreau would have been drawn to a movement that set out to abolish an institution instead of establishing one, but there is more to it than that. Slavery was *the* problem of his time, and he could no more ignore it than he could abandon his personal spiritual quest. In "Civil Disobedience" he expresses the sense of strong moral obligation that bound him to the slavery issue: "If I devote myself to other pursuits and contemplations, I must first see, at least, that I do not pursue them sitting upon another man's shoulders. I must get off him first, that he may pursue his contemplations too" (W, IV, 365). Indeed, Thoreau believed that to ignore the issue would be an impediment to cultivating the divinity within himself:

> Action from principle,—changes things and relations; it is essentially revolutionary, and does not consist wholly with any thing which was. It not only divides states and churches, it divides families; aye, it divides the *individual,* separating the diabolical in him from the divine.
> (W, IV, 367)

Thoreau could not pursue spiritual truths if he thought he was living a diabolical lie; the universal harmony he listened for in nature was interrupted by the sounds of clanking chains. Hence, he spoke out publicly and vociferously against slavery; he aided slaves to escape to freedom in Canada; and he was among the first to defend John Brown after Harpers Ferry in 1859. But never did he officially join any antislavery movement.

Just as the chronic issue of slavery pushed the United States to sectional conflicts, so too did it create in Thoreau conflicts concerning his views of reform. The urgency of the issues caused him to respond with an increased willingness to support the use of resistance as a means of confronting the injustices perpetrated by government. This shift is made readily evident by comparing Thoreau's defense of Brown's raid at Harpers Ferry with an essay Thoreau wrote in 1843 in which he appealed to the individual's faith in universal moral law as a means of reforming the world. In "Paradise (To Be) Regained" Thoreau argued for inner reform and the "incalculable" power of "love" as the most effective method of achieving social ends, but as year after year passed and he saw slavery increasing rather than ending, Thoreau found it necessary to consider other means of reform. Wendell Glick has traced this development:

> For at least eight years—from 1837 ... to 1845 ... he [Thoreau] believed implicitly ... that the reform of society should be intrusted solely to the forces for good within man and the universe ("Thoreau and Radical Abolitionism," p. 105). While Thoreau was at Walden Pond, he and his government had a disagreement [the "Civil Disobedience" episode] which left its mark and hastened the day of his willingness to aid radical Abolitionists in their attempt to destroy it (p. 143). When he left Walden Pond ... the evil which lurked in institutions, he concluded, was more malevolent than he had ever suspected as a youth. It was so malevolent that it would have to be fought by every means available, and that meant, of course, by attempting to decrease the strength of institutions while at the same time appealing to the conscience of man (pp. 133–34). The method of reform from within, which he had advocated so staunchly to 1845, had not been enough to arrest the

trend, any more than the combination of appeals to the
conscience and attacks on institutions to which he re-
sorted after his stay at Walden. The result was that by
the end of the 1850's, Thoreau was in a quandary, and
willing to embrace any method which seemed to have the
least prospect of success (p. 158). Though his close friends
and admirers used the [John Brown] incident in his defense [that through it he fulfilled his social obligations],
had they understood him they would have gone to any
length to play it down. For its real meaning was that
Thoreau's long cherished faith in the adequacy of the
Moral Law to satisfy all man's individual and collective
needs was slipping precariously. (p. 215)

The same Thoreau who has so often been associated with the
nonviolent resistance of Mahatma Gandhi and Martin Luther
King, Jr., clearly went beyond his earlier views of reform in his
championing of Brown. In "A Plea for Captain John Brown" (PE,
133), Thoreau acknowledges that he neither "wish[ed] to kill nor to
be killed, but I can foresee circumstances in which both these
things would be by me unavoidable." He felt no need to apologize
for Brown's violence: "I shall not be forward to think him mistaken
in his method who quickest succeeds to liberate the slave." What
was important was not the method of reform but the goal. "The
question is not about the weapon, but the spirit in which you use
it." Thoreau can reconcile his support of Brown's use of Sharps'
rifles with his own faith in the power of love and moral law only
with paradox, not with logic: he says of Brown that "No man has
appeared in America, as yet, who loved his fellow man so well, and
treated him so tenderly." The power of that "love" is very different
from the kind Thoreau referred to in 1843, and it brings to mind
Thoreau's wary response to philanthropy in *Walden* where he
writes, "If I knew for a certainty that a man was coming to my
house with the conscious design of doing me good, I should run for
my life" (PE, 74).

All of this is not to say, however, that Thoreau totally rejected
the nonviolence and passive resistance that characterized his earlier views on reform. There was only one John Brown in his life.

But it is to say that his views on reform represent another example of the competing ideas that constitute his thought and attitudes. Thoreau's response to politics was essentially apolitical; he was concerned more with the individual than groups, with principles than means, with absolutes than compromises, with virtues than votes. He responded to particular issues on occasion, "but when my task is done, with never failing confidence I devote myself to the infinite again" (J, IX, 205). Even after the Brown episode and on the eve of the Civil War, he wrote to an abolitionist friend on April 10, 1861, that "I do not so much regret the present condition of things in this country (provided I regret it at all) as I do that I ever heard of it." The activist who praised Brown's heroism and direct assault on slavery now urges his reader to ignore "Fort Sumpter, and Old Abe, and all that, for that is just the most fatal, and indeed the only fatal, weapon you can direct against evil ever." (Correspondence, p. 611). Yet, he eventually was in favor of the Civil War, because it suggested to him that the country might be morally regenerated by it. It is evident that if Thoreau was anything, he was radically inconsistent in his approaches to reform, approaches that included passive resistance, violence, and indifference. He knew what kind of world he wanted—one that would be responsive to the worth and dignity of the individual—but he wavered on the question of what means would be most effective in achieving that end. "It is not strategies, after all, that keep his words alive, it is the Prometheus in them, Shelley's Prometheus, who will never make peace with an overlord" (Leo Stoller, "Civil Disobedience: Principle and Politics," p. 41).

\*   \*   \*

Although Thoreau supported John Brown's attempts to incite an insurrection in order to overthrow an unjust state, Thoreau was not, as has sometimes been claimed, an anarchist who rejected all forms of government. His concern was primarily with the necessity of improving government rather than abolishing it. He viewed government as an expedient that was granted authority by the people for the purpose of promoting individual freedom. In "Civil Disobedience" he expresses his hope that one day, "when men are prepared for it," there will be no need for governments at all, but until that day his idealism is tempered: "to speak practically as a citizen, unlike those who call themselves no-government men, I ask for, not at once no government, but *at once* a better government. Let every man make known what kind of government would command his respect, and that will be one step toward obtaining it" (W, IV, 357).

Thoreau acknowledged that certain functions could best be conducted by society rather than by the individual. The individual was always foremost in his thinking, but he could also appreciate the role that government played in matters that did not impinge upon his conscience. "In passage after passage of his published works and journal, Thoreau makes specific proposals for legitimate governmental activity, often proposals for new state or local laws or improvements of existing ones" (John C. Broderick, "Thoreau's Proposals for Legislation," p. 285). Thoreau suggests, for example, compulsory education laws, supplemented by government-sponsored adult education, and he asks that the government improve roads, issue adequate maps, further crime detection, prevent fires, and conserve natural resources. Citing these concerns by no means nominates Thoreau as a candidate for office, but it does lend force to his claim that he sought a "better government."

Less government was better government. Though Thoreau accepted its legitimate functions, he was suspicious of how it operated. As government grew more centralized, the individual became less central; what started out as an expedient servant for the individual became the law and his master. Founded to establish justice, it ended by preserving injustice. The protection of the institution of slavery by the federal, state, and even local governments of Thoreau's own time was to him convincing evidence of the inherent danger, and in his political essays he rang the alarm bell for his fellow citizens.

Under no circumstances would Thoreau accept the idea that a citizen should turn over his conscience to the state and obey any and all laws. Neither votes nor legal precedent could usurp the individual's responsibility and right to choose morality over the state's policy. If the laws of the state conflicted with the Transcendental higher law of the conscience, then it was the individual's duty to obey the higher law within rather than the civil law. "The lawyer's truth is not Truth but consistency, or a consistent expediency" ("Civil Disobedience," W, IV, 384). Unlike the lawyer's truth, Thoreau's was consistent with his faith in higher laws and his belief that they were to be found when an individual examined his conscience, of which statute books were but an imperfect—and sometimes corrupt—reflection. It was imperative that the state adjust its view of the individual instead of the individual relinquishing all authority to the state: "There will never be a really free and enlightened State, until the State comes to recognize the individual as a higher and independent power. . . ." Thoreau goes on in this passage from "Civil Disobedience" to suggest what an ideal state might be:

> I please myself with imagining a State at last which can afford to be just to all men, and to treat the individual with respect as a neighbor; which even would not think it inconsistent with its own repose if a few were to live aloof from it, not meddling with it, nor embraced by it, who fulfilled all the duties of neighbors and fellowmen. A State which bore this kind of fruit, and suffered it to drop off as fast as it ripened, would prepare the way for a still more perfect and glorious State, which also I have imagined, but not yet any where seen. (W, IV, 387)

Thoreau viewed the ideal state, then, as "the benevolent expedient which provided the means for men's individual perfection while forcing no man against his conscience, which promoted social conditions which would make it possible for citizens to disobey if it should overstep its rightful authority, and which one day might realize the perfection of becoming unnecessary" (William A. Herr, "A More Perfect State: Thoreau's Concept of Civil Government," p. 486).

\*    \*    \*

Thoreau's concern for the proper function of government parallels his lifelong concern with the proper use of all things. As he makes clear in *Walden*, he wanted to live economically—to use efficiently the resources available to him—so that he would be the exception to Emerson's generalization that "things are in saddle,/ And ride mankind." Thoreau refused to be owned by property, to be herded by a herd, or to become the tool of his tools. He had in mind a higher use of things so as not to be lowered by them. The simple life that he led provided him with the economic independence that was a prerequisite to the spiritual freedom he sought. He paid no homage to the almighty dollar; when it came to getting a living he never confused means with ends or property with freedom: "In my experience I have found nothing so truly impoverishing as what is called wealth" (J, VIII, 120).

Thoreau's measure of the cost a thing is "the amount of what I will call life which is required to be exchanged for it, immediately or in the long run" *(Walden,* PE, 31). It is this sensibility that informed his refusal to work full-time at any job which would require "sell[ing] both my forenoons and afternoons to society," thereby "neglecting my peculiar calling," because then "there would be nothing left worth living for" (J, II, 141). For a large portion of his adult life he earned his own living by surveying, manufacturing pencils, building chimneys, or even shoveling manure. None of this work distracted him for very long from his "calling" as a writer and thinker. By reducing his wants, he found it was necessary to devote to such labor only a small portion of his time. About six weeks of labor produced funds sufficient to supply his needs for a year, and most of it was performed outdoors.

Thoreau believed in the integrity of work. It should be meaningful rather than perfunctory, an expression of the worker rather than the simple manipulation of the worker. Like Emerson in "The American Scholar," Thoreau saw some of the inherent problems of the division of labor. Visiting Sam Barrett's mill in Concord, he commented: "You come away from the great factory saddened, as if the chief end of man were to make pails; but in the case of the countryman who makes a few by hand, rainy days, the relative importance of human life and of pails is preserved, and you come away thinking of the simple and helpful life of the man" (J, XI, 227). The function of work was not to be reduced to getting a living merely. "For every man . . . should love his work as much as the poet does his" (J, XIII, 20).

Thoreau saw few opportunities for loving one's work in the com-

mercial world he so assiduously avoided (one of the few lapses
being his incongruous and unsuccessful brief efforts to sell sub-
scriptions to the *Agriculturist* in the streets of New York City). Thoreau's contempt for business was in proportion to its tendency to
distract and subvert meaningful work: "In my experience, nothing
is so opposed to poetry—not crime—as business. It is a negation of
life" (J, IV, 162). Business represented to Thoreau all the deadening normality that gave support to a life of quiet desperation. For
Thoreau, being practical meant saving himself instead of money;
his major interest was the private business he transacted at Walden
Pond that earned him a set of values that were independent of the
fluctuations of the marketplace:

> We hear a good deal said about moonshine by so-
> called practical people, and the next day, perchance, we
> hear of their failure, they having been dealing in fancy
> stocks; but there really never is any moonshine of this
> kind in the practice of poets and philosophers; there
> never are any hard times or failures with them, for they
> deal with permanent values. (J, XIV, 284)

Thoreau was not above occasionally feeling buoyed up by a
sinking stock market (see his November 16, 1857, letter to H. G. O.
Blake concerning the financial panic of that year), and yet he
praises the "enterprise and bravery" of commerce in *Walden* (PE,
118–19) for the energy and growth that it represents. As long as
commerce did not ride mankind, it had, like government, a limited
but useful function.

\*    \*    \*

Thoreau preferred to think of man as part and parcel of nature
rather than as an element of any social system. The solitude he
found in nature was fertile ground for the self-culture he nourished
all his life. Though he was alone much of the time, he was not
lonely: "I find it wholesome to be alone the greater part of the
time. To be in company, even with the best, is soon wearisome and
dissipating. I love to be alone. I never found the companion that

was so companionable as solitude" *(Walden,* PE, 135). The charm of this and many similar passages in Thoreau's writings does not entirely remove the chill many readers experience by being made to feel intrusive. There are never any Whitmanesque bear hugs in Thoreau's prose; he never affectionately hooks his arm about our waists to show us the road ahead. But this is not to suggest, as some critics have, that he was hopelessly cold and sour. He had an anti-social streak in him, but it was not informed by misanthropy—although he was an exacting critic of what he took to be meaning-less activities and social mores. Nor was it informed by a faith in the value of a hermit's life. When he traveled through the Maine woods and discovered true hermits living miles from any neighbor, he was appalled. Instead, Thoreau's preference for solitude and his disavowal of society was consciously based on the positive desire for self-renewal:

> You think that I am impoverishing myself by withdraw-ing from man, but in my solitude I have woven for myself a silken web or *chrysalis,* and, nymph-like, shall ere long burst forth a more perfect creature, fitted for a higher society. (J, IX, 246)

Critics who accuse Thoreau of going to Walden because he was a misanthropic hermit who fraudulently urged his readers to be self-reliant while he raided his mother's cookie jar fail to see that their evidence for describing him as a fraud (his almost daily trips to his parents' house, fewer than two miles from the pond, and his friendships in Concord) undercuts their description of him as a misanthropic hermit. Thoreau conceived of his solitude more as a state of mind than as a state of isolation in some distant geograph-ical location. It is reasonable, of course, to disagree with plenty of what Thoreau said and did—he was always uncomfortable with iconoclasts being transformed into icons—but it really is time to turn over his mother's infamous and bottomless, mythic cookie jar to the Concord Antiquarian Society. The argument is too stale not to crumble under scrutiny.

Perhaps the most significant problem that attaches to attempts to describe Thoreau as a fraud is that the argument overlooks what

he genuinely was about. Emerson's essay on "The Transcendentalist" is aimed at characterizing the entire movement, but in doing
so it offers some remarkably apt descriptions that can be used to
describe the nature of Thoreau's solitude and the risks it implied:

> Whoso goes to walk alone, accuses the whole world; he
> declares all to be unfit to be his companions; it is very
> uncivil, nay, insulting; Society will retaliate. Meantime,
> this retirement does not proceed from any whim on the
> part of these separators; but if any one will take pains to
> talk with them, he will find that this part is chosen both
> from temperament and from principle; with some un-
> willingness too, and as a choice of the less of two evils; for
> these persons are not by nature melancholy, sour, and
> unsocial,—they are not stockish or brute,—but joyous, sus-
> ceptible, affectionate; they have even more than others a
> great wish to be loved.

Emerson's description of the Transcendental personality is responsive to both the philosophical and psychological dimensions of
Thoreau's solitude: "They say to themselves, It is better to be alone
than in bad company. And it is really a wish to be met,—the wish
to find society for their hope and religion,—which prompts them to
shun what is called society." Emerson is also accurate in his description of the effect this solitude has upon the individual's relationship to institutions:

> their solitary and fastidious manners not only withdraw
> them from the conversation, but from the labors of the
> world; they are not good citizens, not good members of
> society; unwillingly they bear their part of the public and
> private burdens; they do not willingly share in the public
> charities, in the public religious rites, in the enterprises of
> education, of missions foreign and domestic, in the aboli-
> tion of the slave-trade, or in the temperance society. They
> do not even like to vote.

These passages (and many others in this valuable essay) serve to place Thoreau in a Transcendental context that makes an empathetic understanding of his ideas possible.

\* \* \*

One of the most common stereotypes of Thoreau is that he repudiated civilization and wished to return to a primitive life. Thoreau, however, went to Walden for only two years, and he went there within easy reach of a good many civilized amenities, where he lived in a cabin, not a cave. More important, his purpose was to simplify his life in such a way as to permit and foster the greatest development of his spiritual nature. The emphasis was on reducing his material needs in order to avoid living the "primitive" life that he perceived some of the villagers living because they had sacrificed their humanity for a false economy. From Thoreau's point of view it was conventional society that was primitive, and so he looked to the woods for personal redemption; his purposes were spiritual, not nostalgic. There is a critical difference between escapism and transcendence in intention. Thoreau kept his eye on the woods as a means of intensifying his experiences; he looked inward rather than backward: "Think of the consummate folly of attempting to get away from *here!* When the constant endeavor should be to get nearer and nearer *here*" (J, XI, 275).

Thoreau's acceptance and insistence of the reality of the present moment did not lead him to the conclusion that whatever is, is right. In moments of what might be called cosmic consciousness, Thoreau believed that he, like the artist of Kouroo in *Walden* (PE, 326–27), could transcend the restless and nervous bustling of his time, but more characteristically he criticized the primitive sensibilities that he perceived—even if they masqueraded in the name of civilization, technology, and progress. Industrialization and mechanization were the theme of the day. The railroad reached Concord just before Thoreau moved to Walden Pond, and before his death it had covered most of the eastern half of the United States. Mills were being established on every accessible water privilege in New England. New inventions were pouring into the U.S. Patent Office and on to the market. Paeans in praise of progress were being sung in every direction. Thoreau himself joined in the chorus when he could honestly admit the value of the accomplishments, but frequently he believed that the new inventions were "but improved means to an unimproved end": "We are in great haste to construct a magnetic telegraph from Maine to Texas; but Maine and Texas, it may be, have nothing important to communicate" (*Walden*, PE, 52). These are not the words of a primitivist but those of a person who was concerned about the improvement of the individual members of his civilization rather than the rapid movement of that civilization. Thoreau enjoyed traveling by train to Boston and he appreciated its convenience, but he would not be railroaded.

Thoreau's lifetime was a period of urbanization. Large cities were a comparatively new phenomenon in America. But Thoreau was not pleased with their development. "Almost all our improvements, so called, tend to convert the country into the town," he complained (J, XIV, 57). He avoided cities whenever possible and said that the only places in Boston that appealed to him were the wharves, where he could look at the ocean, and the railroad station, where he could return to Concord. Not surprisingly, the city represented to Thoreau a threat to individuality. In contrast to people in the country, the "city does not *think* much" ("Slavery in Massachusetts," PE, 98). While in New York he found the "pigs in the street . . . the most respectable part of the population. When will the world learn that a million men are of no importance compared with *one* man?" (*Correspondence*, pp. 111–12).

Although Thoreau appreciated some of the resources cities could offer such as museums and libraries, he could never fully appreciate what cities were because he tended to focus upon the natural environment they lacked. Unlike Whitman, who associated energy and vitality with the city, Thoreau sensed weakness; he noted that "artificial, denaturalized persons cannot handle nature without being poisoned. If city-bred girls visit their country cousins,—go a-berrying with them,—they are sure to return covered with blueberry bumps at least" (J, VIII, 448–49). Cities, by separating man from nature, worked an irreparable harm. "At the same time that we exclude mankind from gathering berries in our field, we exclude them from gathering health and happiness. . . . We strike only one more blow at a simple and wholesome relation to nature"

(J, XIV, 56). There is a constant need for the urbanized man to return to nature to fulfill his spiritual needs. The symbol of Romulus and Remus, the founders of Rome, being raised by a wolf, was a favorite in Thoreau's mythology.

Thoreau prescribed as an antidote for the weaknesses caused by citified life an appreciation for wilderness. His concern with man's need for the wild is directly related to his view of civilization as tame, deadening, and commercial rather than the growing, vigorous life to be found in nature. Ultimately, though, the wilderness and culture were complementary rather than antithetical. Thoreau tended to equate one's true self with the wild, untamed nature that needed no artificial cultivating but instead grew on its own.

> No more than in *Walden,* however, did Thoreau relinquish civilization or expect men to go wild: he wanted to preserve the forest and to preserve the wild in man only to keep civilization open on one side and to leave portions of man uncultivated. In the wild he saw the possibility of a higher civilization; here the real self would not have to go to market, but could express itself—its wildness and joy and desire for the liberty to live free from all laws except those of its Maker. Here a man might yet give his genius play and find the nurture he needed to mature *his* fruit. (Sherman Paul, *The Shores of America,* p. 416)

It was almost an inevitable corollary of Thoreau's search for the ideal life that he should become involved in a search for the ideal man; that is, the man in perfect correspondence with nature: "It is the marriage of the soul with Nature that makes the intellect fruitful, that gives birth to imagination" (J, II, 413). Thoreau's fascination with the American Indian was directly related to his interest in the wild. "The charm of the Indian to me is that he stands free and unconstrained in Nature, is her inhabitant and not her guest, and wears her easily and gracefully" (J, I, 253). He spent much time reading about Indians in order to learn "what manner of men they were, how they lived here, their relation to nature, their arts and their customs, their fancies and superstitions" (J, XI, 437). If he could understand the organic integrity of their lives, that understanding might be useful in revitalizing civilized life. They represented a natural standard against which civilization could be measured. Thoreau was primarily concerned with the historical Indian ("the Indian") rather than individual Indians contemporary to him:

> "the Indian" had been a point from which to criticize white American culture, the joyless sabbaths and resignations to joyless work and expensive comforts. "The Indian" meant leisure and health. A synthesis of civilized and savage life could bring renewal. If the ignorant and backward savage was doomed, the reborn white savage or Transcendental Indian could incorporate his virtues, metaphysically eating him as the Indian warrior ate the heart of his enemy. (Robert Sayre, *Thoreau and the American Indians*, p. 213)

Thoreau tended to see the Indians contemporary to him as shadows of what they once were, corrupted by civilization yet incapable of assimilation. He accepted many of the white racial stereotypes about Indians, both favorable and unfavorable. Although, as Robert Sayre has demonstrated, he learned much from his readings and his 1857 encounter with Joe Polis, one of his Maine woods guides, about the realities (rather than the stereotypes) of Indian life, he never fully left those prejudices behind. As late as 1859 he used the Indian as a metaphor for petty duplicity in "A Plea for Captain John Brown." Complaining about newspaper editors who failed to appreciate the principled motivations of Brown, Thoreau writes that "They have got to conceive of a man of faith and of religious principle, and not a politician or an Indian" (PE, 124). Thoreau's placement of a politician and an Indian in the same category is a clear index to his sharing some of the cultural myths of his time; the Indian lacked a spiritual dimension. Readers of Thoreau are aware that he celebrated many Indian values, but "people might [also] reflect on how even an independent, critical person like him was affected by these cultural illusions" (Robert Sayre, *Thoreau and the American Indians,* p. 194). His Indian education was not complete.

Thoreau was led to admire the hunters and trappers of Concord, men such as Haines, Melvin, and Goodwin, who, because of their closeness to nature, were outcasts in the eyes of most Concordians. Twice he speaks of Haines's reminding him of the Indian (J, VI, 233; III, 290). And again he says: "The woodcutter and his practices and experiences are more to be attended to; his accidents, perhaps more than any other's should mark the epochs in the winter day. Now that the Indian is gone, he stands nearest to nature" (J, III, 244). But again, as did the Indian, they had one serious failing: they lacked a spiritual, an aesthetic sense. Nowhere in the past or in the present could Thoreau find his ideal man. He could only hope that such a man would develop in the future. He concentrated therefore upon developing such a man. And consistent with his philosophy, he began with himself.

*       *       *

Thoreau had an abiding interest in education throughout his life, and not surprisingly he tended to focus upon the individual seeking an education rather than the subject matter being learned. Many of the principles he put into practice in his own school anticipated many of those that characterize modern progressive education. He emphasized doing instead of passive indoor studies, local history and nature studies instead of textbook readings of the remote. "Learning by doing" is John Dewey's phrase, but Thoreau put the concept into practice many years before him.

In disciplinary methods Thoreau was equally progressive. He resigned his position in the Concord public schools rather than accept their policy of physical force. To Orestes Brownson he wrote (December 30, 1837), "I have ever been disposed to regard the cowhide as a nonconductor." When he established his own school, he used understanding and an appeal to the moral sense of the child as his principal disciplinary devices: "I would make education a pleasant thing both to the teacher and to the scholar. This discipline, which we allow to be the end of life, should not be one thing in the classroom, and another in the street. We should seek to be fellow students with the pupil, and we should learn as well with him, if we would be most helpful to him" *(Correspondence,* p. 19).

The basis for his educational theory was that the child was innately good and that it was the purpose of the school to foster and stimulate the child's inner development toward perfection. Thoreau was convinced that paradise could be achieved on this earth through the full development of man's potentialities, and so his educational philosophy was aimed in that direction.

Thoreau was consistently critical of the collegiate education of his day. He once remarked to Emerson that Harvard taught all the branches of learning but got to none of the roots. Too much time was spent in studying theory, too little in actual practice: "To my astonishment I was informed on leaving college that I had studied navigation!" he says in *Walden* (PE, 52); "—why, if I had taken one turn down the harbor I should have known more about it." But on the other hand, he did not deny the value of a liberal education: "The learning of trades and professions which is designed to enable men to earn their living, or to fit them for a particular station in life—is *servile"* (J, XIII, 15).

He was critical of college faculties. There were "professors of philosophy, but not philosophers" *(Walden,* PE, 14). They were not interested in searching for truth but lived in the shadow of their established institutions and spent their time defending the status quo. True educators, he believed, should broaden their students' horizons: they should at least teach the students "where the arsenal is, in case they should ever want to use any of its weapons" (J, XIII, 67). All the while he was at Harvard, he wrote his class secretary later, "My spirit yearned for the sympathy of my old and almost forgotten friend Nature."

A further contribution by Thoreau was his interest in adult education, expressed primarily through the lyceum movement of his day. He was an active member of the Concord Lyceum from its founding in 1829 until his death, lecturing before it nineteen times and serving several terms as its curator. In the mid-1840s he was one of the leaders of the successful movement to permit controversial subjects such as abolitionism to be discussed from the lyceum platform. And in *Walden* he urged his fellow townsmen to devote more funds to the lyceum even at the expense of omitting one bridge over a river (PE, 109–10).

\*     \*     \*

Thoreau's emphasis upon self-education and self-discipline has contributed to what is perhaps one of the most popular misconceptions about him. He is often perceived as a rather grim stoic. "He was an ascetic who reveled in self-denial." "He could more easily say no than yes." "He preferred to do without." These are among the most frequent reactions to Thoreau, a misconception popularized by Emerson, who saw Thoreau as "the perfect Stoic." But Thoreau's sister Sophia protested, "Henry never impressed me as the Stoic which Mr. E. represents him" *(Daniel Ricketson and His Friends,* p. 155). Many readers, however, have used Emerson's funeral address to emphasize Thoreau's denials and protests at the expense of the life he affirmed. That Thoreau was a critic of society and a gadfly who satirized its follies is undeniable—and also a large part of his significance to us even today—but his nay-saying is sometimes not recognized as a prelude to his yea-saying. Ultimately, his response to life was extraordinarily positive. He was, after all, a romantic and a Transcendentalist.

There are few writers who have responded more to the texture of life than Thoreau. F. O. Matthiessen went so far as to describe him as "much more of an epicurean than a stoic" *(American Renaissance,* p. 122), a statement that is somehow reasonable if one accepts the broad definition of an epicurean as someone who delights in sensuous pleasure. Thoreau was basically sensuous. "See, hear, smell, taste, etc., while these senses are fresh and pure," he says (J, II, 330). When he denied himself sense stimulation—as often he did—it was owing to his desire to keep his senses "free and pure" for higher levels of perception. Although Thoreau was a Transcendental idealist, his sensuous love of phenomena is evident throughout his writings. Sometimes he sounds almost like Whitman: "My body is all sentient," he says. "As I go here or there, I am tickled by this or that I come in contact with, as if touched by the wires of a battery" (J, VIII, 44). It is this sensuousness that separates Thoreau most from Emerson and that makes him more readable.

It should be emphasized, however, that Thoreau's sentient body was not Whitman's "Body Electric." Thoreau was sensuous, not sensual; clearly he sublimated his sexual identity. Although he refused to be shocked by the sex in Whitman's *Leaves of Grass* and praised the Hindus for their frankness in discussing sexual relations, he had a conventional, Victorian sense of sexual morality. Indeed, at times he was a prig. He was shocked that nature "imitated" the male organs in the *phallus impudicus* fungus; here nature "almost puts herself on a level with those who draw in privies" (J, IX, 115-17). He wrote this despite the fact that he sometimes waded the length of the rivers of Concord completely naked. He berated Channing for telling off-color jokes and added piously, "I lose my respect for the man who can make the mystery of sex the subject of a coarse jest.... I would preserve purity in act and thought, as I would cherish the memory of my mother" (J, III, 406-7). In his own paradoxical way Thoreau believed that "Chastity is the flowering of man." He explains this in his chapter on "Higher Laws": "We are conscious of an animal in us, which awakens in proportion as our higher nature slumbers." This side of man "is reptile and sensual, and perhaps cannot be wholly expelled; like the worms which, even in life and health, occupy our bodies" *(Walden,* PE, 219-20). Thoreau sounds more like St. Paul here than like Whitman. He tends to disassociate love from sex. Perhaps one of the most sensible comments that has been made about Thoreau's sexuality is that whatever it was, it was latent (James Armstrong, "Thoreau as Philosopher of Love," p. 223).

*    *    *

A few weeks before Thoreau died he wrote a letter to Myron Benton (March 21, 1862), saying, "I have not many months to live. ... I may add that I am enjoying existence as much as ever, and regret nothing." It is also worth adding that as he edited some of his writings for publication in those last months, he made no attempt to edit his ideas for consistency or to change his mind. He believed he had lived his life with principle, and if his ideas supported more than one interpretation, then that was life too. Neither his correspondence nor his friends reveals that he regretted anything. He had driven life into a corner and lived it deliberately. There was room for death too.


*Sources for Chapter Four*


The most detailed study of T's developing thought is Sherman Paul, *The Shores of America* (Urbana, 1958); still useful are Joseph Wood Krutch, *HDT* (New York, 1948), and Reginald L. Cook, *Passage to Walden* (1949; 2d ed., containing a "Key to References and Citations," New York, 1966); for specific topics see the indexes to these books. Louis B. Salomon, "The Practical T" *(CE,* 17, 1956, 229–32), refutes eight of the commonest misinterpretations of T's ideas with specific quotations from his writings. But in reply see Wade Thompson, "The Impractical T" *(CE,* 19, 1957, 67–70).

T's Transcendental thought and response to nature are discussed in most of the major studies of his writings. For Transcendental influences on T see Chapter Three. For a succinct overview of Transcendentalism see Alexander Kern, "The Rise of Transcendentalism," in Harry Hayden Clark, ed., *Transitions in American Literary History* (Durham, 1954, pp. 247–314). V. T. Rose, "A Critical Review of the Ideas of HDT" (Univ. of Minnesota, Ph.D., 1972), argues that though T was not a systematic thinker, Transcendentalism was the basis of his world view. T's Transcendental attitude toward life in the 1850s is discussed in J. Lyndon Shanley, "T: Years of Decay and Disappointment?" in Walter Harding, ed., *The T Centennial* (Albany, 1964, pp. 53–64). William L. Howarth, "T, the Journalist" (Univ. of Virginia, Ph.D., 1967), describes T's use of natural details in the late *Journals.* For a useful discussion of T on Mount Ktaadn that includes a brief summary of the views of Sherman Paul, Leo Marx, Charles Anderson, and Leo Stoller see Jonathan Fairbanks, "T: Speaker for Wildness" *(SAQ,* 70, 1971, 487–506). John Jacques, "The Discovery of 'Ktaadn': A Study of T's *The Maine Woods*" (Columbia Univ., Ph.D., 1971), argues that T's experience on Ktaadn did have a lasting impact on him. T's shifting attitudes toward nature are discussed in James McIntosh,

*T as Romantic Naturalist* (Ithaca, 1974); see also Stephen Railton, "T's 'Resurrection of Virtue!' " *(AQ,* 24, 1972, 210–27), and Robert H. DuPree, "From Analogy to Metaphor to Wordplay: T's Shifting View of the Relationship Between Man and Nature" (Auburn Univ., Ph.D., 1975). Mary P. Frederick, "The Idea of Retirement into Nature: Horace, Marvell, T" (Univ. of California, Berkeley, Ph.D., 1977), provides a perspective from literary history. Joel Porte, *Emerson and T* (Middletown, 1965), argues that T's uniqueness as a Transcendentalist is owing to his sensuous and "Lockean" response to nature. This emphasis upon T's sensuousness is connected to his philological interests, particularly in relation to Charles Kraitsir, in Philip F. Gura, "HT and the Wisdom of Words" *(NEQ,* 52, 1979, 38–54). Robert K. Thomas examines T's dialectical approach to matter and spirit in "The Tree and the Stone: Time and Space in the Works of HDT" (Columbia Univ., Ph.D., 1967). Mary G. Bernath, "Substance and Process in T's Universe" (Univ. of Pittsburgh, Ph.D., 1974), discusses T's emphasis upon the senses and "the reality of earth" in his quest for the ideal. Richard J. Schneider, "The Balanced Vision: T's Observations of Nature" (Univ. of California, Santa Barbara, Ph.D., 1973), includes a detailed discussion of T's use of his senses (pp. 29–70). Frederick Garber, *T's Redemptive Imagination* (New York, 1977), argues that T transformed nature into consciousness and that he remained largely separate from nature. See also Joel Porte, "Emerson, T and the Double Consciousness" *(NEQ,* 41, 1968, 40–50).

For studies of T's attitudes toward science, see Raymond Adams, "T's Science" *(Scientific Monthly,* 60, 1945, 379–82); Horace Taylor, "T's Scientific Interests as Seen in His *Journal"* *(McNeese Rev.,* 14, 1963, 45–59); and Nina Baym, "T's View of Science" *(JHI,* 26, 1965, 221–34), who argues that T's Transcendentalism and science were incompatible; see also Richard Schneider (cited above) for an examination of the importance of science and idealism to T. T's view of science is discussed in relationship to his literary art in William W. Nichols, "Science and the Development of T's Art" (Univ. of Missouri, Ph.D., 1966).

For disparaging comments on T's ability as a naturalist, see Francis Allen, *T's Bird-Lore* (Boston, 1925); Fannie Hardy Eckstorm, "T's 'Maine Woods' " *(Atlantic,* 102, 1908, 242–50); W. L.

McAtee, "Adaptationist Naïveté" *(Scientific Monthly*, 48, 1939, 253–55); and John Burroughs, "Another Word on T" in *The Last Harvest* (Boston, 1922, pp. 103–71).

For T as an ecologist, see Philip and Kathryn Whitford, "T, Pioneer Ecologist and Conservationist" *(Scientific Monthly*, 73, 1951, 291–96), and William J. Wolf, *T: Mystic, Prophet, Ecologist* (Philadelphia, 1974, pp. 145–66), who links T's ecological concerns to his religious thought. Walter Harding, "Walden's Man of Science" *(VQR*, 57, 1981, 45–61), explains how the *OED* attributed the "ecology" listing to T and describes T's contributions to natural history studies; for additional studies on the latter, see Joseph Wade, "Some Insects of T's Writings" *(Jour. of the New York Entomological Society*, 35, 1927, 1–21); Kathryn Whitford, "T and the Woodlots of Concord" *(NEQ*, 23, 1950, 291–306), which describes T's findings in his "Succession of Forest Trees"; Alec Lucas, "T, Field Naturalist" *(UTQ*, 23, 1954, 227–32); Robert Henry Welker, "Literary Birdman: HDT," in *Birds & Men* (Cambridge, 1955, pp. 91–115); Lawrence Willson, "T and New England's Weather" *(Weatherwise*, 12, 1959, 91–94); Leo Stoller, "A Note on T's Place in the History of Phenology" *(Isis*, 47, 1956, 172–81); and Donald G. Quick, "T as Limnologist" *(TJQ*, 4, 1972, 13–20). For two studies that connect specific scientific knowledge to his literary art, see Kenneth Walter Cameron, "HT and the *Entomology* of Kirby and Spence" *(ESQ*, 38, 1965, 138–52), and Richard J. Schneider, "Reflections in Walden Pond: T's Optics" *(ESQ*, 21, 1975, 65–75).

The most extensive study of T's relationship to such naturalists as Agassiz, Gray, Darwin, Bartram, Audubon, and White is Kichung Kim, "T's Involvement with Nature: T and the Naturalist Tradition" (Univ. of California, Berkeley, Ph.D., 1969). Kim's discussion of T's preference for Gray over Agassiz appears in "T's Science and Teleology" *(ESQ*, 18, 1972, 125–33). See also John B. Wilson, "Darwin and the Transcendentalists" *(JHI*, 1965, 286–90), and two comparisons of T and Darwin: Loren Eiseley, *The Unexpected Universe* (New York, 1964, pp. 120–46), and Herbert Uhlig, "Improved Means to a Unimproved End" *(TSB* 128).

Studies of Oriental and Christian influences on T's religious thought are cited in the Sources for Chapter Three. A useful discussion of his religious views is John Sylvester Smith, "The Philosophical Naturism of HDT" (Drew Univ., Ph.D., 1948). Raymond Adams summarizes T's attitudes toward an afterlife in "T and Immortality" (SP, 26, 1929, 58–66). For a detailed treatment of T's mysticism, see Charles C. Kopp's two-volume study, "The Mysticism of HDT" (Pennsylvania State Univ., Ph.D., 1963), which argues that T deliberately patterned his life on Christian, Hindu, and Buddhist traditions; see also Michael Keller "HDT: Mystic" (Ball State Univ., Ed.D., 1977), which examines T's mysticism up to the publication of *Walden* by comparing him with other mystics; a revised portion of this appears as "HDT: A Transpersonal View" (*Jour. of Transpersonal Psychology*, 9, 1977, 43–82), which relates T to three stages of "psychospiritual development—Illumination, Dark Night, Unitive Life" (p. 43). For a discussion of T's religious attitudes in the context of modern theology that presents him as "One of the great American mystics and creative religious thinkers" (p. 167), see William J. Wolf, *T: Mystic, Prophet, Ecologist* (cited above). For T's view of Roman Catholics, see Lawrence Willson, "T and Roman Catholicism" (*CHR*, 42, 1956, 157–72). For the Adamic impulse in T, see R. W. B. Lewis, *American Adam* (Chicago, 1955). There still remains to be published a comprehensive and balanced study of T's religious attitudes that places in perspective his use of Eastern and Western religious beliefs and practices.

For an excellent introduction to T's social and political thought in his own words, see Milton Meltzer, ed., *T: People, Principles and Politics* (New York, 1963). A number of interesting essays dealing with the value of T's political ideas have been collected from *MR*, 4, 1962, in John Hicks, ed., *T in Our Season* (Amherst, 1966); several are cited below. To date no book-length comprehensive treatment of T's politics has been published, but there have been several dissertations that provide overviews and discuss his attitudes toward reform; Michael G. Erlich, "Selected Anti-Slavery Speeches of HDT, 1848–1859: A Rhetorical Analysis" (Ohio State Univ., Ph.D., 1970), and Douglas A. Noverr, "T's Development as an Observer and Critic of American Society" (Miami Univ., Ph.D., 1972), relate T's ideas to his art; see also Lauriat Lane, Jr., "The Structure of Protest: T's Polemical Essays" (*HAB*, 20, 1969, 34–40). Two political science dissertations reach differing conclusions

about the value of T's views: Charles M. Evans assesses them nega-
tively in "The Political Theory of HDT: An Exposition and Criticism" (Univ. of Oklahoma, Ph.D., 1973), whereas Glen W.
McKay, "Self-Definition, Conscience, and Growth: The Political
Standpoint of T" (Univ. of California, Santa Barbara, Ph.D.,
1976), describes them favorably. For a discussion that rejects a
political perspective on T, see Lawrence Bowling, "T's Social Criticism as Poetry" *(YR,* 55, 1966, 255–64).

The most detailed study of T's evolving views of reform and his
relationship with the abolitionists is Wendell Glick, "T and Radical Abolitionism" (Northwestern Univ. Ph.D., 1950); see also Nick
Aaron Ford, "HDT, Abolitionist" *(NEQ,* 19, 1946, 359–71). T's
defense of John Brown's violence has generated a number of attacks on T's Transcendental politics; one of the strongest is Vincent Buranelli, "The Case Against T" *(Ethics,* 67, 1957, 257–68);
but see Ralph L. Ketcham, "Reply to Buranelli's Case Against T"
*(Ethics,* 69, 1959, 206–9). Two psychoanalytic readings that dis-
credit T's support of Brown will be found in Hicks, *T in Our Season*
(cited above): Carl Bode, "The Half-Hidden T" (pp. 104–16); and
C. Roland Wagner, "Lucky Fox at Walden" (pp. 117–33). Joseph
De Falco, "T's Ethics and the 'Bloody Revolution' " *(Topic,* 6,
1966, 43–49), praises T's strategic flexibility; Leo Stoller, "Civil
Disobedience: Principle and Politics" (in Hicks, pp. 40–44),
stresses T's principles rather than strategies; see also Edwin S.
Smith, "A T for Today," *Mainstream* (May and April, 1960, 1–24,
42–55). Truman Nelson, "T and John Brown" (in Hicks, pp. 134–
53), believes T abandoned passive resistance in favor of Brown's
heroic revolutionary violence; but Walter Harding, *The Days of HT*
(New York, 1965, pp. 418, 426), sees no radical departure or con-
tradictions in T's support of Brown because it was Brown's "courage and his idealism that T most admired, not his recourse to
violence"; see also Kerry Ahearn, "T and John Brown: What to
Do About Evil" *(TJQ,* 6, 1974, 24–28), and William A. Herr, "T
on Violence" *(TSB* 131). Michael Meyer, "T's Rescue of John
Brown from History," in Joel Myerson, ed., *Studies in the American
Renaissance* (Boston, 1980, forthcoming), demonstrates that T knew
about the charges linking Brown to the Pottawatomie massacre of
1856.

T's attitudes toward government have been widely discussed; a recent and concise summary is William A. Herr, "A More Perfect State: T's Concept of Civil Government" *(MR,* 16, 1975, 470-87). John C. Broderick, "T's Proposals for Legislation" *(AQ,* 7, 1955, 285-90), tempers earlier views of T as an anarchist such as Eunice M. Schuster's "Native American Anarchism" *(Smith College Studies in History,* 17, 1931, 46-51). For a comparative study of T as a social critic, see Taylor Stoehr, *Nay-Saying in Concord: Emerson, Alcott, and T* (Hamden, Ct., 1979). For discussions of particular political essays by T see the Sources for Chapter Two. The most complete survey and discussion of the many commentaries on T's thought related to politics is Michael Meyer, *Several More Lives to Live: T's Political Reputation in America* (Westport, 1977); consult the index for specific topics.

For T's ideas on economics, see Leo Stoller, *After Walden: T's Changing Views on Economic Man* (Stanford, 1957), which discusses T's movement toward a "union of principle and expediency" in his dealings with society. Francis B. Dedmond, "Economic Protest in T's Journals" *(SN,* 26, 1954, 65-76), provides a helpful overview of T's response to the prevailing economy; see also Robin Linstromberg and James Ballowe, "T and Etzler: Alternative Views of Economic Reform" *(Midcontinent Amer. Studies Jour.,* 11, 1970, 20-29). For a comparison of T with the Protestant ethic and capitalism, see Jesse Bier, "Weberism, Franklin, and the Transcendental Style" *(NEQ,* 43, 1970, 179-92); an insightful contrast between T and Franklin is developed by Reginald L. Cook, "Looking for America: A Binocular Vision" *(TJQ,* 8, 1976, 10-17). Herbert F. Smith, "T Among the Classical Economists" *(ESQ,* 23, 1977, 114-22), considers T's chapter on "Economy" in the context of Adam Smith, Malthus, and Ricardo; see also Richard H. Dillman, "T's Humane Economics: A Reflection of Jean-Baptiste Say's Economic Philosophy" *(ESQ,* 25, 1979, 20-25). For a wide-ranging discussion that includes T's economic thought, see Thomas Woodson, "T on Poverty and Magnanimity" *(PMLA,* 85, 1970, 21-34).

Thoreau's ideas on solitude and society have been commented upon by nearly everyone who has written about him. Leon Edel, *"Walden:* The Myth and the Mystery" *(American Scholar,* 44, 1975, 272-81), articulates some of the negative assessments, but see also the rejoinders *(American Scholar,* 44, 1975, 689–91). Joel Porte, "HT: Society and Solitude" *(ESQ,* 19, 1973, 131–40), provides a balanced perspective. Richard Lebeaux, *Young Man T* (Amherst, 1977) offers valuable discussions of both conscious and unconscious reasons for T's withdrawal from society. For a discussion that places T's emphasis upon individual fulfillment in a utopian context, see Northrop Frye, "Varieties of Literary Utopias" *(Daedalus,* 94, 1965, 323–47); for a romantic context, see Michael Hoffman, *The Subversive Vision* (Port Washington, N.Y., 1972, pp. 46–58); and for an Eastern context see Winfield E. Nagley, "T on Attachment, Detachment, and Non-Attachment" *(PE&W,* 3, 1954, 307–20). Leonard Neufeldt describes T's "inner soul" in "The Wild Apple Tree: Possibilities of the Self in T" (Univ. of Illinois, Ph.D., 1966); and Gerald Galgan treats T as an early American social philosopher in "The Self and Society in the Thought of HDT" (Fordham Univ., Ph.D., 1971).

For a discussion of T's views on civilization and primitivism that also includes his views on progress and the pastoral, see John Seelye, "Some Green Thoughts on a Green Theme" *(TriQ,* 23/24, 1972, 576–638), a study that extends and challenges the work of Leo Marx, *The Machine and the Garden* (New York, 1964, pp. 242–65); see also Joseph L. Basile, "Man and Machine in T" (Louisiana State Univ., Ph.D., 1972). Useful earlier studies include H. S. Canby, "T and the Machine Age" *(YR,* 20, 1931, 517–31), and G. Ferris Cronkhite, "The Transcendental Railroad" *(NEQ,* 24, 1951, 306–28). Related to T's ideas about civilization are his attitudes about wilderness and the West. Roderick Nash, *Wilderness and the American Mind* (New Haven, 1967; rev. ed., 1974, pp. 84–95), presents T as one of the first Americans to associate positive values with the wilderness. For T's impressions and use of the West see Lawrence Willson, "The Transcendentalist View of the West" *(WHR,* 14, 1960, 183–91); John Christie, *T as World Traveler* (New York, 1965, pp. 104–17); Edwin Fussell, *Frontier: American Literature and the American West* (Princeton, 1965, pp. 175–231, 327–50); Richard Slotkin, *Regeneration Through Violence: The Mythology of the American Frontier, 1600–1860* (Middletown, 1973, pp. 518–38); and Bradford A. Morgan, "T's Maine Woods: Transcendental Traveler in a Primordial Landscape" (Univ. of Denver, Ph.D., 1978).

For T's interest in the Indian, see Robert Sayre, *T and the Amer-*

*ican Indian* (Princeton, 1977). Another close study is Joan S. Gimlin, "HT and the American Indian" (George Washington Univ., Ph.D., 1974). For discussions of T's use of Indians in *Maine Woods*, see Philip F. Gura, "T's Maine Woods Indians: More Representative Men" *(AL,* 49, 1977, 366–84), and Donald M. Murray, "T's Indians and His Developing Art of Characterization" *(ESQ,* 21, 1975, 222–29). Lauriat Lane, "T's Autumnal Indian" *(CRevAS,* 6, 1975, 228–36), links T's descriptions of Indians to autumn. Leslie A. Fiedler, *The Return of the Vanishing American* (New York, 1968), includes discussions of Indians in *A Week*. See also the studies listed in the Sources for Chapter Three on T's sources in Indian literature. For a detailed study of T's views on another ethnic group—the Irish—see George E. Ryan, "Shanties and Shiftlessness: The Immigrant Irish of HT" *(Eire,* 13, 1978, 54–78.

The most detailed published discussion of T's educational views is Louis B. Salomon, "The Straight-Cut Ditch: T on Education" *(AQ,* 14, 1962, 19–36). Two other useful overviews are Kevin Ryan, "HDT: Critic, Theorist, and Practitioner of Education" *(School Rev.,* 77, 1969, 54–63), and Abraham Blinderman, *American Writers on Education before 1865* (Boston, 1975, pp. 147–50). For a discussion of T's own teaching experiences, see Walter Harding, "HDT, Instructor," *Educational Forum* (29, 1964, 89–97). The most thorough discussion of T's educational theories is Anton M. Huffert, "T as a Teacher, Lecturer, and Educational Thinker" (New York Univ., Ph.D., 1951).

T's views of love, sex, and friendship are described in James Armstrong, "T as Philosopher of Love," in Walter Harding, ed., *HDT: A Profile* (New York, 1971), pp. 222–43); see also Joel Porte, "T on Love: A Lexicon of Hate" *(University Review,* 31, 1964, 111–16). Mary Elkins Moller, "T, Womankind and Sexuality" *(ESQ,* 22, 1976, 122–48), argues that T eventually did acknowledge his own sexuality. Charles R. Anderson, T's Monastic Vows" *(EA,* 22, 1969, 11–20), discusses the chastity passage in "Higher Laws."

For T's views on death, see Mary Elkins Moller, " 'You must First Have Lived': T and the Problem of Death" *(ESQ,* 23, 1977, 226–39), who argues that T had ambivalent ideas about death. T is discussed along with a number of other writers in Thomas G. Couser, "The Shape of Death in American Autobiography" *(HudR,* 31, 1978, 53–66).

# 5.

# Thoreau's Art

The year before Thoreau turned forty, he reaffirmed a belief he held since his early twenties that "My work is writing" (J, IX, 121). He considered his vocation to be writing, and he addressed himself to it with high seriousness. He did so even though he was unable to support himself on the money he earned with his pen. For Thoreau, writing was the fruit of his experiences as well as the grounds for further growth, and he could no more turn away from the literary expressions his life yielded than from life itself.

Thoreau "require[ed] of every writer, first or last, a simple and sincere account of his own life" *(Walden,* PE, 3). He insisted upon this because "He is the truest artist whose life is his material" (J, I, 149). Truth, beauty, and goodness could never be adequately expressed unless they were first lived by the artist who sought to give expression to them. The insights that a writer would present to his reader must be generated from the life he had lived if they were to be convincing. "The theme," he wrote, "is nothing, the life is everything. All that interests the reader is the depth and intensity of the life excited" (J, IX, 121). Thoreau tended to equate life with art. His heroes—"John Brown, Nathaniel Rogers, Wendell Phillips,

Walter Raleigh—all were men in whom the deed became word. In the tributes which he wrote to these men, Thoreau emphasized the quality of their expression, viewing it as inseparable from their acts" (Wendell Glick, "Go Tell It on the Mountain: Thoreau's Vocation as a Writer," p. 166). For Emerson life was a dictionary, a resource; for Thoreau life was an art in itself. If the life that was lived was worthwhile and meaningful, it would yield a universal or mythic significance. Indeed, Thoreau suggests that "The real facts of a poet's life would be of more value to us than any work of his art" (J, X, 131). Given this view, it is not difficult to understand why he wrote journals rather than novels. This attitude may also provide one reason why Thoreau never became an innovative poet like Whitman (quite apart from reasons having to do with their respective talents): "My life hath been the poem I would have writ,/But I could not both live and live to utter it" (J, I, 275). Life, however, did not entirely absorb his art.

Especially in *Walden,* Thoreau both lived and uttered his poem. In the final chapter of that book he provides us with a parable that serves as a succinct gloss on the book, his life, and his attitudes toward art. He tells the story of the artist of Kouroo, an artist who, like Thoreau, was committed to his vocation regardless of the consequences. The artist's commitment to his vocation transforms his very life into an immortal work of art. The work of art he creates—a staff—is relatively unimportant; what is important is the deliberate process to which he devotes himself, a process that his art beautifully expresses. In the parable, if Thoreau's name is substituted for the artist of Kouroo's and if Thoreau's life and prose, particularly *Walden,* are substituted for the artist's staff, then the story clearly illuminates the Transcendental values Thoreau invokes to unite his life with his art. The story is not only illuminating but is also a wonderful expression of the faith, deliberateness, and determination that characterizes Thoreau's life and writings. It is worth quoting in full:

> There was an artist in the city of Kouroo who was disposed to strive after perfection. One day it came into his mind to make a staff. Having considered that in an imperfect work time is an ingredient, but into a perfect

work time does not enter, he said to himself, It shall be perfect in all respects, though I should do nothing else in my life. He proceeded instantly to the forest for wood, being resolved that it should not be made of unsuitable material; and as he searched for and rejected stick after stick, his friends gradually deserted him, for they grew old in their works and died, but he grew not older by a moment. His singleness of purpose and resolution, and his elevated piety, endowed him, without his knowledge, with perennial youth. As he made no compromise with Time, Time kept out of his way, and only sighed at a distance because he could not overcome him. Before he had found a stock in all respects suitable the city of Kouroo was in a hoary ruin, and he sat on one of its mounds to peel the stick. Before he had given it the proper shape the dynasty of Candahars was at an end, and with the point of the stick he wrote the name of the last of that race in the sand, and then resumed his work. By the time he had smoothed and polished the staff Kalpa was no longer the pole-star; and ere he had put on the ferule and the head adorned with precious stones, Brahma had awoke and slumbered many times. But why do I stay to mention these things? When the finishing stroke was put to his work, it suddenly expanded before the eyes of the astonished artist into the fairest of all the creations of Brahma. He had made a new system in making a staff, a world with full and fair proportions; in which, though the old cities and dynasties had passed away, fairer and more glorious ones had taken their places. And now he saw by the heap of shavings still fresh at his feet, that, for him and his work, the former lapse of time had been an illusion, and that no more time had elapsed than is required for a single scintillation from the brain of Brahma to fall on and inflame the tinder of a mortal brain. The material was pure, and his art was pure; how could the result be other than wonderful? (PE, 326–27)

By creating a "new system," by establishing an original relationship to the universe, the artist builds his own permanent world
while lesser worlds collapse and disappear. The disciplined commitment "to strive after perfection" allows the artist to transcend
his own circumstances and all of history. Ultimately, what the
artist creates is not only art but his own infinite identity. Art then
becomes an expression of that infinite identity as well as a means
by which it is achieved.

For Thoreau the great work of art grew out of the great life, a
poetic life. He was fond of describing his life as a poem, but the
great works he wrote were in prose rather than in poetry. For all
his comments on poetry, he tends to discuss it not as a particular
form or genre of literature but as a kind of inspired literature that
allows us a glimpse of the spiritual. Despite the frequent praise he
conferred upon verse, he doubted its ability to sustain as high a
level of thought as prose. In *A Week* he wrote that:

> Great prose of equal elevation, commands our respect
> more than verse, since it implies a more permanent and
> level height, a life more pervaded with the grandeur of
> the thought. The poet often only makes an irruption, like
> a Parthian, and is off again shooting while he retreats;
> but the prose writer has conquered like a Roman, and
> settled colonies. (W, I, 365)

Thoreau was more at home with prose because it was there that he
was able to settle into the detailed factual reality that characterizes
his prose, where "Nature gets thumbed like an old spelling-book"
(J, XI, 274). It is in his prose that "we come to a hard bottom and
rocks in place, which we can call *reality*" (*Walden,* PE, 98). It is
upon this foundation that his literary art is built.

It is almost universally agreed that Thoreau is America's greatest nature writer. It was as a nature writer that he first achieved
fame, and that distinction has remained a significant part of his
reputation. Thoreau had an important influence on the development of the natural history essay. He was "the first of the American writers upon Nature to be concerned with the workmanship of

his product" (Philip M. Hicks, *The Development of the Natural History Essay in American Literature,* p. 88); that is, the first to realize that the natural history essay could be something more than a mere reporting of natural phenomena observed, that it could in fact be a type of belles lettres. He was the first to make the natural history essay "a definite, and separate, literary form as contrasted to the 'Letters' of White and Crèvecoeur, the 'Episodes' of Audubon, the 'Rambles' of Godman, and the various 'Journals' and 'Travels' of earlier writers" (Hicks, pp. 88–89). He established the pattern that most nature writers since his day have followed.

But there are certain characteristics of Thoreau's nature writing that neither his predecessors nor his imitators have ever succeeded in duplicating. He gives his readers a unique sense of immediacy, because he places himself so totally in what he describes. His writing is therefore more intense owing to all of his senses being used to convey what he describes. The richness of his nature writing is the result of his seasoned intimacy with his environment. It is difficult to read very many of Thoreau's descriptions of nature without feeling an urge to go for a walk in the woods.

What makes his nature writing so moving is not only his close observations of nature but also his style. His sensitivity to language serves him whether he is reflecting on autumnal tints, recounting episodes in his life at the pond, exploring philosophical issues, satirizing his neighbors, inveighing against slavery, or championing the heroism of John Brown. His writing "ranges from the lyrical and aspirative to impassioned incisiveness; from mystical transcendentalism to whimsical humor; from description and narration to dramatic action; from poetically evocative writing to cool, meditative monologues" (Reginald Cook, *Passage to Walden,* p. 226). The stylistic qualities that inform his range are particularly appropriate for a writer who steeped himself in nature but who also sought to "look through and beyond her" (J, V, 45).

*     *     *

Thoreau's efforts to have his readers perceive the world freshly are informed by his remarkable and repeated use of figures of speech, which are an important feature of his style. This was his primary means of enabling his readers to move beyond the details he describes to meanings. His reliance upon the full range of figures of speech for special meanings and effects significantly contributes to his success as a writer. Walter Harding (*The Variorum Walden*, pp. xviii–xix) has listed representative examples of some of the figurative language to be found in *Walden*; they include:

> allusions ("twelve labors of Hercules"), metaphors ("No time to be anything but a machine"), rhetorical questions ("Does any divinity stir within him?"), alliteration ("fetch fresh fuel"), analogy ("Man's body is a stove"), puns ("cooked ... *à la mode*"), epanorthosis ("more and richer food, larger and more splendid houses, fine and more abundant clothing"), archaisms ("vert"), parables (about the Indian selling his basket), similes ("grew like exogenous plants"), meiosis ("Not being the owner, but merely a squatter"), anti-strophe ("Men are not so much the keepers of herds as herds are the keepers of men"), oxymoron ("pious slave-breeder"), epizeuxis ("Simplicity, simplicity, simplicity"), anaphora ("one man ... one house ... one vessel"), litotes ("Yet not a few ..."), antithesis ("Why so seeming fast, but deadly slow?"), portmanteau words ("realometer"), metonomy ("My head is hands and feet"), contrast ("Their train of clouds ... going to heaven while the cars are going to Boston"), onomatopoeia ("tr-r-r-oonk"), paradox ("I have a great deal of company in my house; especially in the morning, when nobody calls"), personification ("an elderly dame [nature], too, dwells in my neighborhood"), epistrophe ("This is the house that I built; this is the man that lives in the house that I built"), synecdoche ("asks the black bonnet of the gray coat"), irony ("I felt proud to know that the liberties of Massachusetts and of our father land were in such safe keeping"), apostrophe ("Walden, is it you?"), and hyperbole ("I could sometimes eat a fried rat with a good relish").

It is Thoreau's rich use of figurative language that renders paraphrases of his writings so flat and fundamentally different from the original.

One of the most notable characteristics of Thoreau's style is the concreteness of his diction. Abstractness, abstruseness, and often vapidness were altogether too frequently characteristics of his fellow Transcendentalists' styles—even that of Emerson. But Thoreau's use of language was forceful, direct, and vigorous. For him "The *art* of composition is as simple as the discharge of a bullet from a rifle" ("The Last Days of John Brown," PE, 150–51). The details of the physical world do not evaporate under Thoreau's pen. He typically draws meanings from experience, but he tends to keep the experience in the foreground instead of abandoning it for a generalization. He entitled his most important work *Walden,* not *Nature.* As Albert Gilman and Roger Brown have demonstrated in a comparison of Thoreau's and Emerson's styles, "Thoreau gives us a world well-differentiated, the experience of concrete particulars. Emerson gives us a world processed by abstraction with similarities seen everywhere. It is the difference really between a bean patch and the Over-Soul" ("Personality and Style in Concord" in *Transcendentalism and Its Legacy,* p. 91).

Unlike Thoreau, Emerson never seems to get his shoes muddy. Emerson acknowledged this difference himself in an insightful journal entry for June, 1863. A little more than one year after Thoreau's death he wrote:

> In reading Henry Thoreau's journal, I am very sensible of the vigor of his constitution. That oaken strength which I noted whenever he walked, or worked, or surveyed woodlots, the same unhesitating hand with which a field-laborer accosts a piece of work, which I should shun as a waste of strength, Henry shows in his literary task. He has muscle, and ventures on and performs feats which I am forced to decline. In reading him, I find the same thought, the same spirit that is in me, but he takes a step beyond, and illustrates by excellent images that which I should have conveyed in a sleepy generality.

This vivid passage almost belies the point that Emerson makes, but in general he is correct in distinguishing Thoreau's prose from his own for its straightforward strength and vigor. Although Thoreau was fully capable of writing sleepy generalities, such abstractions are more characteristic of his earliest writings when he was still learning his craft.

Thoreau worked to improve his writing all of his adult life. He knew "How hard one must work to acquire his language,—words by which to express himself!" (J, XI, 137). His education at Harvard provided him with a disciplined beginning as a writer, but he found that the requirements of his art took him beyond academic discipline: "When I read some of the rules for speaking and writing the English language correctly,—as that a sentence must never end with a particle,—and perceive how implicitly even the learned obey it, I think—

> Any fool can make a rule
> And every fool will mind it." (J, XIII, 125)

He insisted that "the first requisite and rule [of grammar] is that expression shall be vital and natural" (J, XI, 386). He rejected arbitrary rules about writing almost as vehemently as he did unjust civil laws; as in all things, he valued freedom and individuality in language.

Although Thoreau admired classical languages, he also saw the importance of continually revitalizing the English language and acknowledging its living, changing nature. He appreciated the colloquial as well as the classic, and if it came down to a choice he preferred life and energy in language over linguistic precedent. Naturalness and simplicity were qualities he found in the homely expressions of everyday language. He praised the "strong, coarse, homely speech which cannot always be found in the dictionary, nor sometimes be heard in polite society, but which brings you very near to the thing itself described" (J, VII, 109). Thoreau found more of value in the simple expressions he heard in talks with some farmers than in the kind of scholarly writing that studied nature but did not evoke any of its truths (J, I, 237). If a person knew something intimately, the language would come naturally enough. Affection had a way of betraying the quality of an experience as well as the style that presented the experience: "I like better the surliness with which the woodchopper speaks of his woods, handling them as indifferently as his axe, than the mealy-mouthed enthusiasm of the lover of nature" (J, I, 237). Good expression was earned expression.

Thoreau believed that working with his hands was an effective means of working on his style. Manual labor reminded him of the importance of getting the job done—saying what he wanted to say without excessive "flourishes." Physical labor was "the best method to remove palaver out of one's style," because such work required economy and purpose. There was no time for the self-conscious excesses produced by writers who had more time on their hands than ideas in their heads. Thoreau's prescription for such writers—particularly politicians and scholars—was a healthy dose of work outdoors. He was often "astonished at the force and precision of style to which busy laboring men, unpracticed in writing, easily attain when they are required to make the effort. It seems as if their sincerity and plainness were the main thing to be taught in schools,—and yet not in the schools, but in the fields, in actual service, I should say" (J, I, 312–13). He understood very well that one could learn to write but that no one could be taught to write.

Thoreau believed that a true artist writes as deliberately as he lives: "The best you can write will be the best you are" (J, I, 225–26). The deeper one's experiences are, the truer one's art will be. In contrast to this is the "writer who does not speak out of a full experience" but who instead "uses torpid words, wooden or lifeless words, such as 'humanitary,' which have a paralysis in their tails" (J, IV, 225). As Thoreau demonstrates in *Walden,* the truth that a writer would convey must be lived before it can be adequately expressed.

\*    \*    \*

The range of Thoreau's vocabulary is impressively broad. He moves easily from colloquialisms to scientific and technical words, from localisms to learned or poetic words. He loved homely, down-to-earth phrases such as "finger-cold," "a jag of wood," "apple-pie order," and "full of the devil." He felt no need to apologize for using the language he heard daily, because it rang true in his ear, an ear attuned to listening for words as signs of natural facts, which in turn were symbols of spiritual facts. Since local natural facts were as much manifestations of the spiritual truths latent in nature as any exotic or remote location, the language used to describe those local natural facts should be related to the immediate environment. Thoreau had little patience with writers who fastidiously avoided "Americanisms" in favor of more established and respectable forms of expression.

> Talk about learning our *letters* and being *literate!* Why, the roots of *letters* are *things*. Natural objects and phenomena are the original symbols or types which express our thoughts and feelings, and yet American scholars having little or no root in the soil, commonly strive with all their might to confine themselves to the imported symbols alone. All the true growth and experience, the living speech, they would fain reject as "Americanisms."
> (J, XII, 389–90)

Thoreau complained that it made no more sense to describe the winding course of the Concord River (originally called the Musketaquid by the Indians) as "meandering" than it would to describe the Meander as "musketaquidding" (J, XII, 390). The relationship between a word and what it described was vitally important to Thoreau, because it had so much to do with the natural expression and integrity he sought to achieve in his writings and life.

Thoreau's affinity for Indian words is an indication of his determination to express himself in language rooted in native soil. He referred to the "muskrat" as "musquash" and wished that Lakeville, Massachusetts, had been named "Assawampsett" or "Sanacus" (J, VIII, 395). His writings are also at home with other words associated primarily with American usage: "clapboards," "baking-kettle," "dinner-horn," "dry goods store," and "poverty-grass" represent merely a handful of them. The Harvard graduate familiar with highly formal writing was also comfortable with colloquialisms such as "tip-top" and "kittlybenders" (the latter term referring to the sport of running over thin bending ice). Not surprisingly, the dialect and localisms that appear in his writings are predominantly those of New England; he chose "angle-worm" for "earthworm" and "devil's needle" for "dragon fly." Although Thoreau regularly employed Americanisms, he did not, like Whitman, attempt to "speak as an American whose home was the entire country." "The American experience in such encompassing terms is never Thoreau's method or mood. At no time does he relinquish the character of a New Englander, the Yankee with his own outlook on life" (Francis E. B. Evans, "The Genuine Word, the Unfolding Sentence: Thoreau's Paths to Truths," p. 88). His identity was linked more to his region than to the nation.

Thoreau's respect for simple, common, and colorful regional language did not inhibit, however, his use of formal, learned words or the scientific terms that reflected his reading. Many readers may feel themselves transported to New England by Thoreau's writings, but perhaps as many have been driven to the dictionary by his use of words such as "sempiternal," "fuscous," "susurrus," "crepusculum," "deliquium," "periplus," "sesquipedalian," "stertorous," "corymb," and "umbelliferous." Thoreau's homely language is sometimes accompanied with difficulties. Moreover, his admiration for down-to-earth phrases did not prevent him from an occasional tendency to use archaic and poetic forms such as "fain," "methinks," "drear," "erelong," "wot," "clomb," and "blowed." And if Thoreau did not find the right word he was looking for in one of the twenty-nine dictionaries and grammars in his personal library, he invented what he needed, whether it was the "moosey" Maine woods or the sound of a loon "looning." He was confident that "intimate knowledge, a deeper experience, will surely originate a word" (J, XII, 390).

Sometimes Thoreau studied words almost as carefully as he examined the woods of Concord, and he made happy discoveries in his word studies just as he did in the woods. He found, for example, that the etymological roots of words nourished their true meanings: "The value of these wild fruits," he wrote, "is not in the mere possession or eating of them, but in the sight or enjoyment of them. The very derivation of the word 'fruit' would suggest this. It is from the Latin *fructus*, meaning that which is *used* or *enjoyed.*" The original Latin root meaning of the word brought him closer to the experience itself—closer to nature, closer to truth. "If it were not so, then going a-berrying and going to market would be nearly synonymous expressions" (J, XIV, 273). Even a variant spelling of a word might yield an insight for a sensitive reader seeking analogies between words and what they describe. Finding in "old books" the word "savages" spelled with an "l" as "salvages," Thoreau felt as if he were "in a wilder country" and closer to "primitive times," because "salvages" reminds him of "the derivation from the word *sylva.* There is some of the wild wood and its bristling branches still left in their langauge. The savages they described are really *salvages,* men of the *woods*" (J, IV, 494). For Thoreau, language itself was a means of discovering truth as well as expressing it.

"Sky water." That is the shortest sentence in *Walden* (PE, 188), and if there are any shorter in all of Thoreau's writing it would not be by much. But there are also very long sentences in *Walden;* one goes for more than 350 words and contains 40 commas, 10 semicolons, and 1 dash (PE, 243–44). Most of Thoreau's sentences do not, of course, resemble these extremes, but the examples do indicate that his sentences, like his vocabulary, are flexible and varied.

If words were at the root of Thoreau's thought, his sentences bore the fruits and seeds. Most critics who have written about his style have commented on the striking quality of his sentences. Even Lowell, who found plenty in Thoreau's writings that he did not like, conceded that "There are sentences of his as perfect as anything in the language." Reginald Cook praised Thoreau as "essentially an aphorist whose unit of writing was the epigrammatic sentence." This categorization of Thoreau as an aphorist may leave the mistaken impression that he was unsuccessful in creating larger units of prose, but Cook's description of why Thoreau's sentences are successful certainly rings true. "Most of his sentences," wrote Cook, are "direct, incisive, spiny, and sanguine, the product of sturdy, keen, affirmative intellection" *(Passage to Walden,* pp. 220–21). All that is needed to confirm Cook's assessment (and the many commentators who in one way or another have made similar statements before and after him) is a quick glance at one of the numerous dictionaries of quotations in which Thoreau is cited for such sentences as: "The mass of men lead lives of quiet desperation"; "Beware of all enterprises that require new clothes"; "We do not ride upon the railroad; it rides upon us"; "I think that we should be men first and subjects afterward"; "Any man more right than his neighbor constitutes a majority of one"; "Some circumstantial evidence is very strong, as when you find a trout in the milk"; and the ubiquitous "If a man does not keep pace with his companions, perhaps it is because he hears a different drummer." Many of Thoreau's sentences are eminently quotable, and they are, therefore, memorable—an effect that was one of his intentions.

The comments Thoreau made about sentence writing emphasize his concern with what is written rather than how it is written. He was not interested in analyzing a sentence in order to determine "if it is long or short, simple or compound, and how many clauses it is composed of"; nor was he interested in assigning it a "place among the sentences you have seen and kept specimens of." He insisted upon focusing on the "meaning of the sentence," because "if you should ever perceive the meaning you would disregard all the rest" (J, XII, 372). This preference for content over form, though it represents Thoreau's ultimate concern in his search for spiritual truths, did not mean, however, that he paid no attention to the form his ideas took.

Thoreau placed a premium upon both the conciseness of a sentence and its suggestiveness. Sentences should be "concentrated and nutty" if they embody truth, and they should "suggest far more than they say [like nature itself]." They should "have an atmosphere about them" so that they "do not merely report an old, but make a new, impression." "That," according to Thoreau, "is the *art* of writing" (J, II, 418). The sentence that transcended itself—by containing the seed of other sentences, or perhaps a chapter, or even an entire volume—was a successful sentence, because it promised a rich harvest of thought: "A well-built sentence, in the rapidity and force with which it works, may be compared to a modern corn planter, which furrows out, drops the seed, and covers it up at one movement" (J, I, 313). Effective sentences, then, were seminal; they were kernels of thought that could generate an individual's growth. For Thoreau, a good sentence was both the fruit of its author's thought and the seed of its reader's new perceptions.

\* \* \*

James Russell Lowell's assertion in 1865 that "Thoreau had no humor" represents a significant misreading of his prose. One of the important elements of Thoreau's style that sensitive readers have always delighted in is his use of humor. To appreciate his humor, it is necessary to recognize the serious playfulness that characterizes Thoreau's use of language. It is a mistake to read him too literally; instead, it is often necessary to penetrate the surface of his prose to understand what he is saying. That is not to argue, however, that Thoreau's prose must be decoded, that we must read between the lines (there is only space there), but it is to say, as he did, that his works must be read deliberately if they are to be read well.

A frequent tribute made about Thoreau's writing is that it seems to improve with each reading, but what has improved, of course, is the reader's sensitivity to Thoreau's style. Those who read him literally never read him twice, because they cannot appreciate his use of puns, understatement, exaggeration, irony, paradox, satire, parody, or his sheer whimsicality. Thoreau's English biographer, Henry Salt, well understood the nature of his problem: "The dangers and demerits of a paradoxical style are sufficiently obvious; and no writer has ever been less careful than Thoreau to safeguard himself against misunderstandings on this score. He has consequently been much misunderstood, and will always be so, save where the reader brings to his task a certain amount of sympathy and kindred sense of humor" (*The Life of Henry D. Thoreau*, p. 263).

Thoreau's comments concerning "Thomas Carlyle and His Works" suggest some of his own reasons for his use of humor and help characterize his own prose: "We should omit a main attraction in these books, if we said nothing of their humor." Humor is an "indispensable pledge of sanity." Without it, "the abstruse thinker may justly be suspected of mysticism, fanaticism, or insanity." Thoreau recognized that "transcendental philosophy needs the leaven of humor to render it light and digestible" (PE, 235). He goes on to suggest the corrective function of his own satire when he explains that "To the thinker, all the institutions of men, as all imperfection, viewed from the point of equanimity, are legitimate subjects of humor" (PE, 236). Thoreau's humor, like Carlyle's, usually had a serious purpose behind it.

As J. Golden Taylor has pointed out, "Humor is a natural and indispensable device of the social critic; historically it has often served to make memorable the critic's denunciations of social follies. A skillful blending of humor almost guarantees against didacticism or sentimentality and gives resiliency and balance. Thoreau particularly would have been at a loss without it" *(Neighbor Thoreau's Critical Humor,* p. 10). Consider, for example, how Thoreau manages in *Walden* to charm the reader into accepting his rigorous simplicity when he rejects a ride in a luxurious railroad car: "I would rather sit on a pumpkin and have it all to myself, than be crowded on a velvet cushion. I would rather ride on earth in an ox cart with a free circulation, than go to heaven in the fancy car of an excursion train and breathe a *malaria* all the way" (PE, 37). A pumpkin and an ox cart? Without the wit in this passage Thoreau's announced preferences would appear to be little more than cranky and eccentric, but the humor clears the air (the bad air of *malaria*) and wins the reader over so that there is at least a free circulation of ideas instead of the reader feeling crowded out by Thoreau's assertions. It is difficult not to feel some affection for so engaging a writer, even though one might disagree with him after reflecting at length upon the hard surfaces of a rounded pumpkin and a bumpy ox cart.

Thoreau employs his comic effects for the serious purpose of encouraging his readers to question the assumptions by which they live. Conventional beliefs are his broadest targets. Here are several examples from *Walden*—on a faith in progress: "We are in great haste to construct a magnetic telegraph from Maine to Texas; but Maine and Texas, it may be, have nothing important to communicate" (PE, 52); on the work ethic: "It is not necessary that a man should earn his living by the sweat of his brow, unless he sweats easier than I do" (PE, 71); on clothing fashions: "We know but few

men, a great many coats and breeches" (PE, 22). Each of these is in
its own way slightly startling because it forces us to reexamine our
assumptions critically.

A central element of Thoreau's verbal wit is his use of wordplay,
a usage related to his fascination with the etymologies of words.
His "puns drive to the radical meanings of things" (Paul, *The
Shores of America*, p. 148): three streets in a village render it "trivial"; "parlors" are for *"parlaver";* a "Nilometer" measures nothing
(as well as a river); the "extravagant" should be "extra vagant."
Often Thoreau's wordplay relies upon the juxtaposition of the
same sounds or multiple meanings of words rather than etymologies: one's belongings, "trappings," become "traps"; an unsuccessful fisherman "belonged to the ancient sect of Coenobites";
Thoreau's "accounts" refer to his personal economy, his journal,
and the writing of *Walden.* Although his puns are occasionally employed to evoke a simple chuckle for those of his readers who, for
instance, belong to the ancient order of "see-no-bites," Thoreau's
humor is characteristically used to evoke a thought as well as a
smile. His use of humor turns out to be strategic, "a way of seeing
two things at once, steadily and clearly. Comedy compares this
with that; it measures human pretensions against human behavior,
human actualities against human possibilities. For Thoreau it is a
way of measuring accurately and fully the ludicrous disparities of
life in Concord in the middle of the nineteenth century" (Edward
L. Galligan, "The Comedian at Walden Pond," p. 37).

Thoreau's fondness for paradox is related to his strategic use of
humor. He frequently employs a paradoxical style (even though
Thoreau criticizes that style in his own writing [J, VI, 165; VII, 7–
8]) to force a reorientation in his readers so that they take a spiritual rather than simply a material view of themselves and their
world. In order to understand what his paradoxes mean it is sometimes necessary to adopt literally his point of view. By adopting
Thoreau's perception, the reader is, in a sense, outmaneuvered by
Thoreau's rhetoric. For example, if a reader is to comprehend the
following passage by getting behind the irony and paradox that
make up its surface, then it is essential to put oneself in Thoreau's
shoes when he writes: "Almost all that my neighbors call good I
believe in my soul to be bad. If I repent of anything, it is of my

good behavior. What demon possessed me that I behave so well?"
(J, II, 137). The mental gymnastics that are necessary to understand why Thoreau "repents" his "good behavior" force the reader
to adopt, at least for the moment, Thoreau's assessment of his
discontented and quietly desperate neighbors. Joseph Moldenhauer has described the dynamics of Thoreau's strategic use of
paradox:

> He "translates" the reader, raising him out of his conven-
> tional frame of reference into a higher one, in which ex-
> treme truths become intelligible. To these ends Thoreau
> employs a rhetoric of powerful exaggeration, antithesis,
> and incongruity. Habitually aware of the "common
> sense," the dulled perception that desperate life produces,
> he could turn the world of his audience upside-down by
> rhetorical means. He . . . challenges ingrained habits of
> thought and action with ennobling alternatives: "Read
> not the Times," he exhorts in "Life Without Principle."
> "Read the Eternities." With all the features of his charac-
> teristic extravagance—hyperbole, wordplay, paradox,
> mock-heroics, loaded questions, and the ironic manipula-
> tion of cliché, proverb, and allusion—Thoreau urges new
> perspectives upon his reader. These rhetorical distortions
> or dislocations . . . are Thoreau's means of waking his
> neighbors up. They exasperate, provoke, tease, and ca-
> jole; they are the chanticleer's call for intellectual morn-
> ing. . . . ("Paradox in Walden," p. 76)

In Thoreau's political essays the call emphasizes not only intellectual morning but intellectual integrity. Thoreau's use of humor
is especially barbed in these essays, and the cuts go a little deeper
owing to his greater sense of urgency. Consider this parody of a
moderate stand on the slavery issue from "Slavery in Massachusetts":

> Do what you will, O Government! with my wife and
> children, my mother and brother, my father and sister, I
> will obey your commands to the letter. It will indeed

grieve me if you hurt them, if you deliver them to over-
seers to be hunted by hounds or to be whipped to death;
but, nevertheless, I will peaceably pursue my chosen calling on this fair earth, until perchance, one day, when I
have put on mourning for them dead, I shall have persuaded you to relent. (PE, 102)

By having a slave (in this case a slave to law) articulate a moderate's point of view, Thoreau renders absurd an argument that previously might have seemed quite reasonable to many readers.
More often than not in Thoreau's writing, if his readers get the
joke they also get the message.

*     *     *

As much as Thoreau was committed to writing as a vocation, he
did not develop a coherent or consistent set of principles dealing
with literary criticism. However, he did record many of his
thoughts about writing. These comments are not systematic or
original, though. He was more concerned with the practice rather
than with the theory of writing. "Thoreau's interest in technique
was normally limited to a concern with his own technique. When
he discusses other writers, his concern is more with emotional impact" (George Craig, "Literary Criticism in the Works of Henry
David Thoreau," p. 141). His judgments about books were centered primarily upon moral values rather than upon literary questions. "A truly good book," he believed, "attracts very little favor
to itself." Instead, a good book brings into focus its reader's response to it: "What I began by reading I must finish by acting" (J,
I, 216). This statement demonstrates that Thoreau was less concerned with how a book worked than that it worked. Moreover,
Thoreau had little to say about literary criticism because, according to Raymond Adams ("Henry Thoreau's Literary Theory and
Criticism"), Wordsworth, Coleridge, Carlyle, and the other early
romanticists had already so well formulated his ideas that he felt
no need of reexpressing them.
    Although he was not an original critical theorist,

Thoreau laid emphases where they had not been laid before. He worked out some of his critical dicta to lengths that had not been attempted hitherto. He was always running some theory down to its ultimate end.

For instance, no other transcendentalist stated the "labor doctrine" so forcefully or persistently, though virtually all transcendentalists held it. . . . No one else spoke so affectionately, so personally of Nature as the ally of the poet, though a hundred critics before Thoreau's time had considered nature as a source of inspiration. . . . Health may long have been the subject of those who sought in some measure to account for genius, but few critics have so consistently demanded health as a basis for true poetry. (Adams, pp. 166–67)

Some of Thoreau's ideas about writing seem to contradict his actual practices. For example, he criticizes a too heavy reliance upon humor, what he calls "getting the laugh" (J, VII, 8), but he employs humor in his most serious writings. Even in "The Last Days of John Brown," prepared for Brown's burial services, Thoreau includes a bit of a laugh when he complains that the Massachusetts legislature, instead of concerning itself with the issues produced by Brown's raid, was occupied with the "liquor-agency question, and indulging in poor jokes on the word 'extension.' " This rebuke does not prevent Thoreau, however, from writing in the next sentence that: "Bad spirits occupied their thoughts" (PE, 149).

To take another example, Thoreau describes the inspired writer as someone who passively accepts the truth that comes to him from God and serves as the medium for that truth: "the unconsciousness of man is the consciousness of God" (J, I, 119). This hardly characterizes Thoreau's typical methods of composition. "Unconsciousness" is not an accurate word to describe the careful and numerous revisions that transformed his field notes to journal entries, and then to lectures, after which they were further polished into essays. His many revisions amply confirm his own awareness that "Nothing goes by luck in composition. It allows of no tricks" (J, I, 225). Thoreau was no stranger to the agonies of reworking a draft over and over: "I wish that I could buy at the shops some kind of india-rubber that would rub out at once all that in my writing which it now costs me so many perusals, so many months if not years, and so much reluctance, to erase" (J, VI, 30). "For practical purposes," as Wade C. Thompson has noted, "Thoreau probably thought of his writing as a happy combination of inspiration and talent, unconscious and conscious work—both of them indispensable" ("The Aesthetic Theory of Henry David Thoreau," p. 8). Thoreau acknowledges this combination himself: "We must walk consciously only part way toward our goal, and then leap in the dark to our success. What we do best or most perfectly is what we have most thoroughly learned by the longest practice, and at length it falls from us without our notice, as a leaf from a tree" (J, XII, 39).

Thoreau's ideas about literature were heavily influenced by organic theories of art. He believed that a true work of art grew naturally from the artist's life and thoughts rather than that it was constructed artificially. A work grew from within outward; its form was inherent in the idea to be expressed and took shape as it grew. What gave form to a work was the character of the artist instead of an external set of literary traditions. The literary result of this organic growth may not yield an immediately recognizable form, but it represents a form nonetheless.

Given his faith in the inevitability of form growing out of the writer's thought, Thoreau apparently felt little need to discuss questions of literary form. "It is surprising," he wrote, "how much, from the habit of regarding writing as an accomplishment, is wasted on form" (J, X, 206). But though he did not discuss in any detail questions of literary form, he clearly was concerned with the problem of giving shape to his own ideas. Early critics of Thoreau's writing, however, frequently criticized him for the formlessness of his works. One of the most thoughtful of the earlier assessments that articulates this point of view is by Fred W. Lorch ("Thoreau and the Organic Principle in Poetry," p. 292):

The tendency toward formlessness inherent in romantic organic doctrine is apparent not only in much of Thoreau's own composition, but in his conception of art and poetry generally; for, though Thoreau points out the ne-

cessity of giving a discourse proper order and arrangement, it is obvious that form in the sense of structural
unity, based upon an harmonious relation of parts to the
whole and of the whole to its parts, was for him a distinctly secondary interest. For a confirmation of this
statement one needs only to remember the almost complete lack of such unity in Thoreau's two best-known
books, *A Week on the Concord and Merrimac Rivers* and *Walden*. In the construction of minor units Thoreau was a
master; but in the larger units he achieved, in the main,
only such unity as arises from a centrality of mood and
an attitude toward life rather than from structure.

In contrast to Lorch's view, much of the criticism on Thoreau
since F. O. Matthiessen's influential *American Renaissance* (1941) has
focused upon his literary craftsmanship and technique, especially
his ability to create unified structures through his use of imagery,
symbol, and myth. These studies have argued that Thoreau was
more than simply a master of the sentence; they argue that he was
a master of literary architectonics. In this context, it is worth noting that while Thoreau was working on the many revisions for
*Walden* he heard a lecture by Channing that he described as one of
the most original and inspired lectures he had ever heard, but
Thoreau also mentions that the lecture "was all genius, no talent,"
because he found it so difficult to follow the succession of powerful
ideas Channing presented. Thoreau reflects on "how much more
glorious" the lecture would have been "if talent were added to
genius" by way of a "just arrangement and development of the
thoughts" (J, III, 249). Thoreau's comments suggest his concern
for the need of a "just arrangement," a structure that would en-
hance rather than inadvertently inhibit the expression of an idea.
*Walden* reveals that Thoreau had in mind more than simply paragraph transitions.

*Walden* is, of course, Thoreau's undisputed masterpiece, and
most structural and organic studies focus upon it. Although, to cite
only two examples, Thoreau employed an overall structural device
in *A Week* by using the seven days of the week for chapter divisions
(even though the journey had actually taken two weeks), and al-

though in *Cape Cod* he unified three separate excursions into one narrative, it is in *Walden* that his structural devices are most integrated and successful.

Thoreau uses time as one means of unifying his experiences at the pond during the two years and two months he was there. He reduces the time to one complete year, thereby using the cycle of the seasons to trace symbolically his spiritual growth. A number of studies have followed Sherman Paul's brilliant discussion of structure in *Walden* (*The Shores of America*, pp. 323–53), but the most intensive reading of *Walden*'s structures is Charles R. Anderson's *The Magic Circle of Walden*, a study that reads Thoreau's book as a poem and "assume[s] that its meaning resides not in its logic but in its language, its structure of images, its symbolism—and is inseparable from them" (p. 17). Anderson's close reading attempts to establish definitively the structural integrity of *Walden;* his reading helps to measure some of the difference in critical approaches between earlier studies that complained of a lack of unity in Thoreau's writings and later ones that stress that Thoreau was a highly conscious artist:

> The overall structure of *Walden* may be likened to that of both a circle and a web. The spider's web is too geometric, but it will serve as a useful analogy to begin with. Walden Pond lies at the center as a symbol of the purity and harmony yearned for by man, though unattainable. Radial lines of wit run out from this, cutting across the attractions of the purely pragmatic or sensual life. And these radials are looped with circle after concentric circle of aspiration toward the ideal life of heaven—which is also mirrored in the central pond. But Thoreau was too much a poet to be content with a mechanical design. These figures—the spider's web and the formal Euclidian circle—are suggestive merely. Like the orientals he sought an asymmetrical pattern that would satisfy the esthetic sense of form and still remain true to the nature of experience, art without the appearance of artifice. (p. 18).

Anderson, unlike Lorch and the earlier generations of critics he represents, argues that there are not very many "works of the creative imagination [which] are more successfully unified" than *Walden* (p. 18).

*    *    *

One of the most-discussed unifying devices in Thoreau's writings is his use of symbolic imagery. Because nature presented itself to Thoreau as a universal language expressive of spiritual truths, he found it both desirable and necessary to use symbols in his writings. The belief that "whatever we see without is a symbol of something within" (J, III, 201) provided him with a method for his writing. His own Transcendental responses to nature created a need for him to use "nature as [the] raw material of tropes and symbols with which to describe his life" (J, V, 135). His works, he hoped, would be read as deliberately as nature itself. In *Walden,* he explains the reason for the necessity of such careful reading while at the same time slightly apologizing for it: "You will pardon some obscurities, for there are more secrets in my trade than in most men's, and yet not voluntarily kept, but inseparable from its very nature. I would gladly tell all that I know about it, and never paint 'No Admittance' on my gate" (PE, 17). Thoreau's writing is heavily metaphorical and symbolical, because such literary devices provided a means by which natural facts could refer to the spiritual. Immediately following this rationale for his use of symbol, Thoreau tells us in what has become a famous passage that he "long ago lost a hound, a bay horse, and a turtle-dove." These symbols have been variously interpreted (Walter Harding's *Variorum Walden* lists many of them, pp. 259–62), and these different interpretations serve to confirm Thoreau's symbolic methods, what he calls his "obscurities."

Far from obscuring his ideas, Thoreau's symbolic imagery is an effective method of expressing them. His Transcendental reflections frequently take the natural forms of the detailed world he describes, and they do so without distorting that world. Many of his ideas are symbolically expressed in images of natural phenomena such as the ponds, rivers, the seasons, the year, the day, the sun, the thaw, fire, ice, the wild, the West, flora and fauna, and various colors. This is the result of his environment, of course, but more importantly it is the result of the way he perceived the nature of language and the world. His imagery, like the phenomena it describes, is evocative of not only the local and the particular but also the universal. Hence, what Thoreau refers to in his writings as "obscurities" are actually latent meanings that patiently wait to be discovered by an alert reader.

Among the more pervasive images found in Thoreau's writing is water imagery. This imagery is used to describe processes of life and growth on a spiritual as well as a physical level. Like Melville, he knew that water was wedded to meditation. Nina Baym finds that:

> Water imagery occurs everywhere in Thoreau's work. It is expressed in images of rivers, brooks, lakes, marshes, waterfalls, rains, dews, and watery ditches. Water is the scene of many of his activities such as bathing, boating, fishing. The lengthy exploratory journeys around which many works are organized always proceed on, beside or towards water. Scarcely a single meditative passage in all the journals develops without employing water metaphors. In its pervasiveness, the image almost loses its character as image and becomes a habit of Thoreau's vocabulary. ("From Metaphysics to Metaphor," pp. 238–39)

This image is also characteristic of the flow of Thoreau's thoughts (the river of thought in *A Week,* for example) and evocative of the spirituality he finds circulating in the universe.

Another significant symbolic image that is found throughout much of Thoreau's writing is the circle. A passage from Thoreau's *Journal* illustrates his use of both water and circle imagery to convey a Transcendental idea:

> Pond.—Nature is constantly original and inventing new patterns, like a mechanic in his shop. ... All things, indeed, are subjected to a rotary motion, either gradual and partial or rapid and complete, from the planet and

system to the simplest shellfish and pebbles on the beach; as if all beauty resulted from an object turning on its own axis, or others turning about it. It establishes a new centre in the universe. As all curves have reference to their centres or foci, so all beauty of character has reference to the soul, and is a graceful gesture of recognition or waving of the body toward it. (J, I, 332)

This passage, along with scores of others, causes Charles Anderson to conclude that "Orbs, spheres, circular paths and flights, daily and seasonal cycles, orbiting stars and ripples on water—all these form an important part of Thoreau's subject matter and provide him with another way of looking at the world." The circular image "ranges from insects to the cosmos and is applied to a great variety of things: animals, plants, ponds, sights, sounds, people" *(The Magic Circle of Walden* p. 214). Although Anderson focuses primarily upon *Walden*, Richard Tuerk has extended this approach to include other works as well. He finds, for example, that "In *A Week* circles are everywhere: stars and planets rotate; wind and water circulate; circular objects dot the landscape; and parts of the landscape arrange themselves in ever-widening circles." These circles form patterns of meaning that help to provide "a momentary glimpse of the whole universe . . . to create visions of eternity and infinity" *(Central Still,* p. 38).

Perhaps the central point to be made concerning Thoreau's symbolic imagery is that it most often makes "reference to the soul" by way of his carefully recording an observed reality. Hence, whether he is recording his observations about water or seasons, celestial bodies or huckleberries, those observations often reflect both the material and the spiritual dimensions of his experience. "If you stand right fronting and face to face to a fact, you will see the sun glimmer on both its surfaces" *(Walden,* PE, 98). If one does not underestimate the value of facts in Thoreau's writings, the meanings surface easily enough. A number of recent detailed studies of his images have further revealed Thoreau's literary artistry. There is still room for more good ones.

One of the very few quantitative approaches to Thoreau's use of images is interesting owing to its suggestiveness. Having restricted his study to similes and metaphors in *Walden,* Richard C. Cook sorted them out in an effort to determine what subjects engaged Thoreau's imagination. By tabulating the images, Cook concluded that approximately "two-fifths of Thoreau's imagery in *Walden* involves nature." Except for the possibility that one might expect the percentage to be somewhat higher, this is not surprising. Among these images, however, he found that the most frequent images of the animal kingdom to appear are, in descending order, "birds, insects, natural habitats, wild quadrupeds, fish, and reptiles." Thoreau's images of the broader elements of nature listed in a descending order of frequency are "weather, water, sky and celestial bodies, land and natural features, and the seasons [including night and day]." Given New England weather, perhaps that is not unusual, but it is curious that "there are more images in *Walden* that involve birds than of any other single phenomenon—including weather—in the whole of Thoreau's nature imagery" ("Thoreau and His Imagery," p. 1). His interest in ornithology (as well as the ethereal nature of birds) helps to account for the frequency of bird imagery, but it is more difficult to explain why the most frequent images of any kind in *Walden* are about "the body and bodily actions. He seems to have been extraordinarily conscious of the metaphoric possibilities of the body, and especially of the face" (p. 2). Even more surprising is that in Thoreau's account of his retreat to the woods "there are more images concerning 1) ships and seafaring than land and natural features, 2) buildings than seasons, 3) music than vegetables, 4) war than fish, 5) jewels than farming, and 6) there are more images concerned with money than with gardening" (p. 2). Although Cook's study is very limited and somewhat subjective, it does suggest some of the interesting questions that *can* arise from a quantitative approach. Thoreau would scorn the idea, but there is at least the possibility that a judicious use of a computer in tactful hands might produce some worthwhile and interesting approaches to Thoreau's style. Such an approach probably would not produce any startling new answers, but it might generate some new questions about Thoreau's style and thereby improve our reading of him—so long as it did not become an improved means to an unimproved end.

\* \* \*

Critics have frequently noted that Transcendental writers had difficulty in creating wholes out of the parts of their works. Thoreau attempted to resolve that problem in some of his works by the use of myth to make "structure itself symbolic" (Sherman Paul, *The Shores of America,* p. 189). Thoreau's extensive use of myth, legend, and fable is evident to any reader who has scanned an annotated edition of *A Week* or *Walden.* (Although there are distinctions to be made among myth, legend, and fable, the term "myth" is used for all three in this discussion.) His frequent mythic allusions are there to extend the meaning of his own particular experiences so that we see them in a larger context. We are continually encouraged to see that his thought and actions have reference to universal experiences, reference, that is, to ourselves.

Although Thoreau wrote more about himself than anyone else, his literary purposes went beyond a simple autobiographical impulse in order to suggest that there were implications in his own story that were relevant to all people. "It is significant that Thoreau revised *Walden* in such a way as to make his own role somewhat less prominent than it is in the original version." Lawrence Buell, "comparing the first and last stages of chapters 1 through 8, which are the most complete in the original . . . sees that the most typical alterations are additions in allusions, literary anecdotes, illustrations, and general discussion" *(Literary Transcendentalism,* p. 309). Such revisions "show the Transcendentalist propensity for universalizing one's own experience" (p. 310). Myth was an important means of achieving that for Thoreau; he makes this clear both in his practice and in his comments about myth.

In a sense, myth, like nature, provided Thoreau with a universal language; they both served as texts of timeless spiritual values. In his efforts to apprehend the reality that surrounded him, Thoreau obviously valued nature above all, but myth also had a high purpose because it helped him to articulate the meanings he found in nature. He complained that he did "not know where to find in any literature, whether ancient or modern, any adequate account of that Nature with which I am acquainted." But, he concluded,

"Mythology comes nearest to it of any" (J, II, 152). Coming from a writer who read so widely about nature, this is high praise.

One use of myth for Thoreau was to provide him with universal models of behavior that would serve to establish a harmonious relationship with nature. Contemporary man had forgotten how to live, but mythology could recall him to his senses. References to myth allowed Thoreau to measure himself and his readers against timeless standards to which he believed we should aspire. His comments on farming in "The Bean-Field" chapter of *Walden* richly illustrate this:

> Ancient poetry and mythology suggest, at least, that husbandry was once a sacred art; but it is pursued with irreverent haste and heedlessness by us, our object being to have large farms and large crops merely. We have no festival, nor procession, nor ceremony, not excepting our Cattle-shows and so called Thanksgivings, by which the farmer expresses a sense of the sacredness of his calling, or is reminded of its sacred origin. It is the premium and the feast which tempt him. He sacrifices not to Ceres and the Terrestrial Jove, but to the infernal Plutus rather. By avarice and selfishness, and a grovelling habit, from which none of us is free, of regarding the soil as property, or the means of acquiring property chiefly, the landscape is deformed, husbandry is degraded with us, and the farmer leads the meanest of lives. He knows Nature but as a robber. Cato says that the profits of agriculture are particularly pious or just . . . and according to Varro the old Romans "called the same earth Mother and Ceres, and thought that they who cultivated it led a pious and useful life, and that they alone were left of the race of King Saturn." (PE, 166)

By invoking these "sacred origin[s]," Thoreau reminds us of what our relationship to the land could be and rebukes us for having degraded that relationship through commercial exploitation. Paradoxically, the use of myth helps us to see what is ultimately real. Thoreau was attached to myths as he was to nature because, Antaeus-like, he drew strength from them. He was strengthened on both an ethical and an artistic level by myth. This also can be seen in "The Bean-Field" chapter where he not only invokes myth but creates one through the "Herculean labor" of tending his beans. This mock-heroic humor does not undercut his serious intention to demonstrate that a harmonious relationship with the earth yields an "immeasurable crop." He was interested in creating his own myths as well as alluding to existing ones.

Thoreau found his primary source of mythmaking in his life close to nature. "Some incidents in my life have seemed far more allegorical than actual . . . they have been like myths or passages in a myth, rather than mere incidents or history which have to wait to become significant" (J, V, 203). He felt "serene and satisfied" at those times in his life "when the events of the day have a mythological character, and the most trivial is symbolical" (J, III, 438). He sometimes found nature itself to be mythopoeic: "If I am overflowing with life, am rich in experience for which I lack expression, then nature will be my language full of poetry—all nature will *fable,* and every natural phenomenon be a myth" (J, V, 135). But more often it was Thoreau himself who "would so state facts that they shall be significant, shall be myths or mythologic" (J, III, 99), for that was his task as a writer and the purpose of his art. He sought to present the universal meanings he discovered in nature through words that would themselves be universally meaningful, words that "may be translated into every language, and not only be read but actually breathed from all human lips;—not be represented on canvas or in marble only, but be carved out of the breath of life itself" *(Walden,* PE, 102). Such was his faith in written words when they took on the significance of the "mythologic" and awakened in readers a spiritual view of things.

Spiritual awakening was Thoreau's goal for himself and his readers. His most important literary effort in achieving these two goals is the story of his spiritual rebirth at the pond. "The skeleton plot of *Walden* is the archetypal monomyth of the hero's retreat from society, his initiation, and final return—as epitomized by Joseph Campbell [*The Hero with a Thousand Faces*]: 'A hero ventures forth from the world of common day into a region of supernatural wonder: fabulous forces are there encountered and a decisive victory is won: the hero comes back from this mysterious adventure with the power to bestow boons on his fellow men' " (Charles Anderson, *The Magic Circle of Walden*, pp. 260–61). The reductive nature of this description should not prohibit an appreciation of the accuracy of its basic outline. The details of Thoreau's writings were local and specific, but the "true cement" of his literary materials and thought was a mixture of his use of myth as well as his use of Concord: "The truth so told has the best advantages of the most abstract statement, for it is not the less universally applicable" (J, III, 334).

\*    \*    \*

In response to the intense efforts by many recent critics to find unifying structures in Thoreau's use of imagery, symbol, and myth, a number of sensitive readers of Thoreau have expressed a concern that such studies, though useful in demonstrating Thoreau's commitment to writing as a vocation, tend to overstate the structural unity to be found in his writings. Lawrence Buell, in a discussion of Thoreau's writings that places some of them in the context of nineteenth-century literary excursions and characterizes his mode of writing as "part sketch, part information, part narrative, part wit, [and] part philosophy," offers a thoughtful caveat concerning formalist readings of Thoreau in the last few decades. Buell observes that:

> the prevailing critical approach to Thoreau carries with it the somewhat misleading implication that literary architectonics was (or should have been) of immense concern to him. In fact, none of his books, not even *Walden*, is very tightly unified, nor probably designed to be, for the romantic excursion is as much a record of events and impressions as it is a poem. Even in the course of so analytical a work as *Walden*, there are all sorts of meanderings and digressions: the song the speaker sings when chopping timber, the length of the diatribe against philanthropy, the inclusion of the "complemental verses," and so forth. It is not that these passages bear no relation

to the overall drift of the book, but that their charm lies
more in their heterogeneity and unpredictableness than
in their contribution to an overarching whole. Like a
Whitman catalogue, Thoreau's writing is to be more appreciated as process than as product, more for its irregu-
lar flow than for any patterns which can be abstracted
from it, although the awareness of such patterns naturally enhances one's pleasure in the work. *(Literary Transcendentalism,* pp. 199–200)

Similarly, Buell argues that *"A Week* is best understood and appreciated when read as a series of epiphanies leading from one to
another by process of association, fitting here and there into larger
patterns, threading back and forth precariously between the infinite and the concrete" (p. 208). James McIntosh has also argued
that "though Thoreau revised and reordered continually, it would
be a mistake to conclude that his works are masterpieces of Byzan-
tine ingenuity, highly finished artistic wholes controlled by the
expert manipulation of structural and stylistic devices" *(Thoreau as
Romantic Naturalist,* p. 45). And Tony Tanner concludes after a
discussion of Thoreau's "sauntering eye" that journal writing "is
really Thoreau's perfect genre since it allows him to set down his
impression in random order; it caters generously for the impulse of
the moment" *(The Reign of Wonder,* pp. 59–60).

Although there are few, if any, contemporary critics who would
characterize Thoreau's writings as totally formless, debate nevertheless continues over the nature of the form that most accurately describes his work. The comments by readers such as Buell
and McIntosh serve as a useful reminder that Thoreau was a nineteenth-century writer rather than a prefiguration of Wallace Stevens. It is clear that modern critical approaches to Thoreau's
writings have enhanced our appreciation of his literary art, but
perhaps such approaches have in some instances exaggerated his
artistic achievements in their zeal to discover form and meaning
everywhere in his writings.

Occasionally, critical interpretations have reflected more upon
the critic's own ingeniousness than upon Thoreau's art. One such

example—an example cited for its resourcefulness as much for its extravagance—offers a reading of that much-interpreted passage in *Walden* where Thoreau describes his having lost a hound, bay horse, and turtle-dove. Approaching the key words in the passage as an anagram, the critic finds that the letters from "hound," "bay horse," and "turtle-dove" yield "Henry D. Thoreau" and, with the letters remaining, "love" and "doubt," plus an "s." From that follows a discussion of the possibilities of there being buried in the passage two readings: "Henry D. Thoreau Loves Doubt" or "Doubts Love." As it turns out, according to the critic, both are possible. The ingenuity of this reading is arresting, but when one reflects upon the appropriateness of reading Thoreau as if he were writing like Vladimir Nabokov, problems emerge. As the critic points out himself, the letters that remain after Thoreau's name are an anagram not only for "love" and "doubt" (plus "s") but also "devout slob." Furthermore, another more obvious possible anagram, which is not pointed out, is the title of the book; *Walden*, which curiously enough, yields "end law." But there is not a shred of evidence to support a claim that Thoreau saw, much less intended, the title or the passage as an anagram. The point of mentioning all this is to note that it is sometimes all too tempting and intriguing to find meaning and patterns in Thoreau's writing even when an approach is obviously inappropriate. The anagrams are there of course, but that does not mean that they were put there. Such a cryptographic approach reminds us that even a clock that has stopped is right twice a day. Thoreau's literary art represents the kind of solid achievement that does not require special pleading to make it significant.

\*     \*     \*

Thoreau's attitude toward the nonliterary arts was informed by his abiding concern with natural beauty rather than formal art. We can search in vain through Thoreau's writings for any extended comments on any of the great masterpieces of painting or sculpture. They were simply outside his ken. For Thoreau "the highest condition of art is artlessness" (J, I, 153), and he found more beauty in an inkblot than in a formal painting (J, I, 119). "The too exquisitely cultured" he avoided as he did the theater (J, IV, 154). He found beauty in reality rather than in its imitations. "What is a gallery in the house to a gallery in the streets!" Thoreau wrote. "I think that there is not a picture-gallery in the country which would be worth so much to us as is the western view under the elms of our main street" (J, XI, 220). He relied upon his own eye, his own perceptions of nature, to create art. Thoreau acknowledged that "It is something to be able to paint a particular picture, or to carve a statue, and so to make a few objects beautiful"; but he believed that "it is far more glorious to carve and paint the very atmosphere and medium through which we look, which morally we can do. To affect the quality of the day, that is the highest of arts" *(Walden,* PE, 90).

The plastic arts did appeal to him a little more than painting, however. He was impressed when he discovered an Indian stone pestle fashioned into the likeness of a bird. It convinced him that the Indian had "so far begun to leave behind him war, and even hunting, and to redeem himself from the savage state" (J, V, 526). But even sculpture, to meet his approval, had to be representative rather than abstract, and the more it was akin to nature, the greater its appeal for him (J, I, 380).

Painting and sculpture failed to move Thoreau because they seemed to him too far removed from the living art he daily experienced. He wanted to establish an intimacy with reality, and so he would not be satisfied with what he took to be a mere representation of it. His commitment to literary art makes clear the reservations he had concerning the arts. The "written word" was for him "something at once more intimate with us and more universal than any other work of art. It is the work of art nearest to life itself" *(Walden,* PE, 102).

Although Thoreau minimized the value of painting and sculpture, his response to music was intense. But, as one might expect, his lifelong interest in music and his frequent reference to various forms of it in his writings were more related to the music he found in nature than to the music of man: "One would think from reading the critics that music was intermittent as a spring in the desert, dependent on some Paganini or Mozart . . . but music is perpetual, and only hearing is intermittent" (J, IX, 245). "One will lose no music by not attending oratorios and operas" (J, II, 379). "I get my new experiences still, not at the opera listening to the Swedish Nightingale [Jenny Lind], but at Beck Stow's Swamp listening to the native wood thrush" (J, IX, 43). Thoreau's "new experiences" were of a Transcendental nature that suggested to him the harmony in the universe and provided yet another symbol of spiritual reality. Kenneth Rhoads has shown how Thoreau's writings reveal that his response to music ranged from the sensuous to the metaphysical. "Music was to him a stimulation to ecstasy and a medium for mystical union wherein he might gain momentary insight into the reality of the divine essence; it was truly transcendental in its nature and function" ("Thoreau: The Ear and the Music," p. 328). In the universal music of nature, God could be heard: "The prophane never hear music; the holy ever hear it. It is God's voice, the divine breath audible" (J, I, 154). Music was for Thoreau a sensuous means of evoking and experiencing the spiritual harmony that vibrated throughout his world.

In addition to music, Thoreau expressed a strong interest in architecture. But whereas music tended to represent a means to the spiritual, architecture represented a manifestation of it. Thoreau's views on architecture are directly related to his ideas about the necessities of life he describes in the "Economy" chapter of *Walden.* As he strove for simplicity and economy in his life, he strove for simplicity and economy in his art. His aesthetic approach to architecture was primarily functional. He demanded an organic functionalism so that the outside was an expression of the inside:

> What of architectural beauty I now see, I know has gradually grown from within outward, out of the necessities and character of the indweller, who is the only builder,— out of some unconscious truthfulness, and nobleness, without ever a thought for the appearance; . . . The most interesting dwellings in this country as the painter knows, are the most unpretending, humble log huts and cottages of the poor commonly; it is the life of the inhabitants

whose shells they are, and not any peculiarity in their surfaces merely, which makes them *picturesque. (Walden,* PE, 47)

Characteristically, Thoreau sought to penetrate the surfaces of things. Architectural form was important only to the extent that it was integrally related and subordinated to its function; hence, form followed function. Thoreau's injunction to "Grow your own house" (J, III, 183) is a telling one, for it suggests the intimate relationship he demanded between form and function.

Functional beauty—as opposed to mere ornamentation—Thoreau appreciated. The functional building, he thought, blended into its background. It was natural for him to suggest that "the architect take a hint from the pyramidal or conical form of the muskrat's house. . . . Something of this form and color, like a large haycock in the meadow, would be in harmony with the scenery" (J, IV, 423). The early American houses were "earth-loving"; they needed "no coping of bricks to catch the eye, no alto or basso relievo" (J, III, 34). In contrast, the Victorian house of Thoreau's own period, with its gingerbread ornamentation and sugarcoating, was offensive to his eye.

Thoreau's approach to architecture is in some respects remarkably similar to the modern ideas of Frank Lloyd Wright and Louis Sullivan. Theodore M. Brown has concluded that Thoreau anticipated a number of modern attitudes: he "framed an architectural program for the United States based upon minimum physical means and maximum human values. Thoreau called for a new domestic architecture, open, flexible, unencumbered, responsive to environment and human sensibility, a physical complement to the spiritual life within" ("Thoreau's Prophetic Architectural Program," p. 20).

\* \* \*

Thoreau's prose, like the man himself, is challenging. He would compromise his talent no more than he would his ideals. He did not write for those who would "vegetate and dissipate their faculties in what is called easy reading" *(Walden,* PE, 104). Though he has sometimes been accused of escaping to the woods, Thoreau never wrote escape literature, because his sense of vocation and high purpose insisted that his writings be provocative. He knew what he was about even if others did not; this is made clear in a letter to the Emersons (July, 8, 1843):

> In writing conversation should be folded many times thick. It is the height of art that on the first perusal plain common sense should appear—on the second severe truth—and on a third beauty—and having these warrants for its depth and reality, we may then enjoy the beauty forever more.

Thoreau's "depth and reality" have always been apparent to his most sensitive readers, and the many critical studies of his prose have explored that depth in detail. Thoreau, however, prepared himself for the worst: "It is enough if I please myself with writing; I am then sure of an audience" (J, I, 345). But the passage of time has indicated that as long as there are readers who admire first-rate prose, Thoreau will have an audience.

*Sources for Chapter Five*

The relationship between T's life and writing is explored most fully in Sherman Paul, *The Shores of America* (Urbana, 1958); see also Wendell Glick, "Go Tell It on the Mountain: T's Vocation as a Writer" (*ESQ,* 19, 1973, 161–69). Gabrielle M. Fitzgerald, "The Writer as Hero, the Writer as Contemplative: T's Divided Self-Image" (Northwestern Univ., Ph.D., 1977), argues that T's style reveals his ambivalent sense of himself as a writer. The autobiographical elements of T's writings are discussed in numerous studies of his work. One of the most helpful is Lawrence Buell, *Literary Transcendentalism: Style and Vision in the American Renaissance* (Ithaca, 1973, pp. 263–333), which discusses *Walden* in the context of a Transcendental autobiographical tradition. *Walden* is compared with *My Bondage and My Freedom* in William W. Nichols, "Individualism and Autobiographical Art: Frederick Douglass and HT"

*(CLAJ*, 16, 1972, 145–58). For T in the context of a modern tradition, see Earl B. Fendelman, "Toward a Third Voice: Autobiographical Form in T, Stein, Adams, and Mailer" (Yale Univ., Ph.D., 1971).

For T's influence on the development of the natural history essay, see Philip M. Hicks, *The Development of the Natural History Essay in American Literature* (Philadelphia, 1924); Richard E. Haymaker, "The Out-of-Door Essay," in his *From Pampas to Hedgerows and Downs: A Study of W. H. Hudson* (New York, 1954, pp. 45–84); and Reginald Cook, "Nature's Eye-Witness," in his *Passage to Walden* (1949; 2nd ed., New York, 1966, pp. 18–51). See also Kichung Kim, "T's Involvement with Nature: T and the Naturalist Tradition" (Univ. of California, Berkeley, Ph.D., 1969).

Walter Harding's representative list of T's figures of speech appears in his introduction to *The Variorum Walden* (New York, 1963). Stylistic differences between T and Emerson are discussed in Albert Gilman and Roger Brown, "Personality and Style in Concord," in Myron Simon and Thornton H. Parsons, eds., *Transcendentalism and Its Legacy* (Ann Arbor, 1966, pp. 87–122); and Donald Ross, Jr., "Emerson and T: A Comparison of Prose Styles" *(Lang&S*, 6, 1973, 185–95); see also his "Composition as a Stylistic Feature" *(Style*, 4, 1970, 1–10), for a linguistic analysis of some stylistic features of T, Emerson, and Carlyle. Francis E. B. Evans, "The Genuine Word, the Unfolding Sentence: T's Paths to Truths" (Purdue Univ., Ph.D., 1976), in addition to discussing T's vocabulary and sentences, includes four appendixes listing learned, scientific, poetic, and local words designed to suggest the range of T's vocabulary. Lee A. Pederson, "Americanisms in T's *Journal" (AL*, 37, 1965, 167–84), lists Americanisms not previously acknowledged by historical dictionaries.

T's efforts to invest his language with scriptural meanings are discussed in Stanley Cavell, *The Senses of Walden* (New York, 1972). Joseph J. Liggera, "T's Heroic Language" (Tufts Univ., Ph.D., 1971), examines T's attempts to create a poetic language expressive of the divinity he found in nature. Thomas Woodson, "T's Prose Style" (Yale Univ., Ph.D., 1963), describes some of the distinctive qualities of his style; a portion of this appears as "The Two Beginnings of *Walden:* A Distinction of Styles" *(ELH*, 35, 1968, 440–73).

See also Herman L. Eisenlohr, "The Development of T's Prose" (Univ. of Pennsylvania, Ph.D., 1966), and Philip W. Eaton, "The Middle Landscape: T's Development in Style and Content" (Arizona State Univ., Ph.D., 1971).

A useful discussion of T's humor is Harold N. Guthrie, "The Humor of T" (Univ. of Iowa, Ph.D., 1953). J. Golden Taylor, *Neighbor T's Critical Humor* (Logan, Utah, 1958), examines T's humor as the chief vehicle of his social criticism on such topics as religion, government, education, and commercialism. Some of T's puns are listed by David Skwire, "A Check List of Wordplays in *Walden*" *(AL,* 31, 1959, 281–89); this is complemented by Donald Ross, Jr., "Verbal Wit and *Walden*" *(ATQ,* 11, 1971, 38–44), which rearranges Skwire's list into linguistic categories for analysis. Joseph Moldenhauer, "The Rhetoric of *Walden*" (Columbia Univ., Ph.D., 1964), provides the lengthiest list of T wordplays in *Walden* along with a briefer checklist of commonplaces and proverbs; "Paradox in *Walden*" and another published portion of this dissertation are cited in the Sources for Chapter Two under *Walden.* See also Russell J. Reaver, "T's Way with Proverbs" *(ATQ,* 1, 1969, 2–7). Michael West uncovers and describes the significance of many covert scatological puns in "Scatology and Eschatology: The Heroic Dimensions of T's Wordplay" *(PMLA,* 89, 1974, 1043–64). West also links T's interest in etymologies and puns with two language theorists in "Charles Kraitsir's Influence upon T's Theory of Language" *(ESQ,* 19, 1973, 262–74) and *"Walden's* Dirty language: T and Walter Whiter's Geocentric Etymological Theories" *(HLB,* 22, 1974, 117–28). A detailed discussion of T's wit appears in Charles R. Anderson, *The Magic Circle of Walden* (New York, 1968, pp. 17–31). For discussions of the comic hero of *Walden,* see Edward L. Galligan, "The Comedian at Walden Pond" *(SAQ,* 69, 1970, 20–37), and Ralph LaRosa, "DHT [sic]: His American Humor" *(SR,* 83, 1975, 602–22). Raymond Adams discusses T's use of the mock-heroic in "T's Mock-Heroics and the American Natural History Writers" *(SP,* 52, 1955, 86–97). The satire in the "Brute Neighbors" chapter of *Walden* is treated in Robert Hodges, "The Functional Satire of T's Hermit and Poet" *(Satire Newsletter,* 8, 1971, 105–8). Rhetorical studies of T's political essays are cited in the Sources for Chapter Four.

Very little has been published on T's literary theories, but two lengthy unpublished studies that remain useful are George D. Craig, "Literary Criticism in the Works of HDT" (Univ. of Utah, Ph.D., 1951), and Raymond Adams, "HT's Literary Theory and Criticism" (Univ. of North Carolina, Ph.D., 1928). T's aesthetic values are discussed in Charles Metzger, *T and Whitman: A Study of Their Esthetics* (Seattle, 1961), and Wade C. Thompson, "The Aesthetic Theory of HDT" (Columbia Univ., Ph.D., 1959). See also Robert J. DeMott, " 'The Eccentric Orbit': Dimensions of the Artistic Process in HDT's Major Writings" (Kent State Univ., Ph.D., 1969).

The background and uses of T's organic form are discussed in Fred W. Lorch, "T and the Organic Principle in Poetry" *(PMLA,* 53, 1938, 286–302). Still provocative are F. O. Matthiessen's comments in *American Renaissance* (New York, 1941, passim). For studies of structure in T's individual works see the Sources for Chapter Two. In addition to the studies listed there on the structure of *Walden* by Shanley, Clapper, Anderson, and Lane, see the following discussion: David Mason Greene, *The Frail Duration: A Key to Symbolic Structure in Walden* (San Diego, 1966); David L. Minter, *The Interpreted Design as a Structural Principle in American Prose* (New Haven, 1969, pp. 86–102); and Kathleen Anne Culver, "Mandala: The Deep Structure of *Walden"* (Univ. of Florida, Ph.D., 1977). Although, as the sources for Chapter Two indicate, there have been some structural approaches to T's other works, the vast majority of them center upon *Walden.* Many of the studies cited below on T's symbols and images also discuss structure.

T's use of symbol is mentioned or discussed in nearly all of the many studies of his literary style since F. O. Matthiessen's *American Renaissance.* Some of the more specific studies follow. Brian R. Harding, " 'Transcendental Symbolism' in the Works of Emerson, T, and Whitman" (Brown Univ., Ph.D., 1971), compares the symbolism common to all three. "A Winter Walk," "Slavery in Massachusetts," and *Walden* are the focus of Walter L. Shear's "T's Imagery and Symbolism" (Univ. of Wisconsin, Ph.D., 1961). William Drake, "The Depth of Walden: T's Symbolism of the Divine in Nature" (Univ. of Arizona, Ph.D., 1967), is a close reading of the *Journal* to 1845, *A Week,* and *Walden.* Melvin E. Lyon,

"Walden Pond as Symbol" *(PMLA,* 82, 1967, 289-300), identifies the pond as *Walden*'s chief symbol and explains its significance to the work as a whole. For an analysis of the railroad cut passage in *Walden* that focuses on its symbolism and organicism, see Michael Orth, "The Prose Style of HDT" *(Lang&S,* 7, 1974, 36-52). Richard Colyer, "T's Color Symbols" *(PMLA,* 86, 1971, 999-1008), examines five colors as major symbols in T's writings: green (organic growth), white (spirituality), blue (meditation), yellow (spiritual cause and material effect), and red (heroism, strength, and spiritual fruition). T's view of the actual West is contrasted with his symbolic use of it in C. A. Tillinghast, "The West of T's Imagination: The Development of a Symbol" *(Thoth,* 6, 1965, 42-50). John T. Irwin, "The Symbol of the Hieroglyphics in the American Renaissance" *(AQ,* 26, 1974, 103-26), provides background information on the interest in Egyptian hieroglyphics during the period. Although Charles Feidelson, Jr., *Symbolism and American Literature* (Chicago, 1953), only touches on T, this study of several major writers contemporary to T provides a helpful context.

The significance of water imagery in T's writing is discussed in Nina Baym, "From Metaphysics to Metaphor: The Image of Water in Emerson and T" *(SIR,* 5, 1966, 231-43). See also Willard H. Bonner, "Mariners and Terreners: Some Aspects of Nautical Imagery in T" *(AL,* 34, 1963, 507-19), which focuses primarily upon sea images; and Bonner's discussion of sailing images in "Captain T: Gubernator to a Piece of Wood" *(NEQ,* 39, 1966, 26-46). A reply to the latter article is in Edwin Stockton, Jr., "HDT, Terrener or Mariner?" *(Radford Rev.,* 20, 1966, 143-54).

Richard Tuerk, *Central Still: Circle and Sphere in T's Prose* (The Hague, 1975), is a detailed treatment of circular imagery in a number of T's works, including early and late writings. A close reading of the function of circles in *Walden* is Charles Anderson, *The Magic Circle of Walden,* pp. 213-42 and passim (cited above). See also Joseph J. Moldenhauer, "Images of Circularity in T's Prose" *(TSLL,* 1, 1959, 245-63), and J. J. Boies, "Circular Imagery in T's *Week" (CE,* 26, 1965, 350-55).

For a quantitative approach to T's imagery see Richard C. Cook, "T and His Imagery: The Anatomy of an Imagination"

*(TSB,* 70, 1960, 1–3); this is a condensation of Cook's master's thesis. A study that develops in detail Cook's notation that the greatest number of nature images in *Walden* refers to birds is Gloria J. Stansberry, "Let Wild Birds Sing: A Study of the Bird Imagery in the Writings of HDT" (Kent State Univ., Ph.D., 1973). For a discussion of T's images of bodily functions see Michael West, "Scatology and Eschatology" (cited above). Howard R. Houston, "Metaphors in *Walden*" (Claremont Graduate School, Ph.D., 1967), is a sensitive reading of T's use of imagery as a means of expanding and unifying elements of the book. More specific studies of T's imagery include: J. Golden Taylor, "T's Sour Grapes" *(PUASAL,* 42, 1965, 38–49); Linda K. Walker, "A Fruitful Profusion: The Wild Berry Motif in T's Journal" (Univ. of Oklahoma, Ph.D., 1976); Theodore Haddin,"Fire and Fire Imagery in T's 'Journal' and 'Walden'" *(SAB,* 41, 1976, 78–89); and Mary L. Kaiser, "Conversing with the Sky: The Imagery of Celestial Bodies in T's Poetry *(TJQ,* 9, 1977, 15–28).

For studies that trace the various sources of T's use of myth, see the Sources for Chapter Three. John C. Broderick, "The Movement of T's Prose" *(AL,* 33, 1961, 133–42), links the typical movement of his paragraphs to the "archetypal Romantic theme of rebirth." Richard Tuerk, "T's Early Versions of a Myth" *(ATQ,* 10, 1971, 32–39), finds the monomyth of the hero's withdrawal, initiation, and return in T's "Natural History of Massachusetts" and "A Walk to Wachusett." Louise C. Kertesz, "A Study of T as Myth Theorist and Myth Maker" (Univ. of Illinois, Ph.D., 1970), employs a modern structuralist approach to myth in *A Week* and *Walden.* Richard Fleck argues that T's concept of mythology was modern in "T as Mythologist" *(RS,* 40, 1972, 195–206). For a discussion of T's attempts to create myth out of the facts of his own life, see Wade C. Thompson, "The Aesthetic Theory of HDT" (cited above, pp. 95–130). John F. Taylor, "A Search for Eden: T's Heroic Quest" (Univ. of Maryland, Ph.D., 1971), offers a Jungian approach to T's "mythic urge" in his life and writings. Peter McInerney, "Edenist Literary Statemanship and the Writings of HT" (Johns Hopkins Univ., Ph.D., 1977), examines T's uses of the myth of Eden as it relates to America. The Orpheus myth is described as an important source of T's imagery in Barbara H. Carson, "Orpheus in New England: Alcott, Emerson, and T" (Johns Hopkins Univ., Ph.D., 1968). Robert D. Richardson, Jr., *Myth and Literature in the American Renaissance* (Bloomington, 1978), provides a valuable historical overview of Emerson's, T's (pp. 90-137), Whitman's, Hawthorne's, and Melville's conscious use of myth in their writings.

Lawrence Buell's *Literary Transcendentalism* includes a valuable discussion of form and meaning in *A Week* and *Walden* and their relationship to Transcendental literary practices contemporary to them. An extensive discussion of T's epiphanic structures is in Carla Mazzini, "Serenade Within the Mind: A Study of Epiphany in Selected Works of HDT" (Univ. of North Carolina, Ph.D., 1977). James McIntosh, *T as Romantic Naturalist: His Shifting Stance Toward Nature* (Ithaca, 1974), argues that what gives form to T's works is the conscious use of polarities that characterize his thought. Tony Tanner, *The Reign of Wonder: Naivety and Reality in American Literature* (Cambridge, 1965, pp. 46-63), is a concise discussion of T's vision and style. For the ingenious cryptographic reading, see Michael Burr, "T's Love and Doubt: An Anagram" *(ATQ,* 24, 1974, 22s-25s).

For a discussion of what music meant to T, see Kenneth W. Rhoads, "T, the Ear and the Music" *AL,* 46, 1974, 313-28), and James V. Kavanaugh, "Music and American Transcendentalism: A Study of Transcendental Pythagoreanism in the Works of HDT, Nathaniel Hawthorne and Charles Ives" (Yale Univ., Ph.D., 1978). For a more general but influential study, see Sherman Paul, "The Wise Silence: Sound as the Agency of Correspondence in T" *(NEQ,* 22, 1949, 511-27). T's anticipation of modern architectural principles is described in Theodore M. Brown, "T's Prophetic Architectural Program" *(NEQ,* 38, 1965, 3-20). For a discussion of T's response to Horatio Greenough's architectural theories, see Charles Metzger, *T and Whitman* (cited above, pp. 28-38), and William J. Griffin, "T's Reactions to Horatio Greenough" *(NEQ,* 30, 1957, 508-12). For a broader context, see Richard P. Adams, "Architecture and the Romantic Tradition: Coleridge to Wright" *(AQ,* 9, 1957, 46-62).

# 6.

# Thoreau's Reputation

One of the most striking phenomena of American literary history has been the gradual growth of Thoreau's reputation. From one who in his own lifetime was dismissed generally as a minor figure and an imitator of Emerson, he has risen to the rank of one of our five or six greatest writers. The growth has been very gradual and not without its setbacks, but it can easily be traced over the years.

Thoreau had to suffer few of the tribulations of the literary lion. Few admirers made pilgrimages to see him. He received only an occasional request for an autograph or a photograph. Few editors asked him to write for them. His services as a lecturer were not in great demand. Indeed, his greatest problem was getting his work into print, getting his writing noticed.

Aside from a brief article printed anonymously in the Concord newspaper, Thoreau first broke into print in the pages of the *Dial*, but only at the strong behest of Emerson and over the protest of the editor, Margaret Fuller. It was only when Emerson took over as editor that any considerable number of his writings appeared in the *Dial*. When the *Dial* floundered, it was chiefly through the good offices of his friend Horace Greeley that Thoreau succeeded in placing any further magazine articles—and even then he found it difficult to collect any pay for his work.

Ironically, the first recognition Thoreau won was in James Russell Lowell, *A Fable for Critics* (1848), wherein Lowell chastised "_____" for not letting "Neighbor Emerson's orchards alone" because "_____ has picked up all the windfalls before." It is almost an academic question which of the blanks refers to Thoreau and which to his friend Ellery Channing, for Lowell is charging both with too much imitation of Emerson.

When Thoreau had completed *A Week,* despite Emerson's efforts he could find no publisher willing to underwrite it, and he was forced to pay the Boston publisher, Munroe, to bring it out. It received few reviews. The two most notable were by Horace Greeley and James Russell Lowell: "Nearly every page is instinct with genuine Poetry except those wherein verse is haltingly attempted. . . . There is a misplaced Pantheistic attack on the Christian Faith," complained the former. The latter declared: "The great charm of Mr. Thoreau's book seems to be, that its being a book at all is a happy fortuity. The door of the portfolio cage has been left open, and the thoughts have flown out of themselves." On October 28, 1853, Munroe notifed Thoreau that of the edition of 1,000 copies, 75 had been given away and only 219 sold. The publishers were returning the remaining 706 copies to clear their shelves.

Although *Walden* was announced in 1849 in the back pages of *A Week,* as "will soon be published" the first book's dismal failure frightened off all publishers. Finally, in 1854 the rising firm of Ticknor & Fields was persuaded to bring it out in an edition of two thousand copies. It received comparatively wider and more favorable notice. Horace Greeley quoted lengthy selections, with words of praise, in an advance notice in the *New York Tribune. Putnam's Monthly Magazine* gave it its first lengthy review (six pages), on the whole favorable, but nonetheless complaining that "although he paints his shanty-life in rose-colored tints, we do not believe he liked it, else why not stick to it?" The *National Anti-Slavery Standard* gave it one of the most understanding reviews it was ever to receive, saying in part: "If men were to follow in Mr. Thoreau's steps, by being more obedient to their loftiest instincts, there would, indeed, be a falling off in the splendor of our houses, in the richness of our furniture and dress, in the luxury of our tables, but how poor are these things in comparison with the new grandeur and beauty which would appear in the souls of men." A number of other reviews appeared in both newspapers and magazines.

In the final years of his life, Thoreau at last began to receive wider recognition. His books and lectures were more widely cited in the public press. He began to receive letters from admirers of his work. But it was Bronson Alcott's essay "The Forester," published just a few weeks before Thoreau's death, that gave him his most sympathetic evaluation—"I had never thought of knowing a man so thoroughly of the country as this friend of mine, and so purely a son of Nature"—although, ironically, Alcott nowhere in it mentioned Thoreau by name.

Little encouragement, however, came to Thoreau from his other fellow townsmen. For the most part they looked upon him as a crank and did not hesitate to tell him so to his face. Far more memorable to them than his life at Walden or his writings was the fact that he once let a campfire get out of control and burn down a woodlot. They were willing to purchase his services as a surveyor. "I am frequently invited to survey farms in a rude manner, a very [sic] and insignificant labor, though I manage to get more out of it than my employers; but I am never invited by the community to do anything quite worth the while to do," he complained in his *Journal* (IV, 252). They were willing to listen to his lectures before the Concord Lyceum—since he did not charge for his services. They admitted the pencils he manufactured were the best in America, although they could not understand why he did not devote himself to the business and make himself a fortune. In his last years they began to recognize him as a local authority on natural history and consulted him when they ran across any strange or unusual phenomenon. Just before Thoreau's death, Bronson Alcott, who was then superintendent of the Concord schools, persuaded the town authorities to ask Thoreau to compile an "Atlas of Concord" for use in the public schools, but he was too ill to attempt the project.

Ironically, the first turning point in the growth of Thoreau's fame coincided approximately with his death in 1862. For one so comparatively little known, Thoreau received many eulogies. Obituaries appeared in many newspapers and magazines, both local and national. Of these, Emerson's funeral address was unquestionably the most influential in forming Thoreau's posthumous reputation. Although it was written with the highest motives, it emphasized Thoreau's negative rather than positive characteristics—"He was a protestant à outrance, and few lives contained so many renunciations"—and in the long run did more harm than good.

Just before his death Thoreau devoted his time to revising many of his lectures for publication. Four of these appeared in the *Atlantic Monthly* for 1862, two in 1863, and two in 1864. *Walden*, out of print since 1859, went into its second printing (280 copies) in 1862, its third printing in 1863 (again 280 copies), and continued to be reissued almost annually from then on. The stillborn first edition of *A Week* was reissued by Ticknor & Fields in 1862 and reprinted in a revised edition in 1867.

In 1863, his sister Sophia collected many of his essays in a volume entitled *Excursions*. In 1864, with Ellery Channing, she edited *The Maine Woods*. In 1865, they edited *Cape Cod*, and that same year Emerson edited the *Letters to Various Persons*. In 1866, *A Yankee in Canada with Anti-Slavery and Reform Papers* was issued. Thus, in the four years after Thoreau's death, five new volumes of his works were published.

Once again, however, Emerson's editorial hand was unfortunate. In editing Thoreau's letters, he deliberately deleted any letters or portions thereof that showed Thoreau's warmth and friendliness and concentrated more on his austere side, wishing to emphasize his stoicism, thinking that to be his greatest claim to fame. Sophia Thoreau protested, when she saw the manuscript, that she did not recognize her brother in the volume. The publisher worked out a compromise wherein a few deletions were restored. But neither Emerson nor Sophia were happy with the result. The book served only to confirm the popular opinion that Thoreau had little warmth in his personality.

It has often been assumed that the publication of these posthumous volumes attracted little notice. But research continues to turn up more and more reviews and critical notices, and Ticknor &

Fields and its successors found it worthwhile to reprint all five
volumes regularly.

Unfortunately, the most influential of the numerous reviews of
this period was by James Russell Lowell. Ostensibly it was a review
of the *Letters,* but actually it was an essay on Thoreau and his
works. Lowell's whole philosophy of life was such that it was impossible for him to understand or appreciate Thoreau. And apparently after their quarrel over the publication of "Chesuncook" in
the *Atlantic Monthly* for July, 1858, Lowell became embittered. He
repeated his charge that Thoreau was "among the pistillate plants
kindled to fruitage by the Emersonian pollen." He thought Thoreau "was not by nature an observer," that he "had not a healthy
mind," and that he "had no humor." It is true that in his closing
sentences Lowell said: "There are sentences of his as perfect as
anything in the language," but the overwhelming effect of the essay is negative. Since Lowell was accepted as the leading critic of
his day, his essay had tremendous influence; probably it postponed
a true appreciation of Thoreau for a generation or more.

There was a new surge of interest in Thoreau in the 1880s when
H. G. O. Blake of Worcester, Thoreau's most devoted disciple and
the inheritor of his manuscripts, began publishing the first extended series of excerpts from the *Journal* in four volumes entitled
*Early Spring in Massachusetts* (1881), *Summer* (1884), *Winter* (1887),
and *Autumn* (1892). Blake tended to emphasize Thoreau's nature
writing at the expense of his social criticism. It proved to be the
right choice. The publication of these volumes coincided with the
end of the American frontier and the great upsurge of interest in
nature. Thoreau's writings found a popularity they had never enjoyed before.

In 1893 Houghton Mifflin, Thoreau's hereditary publishers,
found the demand for his works sufficient to justify the issuing of
the first collected edition, the ten-volume Riverside Edition, and in
1894 they added *Familiar Letters,* edited by F. B. Sanborn, greatly
enlarging Emerson's earlier volume, although if anything, sinking
beneath it in editorial mistreatment. It was about at this time that
Sanborn began thinking of himself as the sole guardian of Thoreau's fame, and he began pouring through the presses, books,
magazines, and newspapers, a torrent of material. Sanborn's work

did serve, undoubtedly, to increase the recognition of Thoreau, but Sanborn was so arbitrary and so careless in his writing that he has been the bane ever since of those who searched for accuracy and authenticity. Among the earliest to protest Sanborn's methods were Fred Hosmer, Horace Hosmer, Samuel Arthur Jones, and E. B. Hill. Fred Hosmer was a dry-goods clerk in Concord; Horace Hosmer, once a pupil in Thoreau's school in Concord, resided in nearby Acton. Jones was on the faculty of the medical school at the University of Michigan, and Hill was a Detroit newspaperman. Fred Hosmer searched the attics of Concord and gathered together a massive collection of Thoreauviana when few others thought it of any importance or value. (It is now housed in the Concord Free Public Library, the gift of his heirs.) The two Hosmers, at Jones's instigation, searched out the facts about many important events in Thoreau's life while there were still among those living many who had known him well. Jones and Hill saw to it that these facts got into print before they were forgotten.

The academy, not unexpectedly, was slow to recognize Thoreau. For years college and high school textbooks of American literature dismissed him as a minor disciple and imitator of Emerson. With one surprising exception, he was not considered worthy of doctoral research until Raymond Adams's pioneering dissertation, "Henry Thoreau's Literary Theories and Criticism" (University of North Carolina) of 1928. (The exception was Ella Knapp, "A Study of Thoreau," University of Michigan, 1899. But since all copies of that work seem to have disappeared, little is known about it.) By the 1940s there was an average of one dissertation a year on Thoreau; by the late 1950s, two; and currently, three.

Just after the turn of the century, Francis H. Allen, a young editor at Houghton Mifflin, persuaded his firm against their better judgment to issue a new twenty-volume collection of Thoreau's writings including, for the first time, a fourteen-volume nearly complete transcription of the *Journal.* Although Allen himself supervised the editing of the *Journal,* credit was long given only to the then better-known Bradford Torrey. To everyone's pleasant surprise, the edition sold out before publication. For the first time readers were able to see that natural history was not the sole concern of the *Journal,* that Thoreau commented on his neighbors as frequently as on the flora and fauna of Concord, and that he was also concerned with social and philosophical issues.

In 1910 the copyright of *Walden* expired, and many other publishers joined Houghton Mifflin in issuing editions of the book. For the first time there were textbook editions aimed at schools and colleges. But Houghton Mifflin maintained its superiority by issuing the first well-annotated edition, edited by Francis Allen. In 1917 the centennial of Thoreau's birth was comparatively little noted. A few books were published and a couple of magazine notices, but the only commemorative meeting was a small session held belatedly in October in Concord. In the long run, perhaps the most influential essay of the period so far as Thoreau's reputation was concerned was John Macy's chapter on Thoreau in his *Spirit of American Literature* (New York, 1908), which was one of the earliest to present him as a social philosopher.

As Michael Meyer has said, "The social and political climate of the 1920's was not conducive to the growth of Thoreau's reputation" *(Several More Lives to Live,* p. 17). The conservative politics of the era and the materialism engendered by the stock market boom fostered an attitude quite foreign to Thoreau's ideas. Although the New Humanists Norman Foerster and Paul Elmer More found some aspects of Thoreau admirable, they were ill at ease with his romanticism and his radicalism. It was not until Vernon L. Parrington's monumental and highly influential *Main Currents in American Thought* (1927) that Thoreau found a truly sympathetic spokesman in the decade—and Parrington's greatest impact was delayed into the 1930s.

It was in the depression years of the 1930s that Thoreau first really came into his own. A friend of ours once commented, "Thoreau is the only author I know of that I can read without a nickel in my pocket and not feel insulted." Certainly the simple life forced upon people by financial necessity through those years turned many of them to reading Thoreau with a new insight, and for the first time Thoreau was treated generally as a social philosopher rather than simply as a nature writer.

With the growth of fascism on the Continent, many turned to Thoreau's independent individualism as an antidote. Marxists, in the days of the Popular Front, made some attempt to accommodate Thoreau to their theories, but could come up with little more than that Thoreau at Walden was a good example of "individual communism." Henry Seidel Canby was perhaps the chief spokesman for Thoreau in the decade. His numerous essays, editorials, and reviews on Thoreau helped to popularize the man, and his biography, *Thoreau* (1939), was the first to reach the best-seller lists. We also at this time saw the beginnings of a nostalgic view of Thoreau that reflected a desire to escape from the complexities of modern life into the simplicity of the past. E. B. White's several essays are typical of this viewpoint.

When the depression was over, the interest in Thoreau did not fade, as many thought it might. In the late 1930s Raymond Adams of the University of North Carolina began occasional publication of a privately circulated "Thoreau Newsletter." And in 1941 a small group established the Thoreau Society, which since that time has held annual meetings in Concord and published a quarterly bulletin and occasional booklets to a membership that now numbers more than a thousand scattered not only over the United States but in foreign countries on at least five continents—the largest society of its kind devoted to an American author.

F. O. Matthiessen's monumental *American Renaissance* (New York, 1941) engendered a multitude of dissertations on Thoreau over the next twenty-five years, most of them concerned (as Matthiessen himself was) with Thoreau as a literary craftsman. Unfortunately, few of them displayed Matthiessen's insight and some were downright inane.

World War II seemed to have little impact one way or another on Thoreau's reputation, but the 1945 centennial of his going to Walden was much more widely marked in essays and commemorative meetings than had been the centennial of his birth in 1917. (Curiously, the centennial of Thoreau's jailing in 1946 and of the publication of "Civil Disobedience" in 1949 both slipped by almost unnoticed.) Although Houghton Mifflin had never bothered to renew the copyright on Thoreau's *Journal* when it expired in 1934, by 1948 they found enough demand to reissue it in a separate fourteen-volume set.

Although the 1950s was a period of political conservatism, Thoreau's popularity did not abate in the least. It is true that the notorious Senator Joseph McCarthy did succeed in having an anthology of American literature removed from the shelves in United States Information Service libraries all over the world in part because it included Thoreau's "Civil Disobedience," but it is notable that one of the earliest strong protests against McCarthyism was a full-page ad in the *New York Times* for January 15, 1951, sponsored by seventeen nationally known writers, artists, and scholars such as Mark Van Doren, Arthur Miller, and Nelson Algren, featuring a drawing of Thoreau in jail, and asking Americans to speak out against bigotry as Thoreau once had from jail. Matthiessen's impact flourished in this decade, and a great deal of the interest in Thoreau centered on his craftsmanship. It is notable that Sherman Paul's *Shores of America* (1958), still undoubtedly the major volume of criticism on Thoreau, almost completely ignored Thoreau's interest in either natural history or social criticism and focused on his artistry.

It was in the 1960s that Thoreau reached the height of his popularity. When the first edition of this *Handbook* was published in 1959, it cited the fact that Thoreau still lacked "household" recognition. He had not been elected to the Hall of Fame. No postage stamps had ever been issued in his name. To the average man in the street he was little more than a name. But in 1960 he was elected to the Hall of Fame, and in 1967 (commemorating the 150th anniversary of his birth) a Thoreau postage stamp was issued. But what is more, he became one of the most quoted of American authors on posters, calendars, greeting cards, and even in the comic strips. Such phrases as "different drummer" and "lives of quiet desperation" became commonplaces.

Interest in Thoreau came from many sources. Dr. Martin Luther King, Jr., and his followers in their fight against segregation in the South frequently cited Thoreau as one of their major sources of inspiration. The "beat generation" of writers—Allen Ginsberg, Jack Kerouac, and Gary Snyder, among them—praised his writing. The rapidly growing ecology movement led by the Sierra Club and Friends of the Earth gave him a high place in their pantheon as one of the earliest American conservationists. The hippies evoked his philosophy of the simple life. The yippies extolled his "anarchism." As the war in Vietnam became more and more unpopular

with the American people, Thoreau's "Civil Disobedience" became one of the most widely quoted of American historical documents and was even reissued in an "updated" version by
substituting "Vietnam" for "War with Mexico" throughout.
Jerome Lawrence and Robert E. Lee, two of the country's most
popular playwrights, collaborated on *The Night Thoreau Spent in Jail*
(New York, 1970), making of it a powerful antiwar protest that
immediately became the most popular play in the college and
community playhouse circuits, and it was performed more frequently, its authors claimed, than any other play in history.

Interest in academia in Thoreau continued to increase. Doctoral
dissertations on Thoreau became commonplace, though unfortunately a large number of them were so highly specialized that they
are likely to be of interest only to members of the dissertation
committee. Others seemed so fabricated that we suspect them of
being of the same material as the emperor's clothes. But this is not
to say they are all a waste of time. Indeed there have been some
outstanding ones, as has been indicated by the citations throughout this book.

In the mid-1960s, through the cooperation of the National Endowment for the Humanities and the Modern Language Association work was begun on a full new edition of Thoreau's writings.
As yet only four volumes have appeared, but eventually there will
be approximately twenty-five. These are being edited by a group of
outstanding Thoreau scholars who are applying the latest techniques of bibliographical and scholarly research. As a result, for
the first time we are seeing some of Thoreau's works as he intended
them to appear, and as a bonus we are seeing a number of hitherto
unpublished works. Our only caveat is that bibliographic theorists
for a time controlled the NEH-MLA projects and imposed rules
that wasted much time and space in counting commas and chart-
ing end-of-line hyphens, time, and space that might better have
been devoted to more helpful annotations.

In the mid and late 1970s there seems to be a scholarly trend
toward psychological approaches to Thoreau, owing to a feeling
that the traditional biographical approaches have exhausted available materials and that if we are to understand Thoreau more
fully, we must explore other techniques. Most notable of course is

Richard Lebeaux, *Young Man Thoreau* (Amherst, 1977). But there are further studies in these directions under way.

After the great peak of excitement in the late 1960s and early 1970s, widespread interest in Thoreau has tapered off slightly. Publishers are not issuing quite as many new editions of *Walden* or of "Civil Disobedience" as they were. They have even dropped the Thoreau volumes from several of the mass-selling paperback series of classics. Fewer books on Thoreau have appeared in the 1970s than in the 1960s. Nonetheless he continues to be quoted as widely as ever—perhaps there has even been a slight increase in citation of his words. But, paradoxically, he is cited less by the radicals and more by the establishment. The Franklin Mint, purveyors of useless luxuries to the superpatriotic and the superrich, announced they would issue a morocco-bound, gilt-edged limited edition of *Walden.* When the manuscripts that he had so much difficulty in persuading editors and publishers to accept become available, they sell usually for $1,000 or more a page—far more than he succeeded in earning from his writing in his entire lifetime. When the copy of the first edition of *Walden* that Thoreau presented to Emerson came on to the market in the fall of 1978, it was bid up and sold for $72,400. The next thing we know, Harvard will be getting around to recognizing its alumnus—and will probably set up the Henry David Thoreau chair of management science. Thoreau the nonconformist is rapidly becoming acceptable. Unfortunately, in the process he is sometimes homogenized beyond recognition.

\*    \*    \*

The path of Thoreau's fame can also be charted through the histories of American literature. During his own lifetime he was accorded recognition in only one: Evert and George Duyckinck, *Cyclopaedia of American Literature* (1855), in which *A Week* and *Walden* were described as "two of the most noticeable books in American literature on the score of a certain quaint study of natural history and scenery."

It was 1870 before he was noticed again, and then in Rufus Wilmot Griswold, *The Prose Writers of America,* where he was described as a "wayward genius." In 1872, however, John Hart, in *A*

*Manual of American Literature,* said: "With Thoreau's wonderfully acute power of observation, and his fine taste and skill in word-painting, he might have made a first-class naturalist. His works are to the last degree original and quaint." In 1878 Charles F. Richardson continued the emphasis on Thoreau's nature writing by saying, *"Walden* is his best book; but in seven other volumes he carries the reader straight to Nature's heart." In 1879 Thomas Wentworth Higginson, in his *Short Studies of American Authors,* declared that *Walden* was "the only book yet written in America, to my thinking, that bears an annual perusal" and added that "the impression that Thoreau was but a minor Emerson will in time pass away."

In 1882 John Nichol, in *American Literature,* dismissed Thoreau as "little else than water added to the wine of Emerson and Lowell." In 1886 Charles F. Richardson, despite his earlier praise, said in *American Literature* that he considered Thoreau "inferior to Emerson in every trait of character and in every element of genius." Henry A. Beers, in *An Outline Sketch of American Letters* (1887), continued the condemnation by stating, "The most distinctive note in Thoreau is his inhumanity." Albert Smyth, in his *American Literature* (1889), said, "He was the most original character among his distinguished townspeople, and has as permanent a place in literature as any of them."

In 1891 Julian Hawthorne and Leonard Lemmon, in *American Literature,* wrote a lengthy and violent diatribe against Thoreau, denouncing him as "bilious," "defiant," "stealthy," "egotistical," and "disagreeable." They saw his writings as chiefly Emersonian, "thinly overspread with Thoreau." In 1893 Francis Underwood, in *The Builders of American Literature,* said, "Whatever we may think of the eccentric man and his philosophy of living, we acknowledge a great debt to him for his fresh and delightful books." In 1894 Mildred Rutherford, in *American Authors,* said, "He was a naturalist, and his life and work are of consequence as having given an impulse in that direction." In that same year Mildred Cabell Watkins dismissed him in one paragraph of *American Literature* as "eccentric." However, in 1896, Brander Matthews, in *An Introduction to the Study of American Literature,* concluded a lengthy and favorable evaluation of Thoreau: "He was above all an artist in words, a ruler of the vocabulary, a master phrase-maker." In that same year Fred Lewis Pattee, in *A History of American Literature,* presented a primarily negative picture of Thoreau, although he did admit that "no other writer has done more for the independence of American thought." Katherine Lee Bates, in *American Literature* (1897), discussed Thoreau as a nature writer and said of him, "Not the best of his disciples . . . can reach his upper notes." In that same year F. V. N. Painter, in *Introduction to American Literature,* dismissed him in two sentences as "a recluse and observer of nature." In 1898 Henry S. Pancoast, in *An Introduction to American Literature,* dismissed Thoreau as "Emerson's eccentric disciple." Although Donald G. Mitchell, in *American Lands and Letters* (1899), devoted considerable space to Thoreau, he was on the whole disparaging and decided that Thoreau was not a first-rate essayist, poet, or scientist.

In 1900, in *A Literary History of America,* Barrett Wendell admitted that Thoreau was "in his own way a literary artist of unusual merit," although he thought him "eccentric" and "unpractically individual," and classified him among "the lesser men of Concord." In that same year Walter Bronson, in *A Short History of American Literature,* said, "On the whole, Thoreau must be classed with the minor American authors." Alphonso G. Newcomer, in *American Literature* (1901), devoted a surprisingly large amount of space to Thoreau, and on the whole was sympathetic, although he commented, "Not many of us will care to accept the philosophy of *Walden,* so extreme is it," and finally came to the conclusion: "The parts of Thoreau's work upon which his fame rests most securely to-day are his nature studies." In 1902 William C. Lawton, in *Introduction to the Study of American Literature,* said: "He . . . has taken an honored place beside, yet apart from, Emerson himself, among the authors whom the world cannot now spare, and apparently will not soon suffer to be forgotten." In a generally skeptical account of Thoreau's life in *American Literature in the Colonial and National Periods* (1902), Lorenzo Sears said: "A great part of his charm as a writer is the naïve simplicity with which he describes things as new that several other observers were already familiar with." In that same year William Cranston Lawton, in *Introduction to the Study of American Literature,* considered Thoreau's life at Walden "an interesting failure," but thought that he "is interesting chiefly for his originality, not for his loyalty to Emerson." In 1903 T. W. Higginson and H. W. Boynton, in *A Reader's History of American Literature*, said, "Time is rapidly melting away the dross from his writings, and exhibiting their gold." William P. Trent, in *A History of American Literature* (1903), affirmed that "it is as a writer rather than as a thinker or observer that Thoreau deserves heartiest admiration." In 1908 John Macy, in what is often termed one of the most influential books in the field, *The Spirit of American Literature*, wrote, "Thoreau's vision shot beyond the horizon which bounded and still bounds the sight even of that part of the world which fancies itself liberal and emancipated." Abby Willis Howes, in *A Primer of American Literature* (1909), thought Thoreau "a man of true and rare genius."

In 1910 William Morton Payne, in *Leading American Essayists*, said of Thoreau: "When we look back toward his life from our present twentieth century point of vantage, it is easily seen that he was the principal figure among those who lived in the circle of Emerson's radiance and felt directly the inspiration of his example." In the next year Reuben P. Halleck, in *History of American Literature*, said: "In spite of some Utopian philosophy and too much insistence on the self-sufficiency of the individual, *Walden* has proved a regenerative force in the lives of many readers who have not passed their plastic stage." In 1912 W. P. Trent and John Erskine wrote in *Great American Writers:* "If we should compare the influence of any one of Emerson's book with the influence of *Walden* upon thought in America and Europe, the result would show in Thoreau an astonishing power of fertilizing other minds." Said William Cairns, in *A History of American Literature* (1912): "Though his eccentricities prevent him from ranking with the greatest American essayists, he has a unique charm for many readers, and his place in American literature seems secure." William J. Long, in *American Literature* (1913), suggested since "Thoreau's oddity has received perhaps too much attention, to the neglect of his better qualities," that "the beginner ... make the acquaintance of the man himself rather than of his critics or biographers." In 1914 Adaline May Conway, in *The Essay in American Literature*, said, "As a stylist we have no more admirable writer in our American literature." In 1915 Fred Lewis Pattee, in *A History of American Literature*

*Since 1870,* reflected a change from his opinion of nearly twenty years before when he said: "His rehabilitation has come solely because of that element condemned by Lowell as a certain 'modern sentimentalism about Nature.' . . . It was because he brought to the study of Nature a new manner." In 1918 Bliss Perry, in *The American Spirit in Literature,* commented: "To the student of American thought Thoreau's prime value lies in the courage and consistency with which he endeavored to realize the gospel of Transcendentalism in his own inner life." In that same year, although Archibald MacMechan devoted a whole chapter to Thoreau in the *Cambridge History of American Literature,* he epitomized his attitude: "The truth is that Thoreau with all his genuine appreciation of the classics never learned their lessons of proportion, restraint, 'nothing too much.' " In 1919 Percy Boynton, in *A History of American Literature,* rounded off the decade with the comment: "As a citizen and as a critic of society, Thoreau lacked the sturdy Puritan conscience which is the bone and sinew of Emerson's character."

In 1926 Stanley T. Williams, in *The American Spirit in Letters,* for Yale University's "Chronicles of America" series, said, "Thoreau is the high-water mark of New England Transcendentalism." In the next year V. L. Parrington, in his epoch-making *Main Currents in American Thought,* discussing primarily Thoreau's economic theory, concluded, "One of the greatest names in American literature is the name of Henry Thoreau." Yet in that same year Lucy Hazard, in *The Frontier in American Literature,* wrote: *"Walden* is fascinating as the adventure of a solitary pioneer; it is fallacious as the guidebook for a general migration. An idyll of the golden age of transcendentalism, it is an ineffectual protest against the gilded age of industrialism." E. E. Leisy, in *American Literature* (1929), wrote: "His tonic simplification of life is giving him a fresh vogue, and it seems that the village crank who wrote with aboriginal vigor is at last coming into his own."

Russell Blankenship, in *American Literature as an Expression of the National Mind* (1931), devoted only one page to Thoreau as a nature writer, but ten pages to his social theory. He thought "Civil Disobedience" the "capstone of Thoreau's works" and stressed that his life, rather than being negative, "was one long-drawn affirmative." In that same year Gilbert Seldes, in John Macy, *American Writers on*

*American Literature,* thought that Thoreau's "importance to us then is in the assertion that wisdom, nobility, the things of the spirit exist to gratify man and make him truly complete and happy." Yet that same year Constance Rourke, in *American Humor,* said: "He produced no philosophy, though he obviously intended to construct a philosophy. . . . He is read for the aphorism or the brief description." In 1932 Grant C. Knight, in *American Literature and Culture,* felt that "no American means more to our times than Thoreau." In the same year Ludwig Lewisohn, in *Expression in America,* after condemning Thoreau's comments on chastity and sensuality as too puritanical, decided that "Thoreau . . . must be saved in spite of his limitations." In 1933 Ralph Boas and Katherine Burton, in *Social Backgrounds of American Literature,* affirmed that *"Walden* is one of the few American classics which have achieved international fame." Carl Van Doren, in *What Is American Literature?* (1933), wrote: "In the long run he has become what he was from the first: a hero of the mind, not legendary or abstract but concrete and positive." And Stanley T. Williams, in *American Literature* (1933), said, "Proleptic, he expressed a mood of our civilization which today is vocal indeed." In 1936 Percy Boynton, in *Literature and American Life,* wrote that Thoreau was "a master of invective, passionately assailing the foes of human liberty," and Walter Fuller Taylor, in *A History of American Letters,* concluded that "historically, it is evident that Thoreau represents the extreme reach in America of (1) the romantic return to nature, and (2) romantic individualism." Bernard Smith, in *Forces in American Criticism* (1939), declared that Thoreau "was the first American to urge the union of labor and art—an ideal which has become a catalytic influence in modern letters."

In 1940 G. Harrison Orians, in *A Short History of American Literature,* asserted that "though Thoreau did not make an impression on his age, he became one of the notable voices of the 'Golden Day.'" James Hart, in the *Oxford Companion to American Literature* (1941), said: "His observations of nature were distinguished not merely by his scientific knowledge, which was occasionally erroneous, but by his all-inclusive love of life." In *American Idealism* (1943) Floyd Stovall declared: "The greatest single contribution of Thoreau to American idealism was his uncompromising individualism, and the next greatest was his enthusiasm for nature." W. Tasker Witham, in the *Panorama of American Literature* (1947), decided that Thoreau was "the greatest of the Concord group next to Emerson." One of the significant indications of the tremendous rise in Thoreau's prestige among literary critics is Townsend Scudder's essay in Spiller, Thorp, Johnson, and Canby, *Literary History of the United States* (1948), which concludes, "Thoreau has become one of America's great." Decidedly in contrast to that is Arthur Hobson Quinn's decision in *The Literature of the American People* (1951) that "Thoreau will probably remain one of those figures in our literature that represent an acquired taste, and a reputation based largely upon one book, *Walden.*" Far more typical of current opinion was the decision of the American Literature Group of the Modern Language Association to include Thoreau in its bibliographical survey of our outstanding authors, *Eight American Authors,* first published in 1957.

Leon Howard, in *Literature and the American Tradition* (1960), thought Thoreau "wanted to reform the world by opening men's eyes to their own potentialities rather than by changing social conditions; but his method was by example rather than by evangelism." Wilson O. Clough, in *The Necessary Earth* (1964), assessed that Thoreau's "outspoken phrases can provoke us not only to personal revaluations; they can suggest that a Thoreau is a measure of how free a society is or can be. That State which can afford a Thoreau is free." Edwin Fussell, in discussing "American Literature and the American West" in *Frontier* (1965), asserts, "The average American went West (when he had the money), in hope of improving his economic status. Thoreau went to Walden, his personal West, to embrace voluntary poverty." "Thoreau's work does convey a sense of the sheer reality which surrounds a man, and which a man may rediscover by taking 'a new and absolute view of things,'" says Tony Tanner in *The Reign of Wonder: Naivety and Reality in American Literature* (1965). Richard Poirier, concerned in *A World Elsewhere* (1966) with Thoreau's style, laments that "No one has sufficiently demonstrated its truly dazzling inventiveness and originality." Martin S. Day, in *History of American Literature* (1970), says, "Thoreau does not preach withdrawal from the responsibilities of civilization, he urges a spiritual awakening to the fullness and variety of life's possibilities." Thus once again we have seen that Thoreau was first dismissed as an eccentric and a minor disciple of Emerson, then accepted as a nature writer, and finally granted a place among the greatest of American authors both as a stylist and thinker.

*  *  *

Thoreau's reputation abroad followed a somewhat different pattern. A few copies of Thoreau's books and some of his articles found their way to England during his lifetime and found generally a mildly favorable reception. George Eliot even wrote a brief notice of *Walden* for the *Westminster Review*. Although A. H. Japp's *Thoreau: His Life and Aims* was published in London in 1878 (under the pseudonym of H. A. Page), it was too uncritical and eulogistic to attract much attention. In 1880 Robert Louis Stevenson published his "Henry David Thoreau: His Character and Opinions" denouncing Thoreau as a "skulker." It made little difference that six years later Stevenson recanted and admitted he had based his statements on insufficient evidence and that Thoreau had been one of the most powerful influences on his own writing; it was the earlier statement that prevailed and prejudiced many against Thoreau.

There was, however, a flowering of interest in Thoreau in the last decades of the century. Walter Scott issued the first true English edition of *Walden* in 1886. Other volumes followed rapidly, so that by 1900 there were at least twenty editions of Thoreau's books in print in the British Isles. Henry Salt's fine biography appeared in 1890.

It was, however, the Fabians and early Labour party members who really popularized Thoreau in England. Robert Blatchford, whose *Merrie England*, with a sale of two million copies, was the first Labour party best-seller, began his book with the injunction that if his readers first read *Walden*, they would more easily understand his book, and confessed that he slept with *Walden* under his pillow. Many local units of the Labour party were called Walden Clubs. Inexpensive paperbound editions of *Walden* and *Civil Disobedience* were distributed with the party's blessing. William Archer, the translator of Ibsen, lived from 1890 to 1895 near Ockham, Surrey, in a cottage he called Walden. Edward Carpenter confessed that *Walden* served "to make me uncomfortable for some years" and frequently quoted from it in *Towards Democracy*. *The Eagle and the Serpent*, a "little magazine" published in London from 1898 to 1902, was dedicated to "the philosophy of life enunciated by Nietzsche, Emerson, Stirner, Thoreau and Goethe." In Ireland, William Butler Yeats, inspired by his father's reading of *Walden*, wrote one of his most beloved poems, "The Lake Isle of Innisfree."

The centenary of Thoreau's birth was celebrated in London in 1917 at a public meeting at which W. H. Hudson proclaimed that "when the bicentenary comes around . . . he will be regarded as . . . one without master or mate . . . and who was in the foremost ranks of the prophets." The London *Bookman* devoted a whole issue to Thoreau, including a long reminiscent essay by Emerson's son Edward. Unfortunately, however, by the end of World War I, British interest in Thoreau withered away and has never been revived. He is now probably one of the most neglected major American authors in England.

Outside the English-speaking world Thoreau first attracted attention in Germany. *Walden* appeared in a fine translation by Emma Emmerich in 1897 (which is still in print today) and has been translated at least four other times. A translation of *Winter* appeared in 1900 and *Spring* in 1947. Translations of various essays have appeared from time to time. A number of articles about him appeared in the press in the years before World War I, and two pamphlet-sized biographies—one by A. Prinzinger in 1895 and one by Karl Knortz in 1899. Between the wars there was a long silence; Thoreau's ideas and Nazism were completely incompatible. But by the 1950s there was a revival of interest, and since then translations, articles, and doctoral dissertations have appeared regularly.

Elsewhere on the Continent interest in Thoreau has been sporadic. A translation of *Walden* into French appeared in 1922 and another in the 1960s. Leon Bazalgette's fictionized biography appeared in 1924. In the 1960s there was an active "Friends of Thoreau" group in Paris that sponsored a goodly number of publications by and about Thoreau. Since World War II translations of *Walden* have appeared in Denmark, Norway, Sweden, Finland, Italy, Czechoslovakia (there had been earlier ones there in 1924 and 1933), and Greece. A translation did not appear in Spain until after the Franco regime ended in the 1970s, although Spanish translations had appeared in 1945 and 1949 in South America. A Portuguese translation appeared in Brazil in 1953. A Dutch translation had appeared as early as 1902, sponsored by Frederick van Eeden, who had established a utopian community named Walden on the outskirts of Amsterdam in 1897. *Walden* had been translated into Russian in 1900 and 1910, before the Russian Revolution. Both Tolstoy and Chekov read Thoreau with interest and recommended him to their friends. In recent years there has been a good deal of interest in Thoreau in Soviet Russia. *Walden* has been retranslated, and a number of doctoral dissertations have been written about him.

Gandhi's interest in Thoreau is so well known that it hardly needs rehearsing. He is said to have carried a copy of "Civil Disobedience" with him wherever he went in later years. Thoreau's name is often referred to in Gandhi's collected works. After Gandhi's death, the Indian government sponsored translations of *Walden* into fifteen different Indian languages. *Walden* has also been translated into both Hebrew and Arabic in recent years. There have been several Chinese translations. Japanese interest has been phenomenal. Many there find a kinship between Thoreau and Zen. *Walden* has been translated at least fifteen times (once as early as 1911) and many of his other works as well. Scholarly articles in Japanese on Thoreau number in the hundreds, and there has been an active Thoreau Society, meeting usually twice a year, since 1965. In recent years there have been more editions of *Walden* available in Tokyo than in New York City. In short, *Walden* is now available in nearly every major modern language.

Thoreau has taken a full century to achieve recognition. In American literature only Herman Melville has climbed more spectacularly the heights of literary fame from obscurity. In his own lifetime Thoreau was almost invariably dismissed as an eccentric and unimportant imitator òf Emerson. Today he overshadows Emerson. We Americans are prone to compiling lists of the five, the ten, the twenty-five, the fifty, or the hundred greatest authors. And no such list in recent years fails to place Thoreau near the top.

### Sources for Chapter Six

The most useful survey of T criticism over the years is Wendell Glick, *The Recognition of HDT* (Ann Arbor, 1969). It reprints with commentary forty-five critical essays on T from 1848 to 1966. A smaller but similar collection is Walter Harding, *T: A Century of Criticism* (Dallas, 1954). Samuel A. Jones, *Pertaining to T* (Detroit, 1901), gathers many of the important critical essays that appeared in T's lifetime or shortly thereafter. Sherman Paul, *T: A Collection of Critical Essays,* gathers fourteen twentieth-century essays. Other collections include John Hicks, *T in Our Season* (Amherst, 1966; originally published as *TSB* XVII); J. Golden Taylor, *The Western T Centenary (TSB* XIX); Walter Harding, *The T Centennial* (Albany, 1964); and Walter Harding, George Brenner and Paul A. Doyle, *HDT: Studies and Commentaries* (Rutherford, 1972). See also Randall Stewart, "The Growth of T's Reputation" *(CE,* 7, 1946, 208–14), and Gilbert P. Coleman, "T and His Critics" *(Dial,* 40, 1906, 352–56).

Fuller bibliographical details for the various books and articles cited in the chapter follow. T's reliance upon Emerson is charged in James Russell Lowell, *A Fable for Critics* (New York, 1848). See also E. J. Nichols, "Identification of Characters in Lowell's *A Fable for Critics" (AL,* 4, 1932, 191–94). Greeley's review of *A Week* (sometimes mistakenly attributed to George Ripley) appeared in the *New York Tribune* for June 13, 1849, and Lowell's in the *Mass. Quart. Rev.* (3, 1849, 40–51). For "The First Year's Sales of T's *Walden,"* see Walter Harding *(TSB* 117). Greeley's notice of *Walden* appeared in the *New York Tribune* for July 29, 1854. *Putnam's* review, by Charles Frederick Briggs, appears in 4, 1854, 443–48; the *National Anti-Slavery Standard* review on December 16, 1854; Bronson Alcott, "The Forester," in the *Atlantic* (9, 1862, 443–45). For Alcott's plans, see Anton Huffert, "Alcott on T's *Atlas of Concord" (TSB* 56). Hazel J. Pfennig, "Periodical Literary Criticism (1800–1865)" (New York Univ., Ph.D., 1932, pp. 210–47), includes a selection of and discussion of periodical reviews of T's lifetime and early posthumous works. Emerson's funeral sermon is reprinted in most collections of his works and is also often used as an introduction to collections of T's works. For Emerson's misediting of T's letters and the ensuing controversy, see Walter Harding and Carl Bode, eds., *The Correspondence of HDT* (New York, 1958, p. xiii). A good many of the reviews of T's posthumous books are evaluated in John C. Broderick, "American Reviews of T's Posthumous Books, 1863–1866" *(UTSE,* 34, 1955, 125–39). For the sales records of his posthumous books, see Walter Harding, "The Early Printing Records of T's Books" *(ATQ,* 11, 1971, 44–59). Lowell's essay first appeared in the *North Amer. Rev.* (101, 1865, 597–608) and has been frequently reprinted. For details of the Sanborn-Jones-Hosmer controversy, see Horace Hosmer, *Remembrances of Concord and the Thoreaus,* edited by George Hendrick (Urbana, 1977), incidentally one of the most delightful books of Thoreauviana. Hendrick and Fritz Oehlschlaeger are currently involved in editing a great many other important papers in the Samuel Arthur Jones Collection at the University of Illinois Library, and they should be appearing in the near future. See also the equally important Alfred Hosmer collection in the Concord Free Public Library. For Francis Allen's editorial experiences, see his *T's Editors: History and Reminiscence (TSB* VII). Another good insight into Thoreau's reputation in the late nineteenth century and the gathering then of his early disciples is provided by Anna and Walton Ricketson, *Daniel Ricketson and His Friends* (New Bedford, 1910). For an enumeration of 132 different editions of *Walden,* see Walter Harding, *A Centennial Check-List of Editions of HDT's Walden* (Charlottesville, 1954).

For a survey of twentieth-century criticism of T, see Michael Meyer, *Several More Lives to Live: T's Political Reputation in America* (Westport, 1977). See also Richard Ruland, *The Rediscovery of American Literature* (Cambridge, 1967), and Theodore Haddin, "The Changing Image of HT: The Emergence of the Literary Artist" (Univ. of Michigan, Ph.D., 1968). For a dissent against some of the criticism of the 1960s, see Hubert Hoeltje, "Misconceptions in Current T Criticism" *(PQ,* 47, 1968, 563–70).

The most extensive survey of T's reputation abroad is Eugene Timpe, ed., *T Abroad* (Hamden, 1971). See also Walter Harding,

"T's Fame Abroad," in *Boston Pub. Lib. Quart.* (9, 1959, 94–101). George Eliot's notice appeared in the *Westminster Rev.* (65, 1856, 302–3); Stevenson's "HDT: His Character and Opinions" in *Cornhill Magazine* (41, 1880, 665–82) and his recantation in *Familiar Studies of Men and Books* (London, 1886). Henry Salt's interest in T is delineated in George Hendrick, *Henry Salt: Humanitarian Reformer and Man of Letters* (Urbana, 1977). The best account of T's popularity in England at the turn of the century is George Hendrick, "Henry S. Salt and the Late Victorian Socialists, and T" *(NEQ, 50, 1977, 409–22).* The June, 1917, number of the London *Bookman* (52, 75–104) is devoted to T. James F. Lacey, "HDT in German Criticism 1881–1965" (New York Univ., Ph.D., 1968), is a model upon which we wish other dissertations on T's reputation in Japan, India, Russia, and elsewhere might well be based. It not only summarizes and evaluates all the pertinent books and articles but also the German doctoral dissertations on T and evaluates the accuracy of all the book-length German translations of T. The authoritative study of T's influence on Gandhi is George Hendrick, "T and Gandhi" (Univ. of Texas, Ph.D., 1954). See also his "The Influence of T's 'Civil Disobedience' on Gandhi's Satyagraha" *(NEQ,* 29, 1956, 462–71). His "Gandhiana at TxU" *(LCUT,* 5, 1954, 43–47) adds important bibliographical details.

# Bibliographies

Students of Thoreau are fortunate in that there are available good bibliographies of both his works and the writings about him. Francis H. Allen, *Bibliography of Henry David Thoreau* (Boston, 1908), supersedes all earlier works. J. S. Wade, "A Contribution to a Bibliography from 1909 to 1936 of Henry David Thoreau" (*Jour. of the New York Entomological Society*, 47, 1939, 163–203), and William White, *A Henry David Thoreau Bibliography 1908–1937* (Boston, 1939), duplicate each other in a large measure, but each contains material not in the other. They are both supplemented by Philip E. Burham and Carvel Collins, "Contribution to a Bibliography of Thoreau, 1938–1945" (*BB*, 19, 1946, 16–18, 37–40). Since 1941 a running bibliography has appeared in each issue of the quarterly *Thoreau Society Bulletin*. These have been gathered into Walter Harding and Jean Cameron Advena, *A Bibliography of the Thoreau Society Bulletin Bibliographies 1941–1969* (Troy, 1971). A more selective listing is Christopher A. Hildenbrand, *A Bibliography of Scholarship about Henry David Thoreau (1940–1967) (Fort Hays Studies: Bibliography Series* No. 3, 1967).

Specialized bibliographies include Walter Harding, "A Bibliography of Thoreau in Poetry, Fiction and Drama" *(BB,* 18, 1943, 15–18); Harding, *A Centennial Check-List of the Editions of Henry David Thoreau's Walden* (Charlottesville, 1954); and Harding, *Thoreau's Library* (Charlottesville, 1957).

Catalogues of Thoreau manuscripts are listed among the Sources for Chapter Two.

Raymond Borst is at work on a primary bibliography of Thoreau for the University of Pittsburgh series in Bibliography.

\*   \*   \*

Thoreau is now so fully "bibliographied" that there is a real need for a selective annotated secondary bibliography to guide the student through the great morass of duplicative and redundant material. The most recent selective and annotated bibliography is Lewis Leary, "Henry David Thoreau," in James Woodress, ed., *Eight American Authors* (New York, 1971, pp. 129–71). *American Literary Scholarship: An Annual* (Duke Univ. Press, 1963–     ) includes a bibliographical essay on Transcendentalism that evaluates most of the year's work on Thoreau.

Thoreau scholars should be aware of three different quarterly periodicals devoted to Thoreau: *The Thoreau Society Bulletin* (1941–     ), Walter Harding, ed., State University College, Geneseo, New York 14454; *The Concord Saunterer* (1966–     ), Anne McGrath, ed., The Thoreau Lyceum, 156 Belknap Street, Concord, Mass. 01742; and the *Thoreau Journal Quarterly* (1969–     ), Marie Urbanski, ed., English Department, University of Maine, Orono, Maine 04473.

# Index

Abernethy Library (Middlebury, Vt.), 90
Abolitionism, 12-13, 28, 39, 40-42, 48-49, 56-58, 80, 83, 85-86, 107, 108, 110, 120, 132-37, 155-57
Academic reputation of HDT, 207-19
Adams, Alexander, 87
Adams, Henry, 196
Adams, Raymond, 1, 25, 26, 28, 60, 79, 80, 82, 153, 155, 177, 178, 197, 198, 207, 209
Adams, Richard P., 51, 201
Advena, Jean Cameron, 225
Aelian, 95
Aeschylus, 35, 95
*Aesthetic Papers,* 9, 41
Aesthetics, HDT's: architecture, 193-94, 201; literature, 160-63, 177-79, 195, 198; music, 192-93, 201; painting and sculpture, 191-92
"After the Death of John Brown." *See* "Martyrdom of John Brown"
Agassiz, Louis, 11, 154
Ahearn, Kerry, 156
Aitteon, Joe, 65
Albrecht, Robert, 83, 85
Alcott, A. Bronson, 6, 13, 15, 27, 41, 73, 74, 80, 110, 157, 204, 222
Alcott, Louisa May, 28
Algren, Nelson, 210
"Allegash and the East Branch, The," 63, 64, 87
Allen, Francis H., 20, 29, 35, 51, 63, 66, 73, 83, 86, 89, 153, 207-08, 223, 225

Allen, Phineas, 2, 106, 118
American literature: HDT in histories of, 212-19; HDT's interest in, 102-03, 117
American Men of Letters (series), 17
*American Renaissance,* 209. *See also* Matthiessen, F.O.
"American Scholar, The" (Emerson), 108, 140
Americanisms, HDT's use of, 169-70, 196
Anacreon, 36, 95
"Anacreontics," 79
Anagrams in *Walden,* 191, 201
Anarchism, 81, 137-39, 157, 210
Ancestry, 1, 25
Anderson, Charles R., 84, 152, 159, 181, 184, 189, 197, 199
Antaeus, 187-88
*Antigone* (Sophocles), 41, 95
Antislavery. *See* Abolitionism
Archer, William, 219
Architecture, 193-94, 201
Aristotle, 95, 128
Armstrong, James, 151, 159
Arnold, Matthew, 100
Arnold, William Harris, 90
Arrest, HDT's 27, 40-41, 108
Art. *See* Aesthetics
Artist of Kouroo. *See* Kouroo
Association for the Advancement of Science, 11, 128, 132
Atkinson, J. Brooks, 24
*Atlantic Monthly,* 14, 15, 16, 60-67 *passim,* 205

227

"Atlas of Concord," 204, 222
Audubon, J. J., 128, 154, 164
Augustine, Saint, 120
"Aulus Persius Flaccus," 37, 79
Austin, James, 28
Autobiographical impulse, 160-63, 195-96
*Autumn*, 10, 73, 206
"Autumnal Tints," 61, 86

Bacon, Sir Francis, 100, 116
Baker, Gail, 82
Ballou, Ellen, 28
Ballowe, James, 79, 157
Barrett, Sam, 140
Bartram, William, 59, 154
Basile, Joseph, 158
Bates, Katherine Lee, 214
Baym, Nina, 153, 183, 199
Bazalgette, Leon, 29, 220
"Bean-Field, The," 187-88
Beat generation, 210
Bedau, Hugo Adam, 81
Beers, Henry A., 213
Bellew, F. A. T., 133
Benson, Adolph B., 116
Benton, Myron, 151
Berg Collection, 90. *See also* New York
    Public Library
Berkshire Mountains, 26
Berneth, Mary G., 153
Berry, Edmund, 47, 83
Berryman, Charles, 119
"Best Criticism, The," 76
*Bhagavad Gita*, 93, 94, 113, 114. *See also*
    Oriental literature
Bhatia, Kamala, 113
Bible, 100, 117
Bier, Jesse, 157
Biographies of HDT, 15-25; juvenile, 30;
    pictorial, 30
Birds: HDT on, 89; imagery of, 200
Bishop, Jonathan, 82
Blake, Harrison Gray Otis, 10, 13, 14, 46,
    48, 56, 60, 69, 73, 74, 93, 141, 206
Blanding, Thomas, 74, 76, 89, 116
Blankenship, Russell, 216
Blatchford, Robert, 219
Blinderman, Abraham, 159
Boas, Ralph, 217
Bode, Carl, 30, 88, 89, 116, 156, 223
Boies, J. J., 199
Boller, Paul F., Jr., 119, 132
Bond, Brian, 82
Bonner, Willard H., 116, 119
*Bookman* (London), 220
Borst, Raymond, 226
*Boston Miscellany*, 35
Boston Society of Natural History, 11, 129
Botany, 128-29
Boudreau, Gordon V., 117, 120
Bowling, Lawrence, 156
Boynton, H. W., 215

Boynton, Percy, 216, 217
Bradford, Robert, 27
Brazil, 221
Brenner, George, 222
Briggs, Charles Frederick, 222
British Labour Party, 42, 219
Broderick, John C., 27, 51, 80, 85, 98, 116,
    157, 200, 223
Bronson, Walter, 214
Brook Farm, 134
Brooks, Van Wyck, 29
Brown, John, 13, 28, 39, 56-58, 85-86, 108,
    120, 135-37, 156, 160, 178
Brown, Roger, 166, 196
Brown, Theodore M., 194, 201
Browne, Sir Thomas, 98-99, 100, 116
Brownson, Orestes, 3, 97, 109, 119, 148
Budge, M. A., 116
Buell, Lawrence, 186, 189-90, 195, 201
Buranelli, Vincent, 156
Burham, Philip E., 225
Burns, Anthony, 48
Burns, John R., 100, 117
Burr, Michael, 201
Burroughs, John, 53, 56, 86, 154
Burton, Katherine, 217
Business, HDT on, 124, 141, 187, 197. *See also*
    Franklin, Benjamin
Byron, George Gordon, 101

Cabin, HDT's, 27, 55, 85
Cabot, James Elliot, 11
Cady, Lyman V., 114
Cairns, William, 215
Cameron, Kenneth Walter, 26, 27, 28, 78,
    83, 88, 90, 111, 115, 116, 119, 154
Campbell, George, 119
Campbell, Joseph, 118
Canadian notebook, 47, 76, 83
Canby, Henry Seidel, 4, 5, 21-22, 24, 29, 66,
    75, 91, 158, 209
Cape Cod (Mass.), 9, 112
*Cape Cod*, 32, 65, 66-69, 87-88, 181, 205
Capitalism, 157. *See also* Economic thought
Carlyle, Thomas, 40, 51, 97, 101, 109, 177,
    196. *See also* "Thomas Carlyle and His
    Works"
Carpenter, Edward, 220
Carroll, Mary Suzanne, 81
Carson, Barbara H., 201
Catholicism. *See* Roman Catholicism
Cato, 95
Catskill Mountains, 26
Cavell, Stanley, 84, 196
Chalmers, Alexander, 98
Chamberlain, Allen, 28
Channing, Edward Tyrrel, 32, 33
Channing, Rev. William Ellery (the elder),
    7
Channing, William Ellery (the younger) 7,
    11, 14, 15-17, 27, 29, 46, 47, 54, 63, 66, 72,
    89, 98, 151, 180, 203, 205

"Chastity and Sensuality," 46, 82
Chaucer, Geoffrey, 99, 116
Chekov, Anton, 221
Chen, David T. Y., 114
"Chesuncook," 63, 64, 65, 87, 206
"Chinese Four Books," 37, 79, 93
*Chinese Four Books,* 114
Chinese literature. *See* Oriental literature
Cholmondeley, Thomas, 12, 13, 28, 93, 113
Christianity, 44, 203. *See also* Religion
Christie, John Aldrich, 81, 104, 118, 158
Christy, Arthur, 45, 82, 90, 94, 113
Chuang Tzu, 114
Cities, HDT on, 124, 145-46
"Civil Disobedience" (essay and action), 8-
    9, 27, 40-42, 49, 56, 57, 60, 80-81, 138-39,
    156, 157, 209, 210-11, 212, 216, 219, 221
Civil Rights Movement (1960s), 42, 210-11
Civil War, 137
Civilization, HDT on, 54, 55, 66, 141-42, 144-
    47, 158
Classbook autobiographical sketch, 33
Clapper, Ronald, 50, 83
Clark, Harry Hayden, 119, 152
Clergy, HDT on, 130-31. *See also* Religion
Clough, Wilson O., 218
Coleman, Gilbert P., 222
Coleridge, Samuel Taylor, 97, 101, 177, 201
*Collected Poems of Henry Thoreau,* 69-71, 88. *See*
    *also* Poems
College essays, 17, 20, 32-34, 78
Collie, David, 113
Collins, Carvel, 225
Collins, James, 55
Columella, 95
Colyer, Richard, 199
Commencement exercise, 33
Commerce. *See* Business, Economic thought
Commonplace books, 76, 90, 92, 99
*Commonwealth* (Boston), 15
Concord, Massachusetts, 7, 60, 86, 111, 117,
    204; maps of, 25, 77
Concord Academy, 2, 4, 26, 92, 94, 106, 115,
    118
Concord Antiquarian Society, 90
Concord Free Public Library, 90, 207, 223
Concord Lyceum, 2, 8, 9, 13, 27, 36, 39, 40,
    41, 46, 61, 66, 75, 80, 100, 110, 149-50,
    204
*Concord Saunterer, The,* 226
*Consciousness in Concord,* 74, 89
Conservation. *See* Ecology
Conservatives, HDT on, 133
Continental literature, 97-98
"Conversation," 72, 76
Conway, Adaline May, 215
Cook, Reginald L., 52, 84, 90, 115, 118, 152,
    157, 171, 185, 196, 199
Cooke, George W., 26
Cooper, James Fenimore, 102
*Correspondence of Henry David Thoreau, The,* 88
Cosbey, Robert, 87

Cosman, Max, 25, 27
"Country Walking," 16, 89. *See also* "Walks
    and Talks in Concord"
Couser, Thomas, G., 159
Craig, George, 177, 198
Creativity, the development of HDT's, 23
Crèvecoeur, Hector St. John de, 164
Cronkhite, G. Ferris, 158
Cruickshank, Helen, 89
Cryder, M. E., 83
Culver, Kathleen Anne, 198
Curtis, George William, 46, 67
Czechoslovakia, 221

Daniel, Samuel, 117
Dante, 98, 116
"Dark Ages," 37, 79
Darwin, Charles, 104, 154
Davies, Barrie, 83
Day, Martin S., 218
Death: HDT on, 68, 159; HDT's, 14-15, 28,
    151-52, 204-05
Dedmond, Francis, 157
Deevey, Edward S., 59, 85, 86
DeFalco, Joseph, 79, 156
Defoe, Daniel, 100
Democratic party, 134
*Democratic Review,* 36, 38
DeMott, Robert, J., 114, 198
Denmark, 221
Depression, HDT's reputation during, 208
DeQuincey, Thomas, 101
Derleth, August, 30
"Devil, The," 76
Dewey, John, 148
*Dial, The,* 5, 10, 12, 26, 32-39 *passim,* 43, 68,
    79, 93, 114, 202
Dickens, Charles, 101
"Died," 34, 78
Dillman, Richard H., 119, 157
"Dispersion of Seeds, The," 75
Doctoral dissertations on HDT, vii, 207, 209,
    211, 220
Donatello (Hawthorne's *Marble Faun*), 6
Donne, John, 98-99
Douglass, Frederick, 56, 195
Doyle, Paul A., 222
Drake, William, 74, 77, 120, 198
Drama, HDT in, 226
Drinnon, Richard, 81, 118
Dryden, John, 100
Dunbar, Asa, 1
Dunbar, Marianne, 25
Dunn, Esther Cloudman, 99, 116
DuPree, Robert H., 153
Duyckinck, Evert, and George, 212
Dwight, Timothy, 59

*Eagle and the Serpent,* 220
"Eagleswood" (Perth Amboy, N.J.), 13, 28
*Early Essays and Miscellanies,* 36, 78, 79, 80, 82
*Early Spring in Massachusetts,* 10, 73, 206

Eaton, Philip W., 197
Eckstorm, Fannie H., 65, 86, 87, 153
Ecology, 59, 86, 129, 154, 210
Economic thought, 107, 139-41, 157
Edel, Leon, 30, 157
Education: HDT's, 2-3, 26, 32-34, 105, 118, 149; HDT's views on, 148-50, 197. *See also* Harvard University
Edwards, Jonathan, 120
Eeden, Frederick van, 221
Eisely, Loren, 154
Eisenlohr, Herman L., 197
Eliot, George, 219, 224
Emerson, Edward, 3, 9, 19-20, 29, 220
Emerson, Lidian, 5, 21-22
Emerson, Ralph Waldo, 9, 10, 11, 16, 21, 30, 37, 38, 39, 42, 46, 50, 54, 56, 66, 70, 72, 79, 88, 89, 97, 100, 117, 120, 121, 157, 161, 203, 206, 212-223 *passim;* eulogy for HDT, 15, 19, 65; friendship with HDT, 5-6, 8, 22, 26, 33, 40, 81, 202; influence on HDT, 93, 98, 103, 107-09, 111, 119, 140, 207; influence on HDT's reputation, 19, 24, 69, 150, 205; style compared with HDT's, 51, 108, 166-67, 196, 198, 199, 201; on Transcendental individualism, and HDT, 143-44
Emerson, Waldo, 5
Emerson, William, 6
Emmerich, Emma, 220
England, HDT's reputation in, 219-20, 224
English literature, HDT on, 98-101, 116-17
Epiphanic structure, 201
Erikson, Erik, 23, 30, 119
Erlich, Michael G., 81, 155
Erskine, John, 215
"Ethnical Scriptures," 37, 93
Etzler, J. A., 38, 79
Eulau, Heinz, 81
European literature, HDT on, 97-98, 115-16
Evans, Charles M., 156
Evans, Francis E. B., 170, 196
Excursions (HDT's), 9, 14, 26, 28, 35, 42-43, 46-47, 63-69, 74, 82, 83, 87, 88, 104, 118
"Excursion to Canada, An" 46, 47, 82
*Excursions,* 63, 78, 82, 86, 205

Fabians, 219
Fable, 115
*Fable for Critics, A* (Lowell), 203, 222
Fairbanks, Jonathan, 86, 126, 152
Falk, Robert, 120
"Fall of the Leaf, The," 75
*Familiar Letters,* 69, 88
Family (HDT's), 1-2, 23, 25, 26, 107
Farming, HDT on, 187
Fascism, 208
Feidelson, Charles, Jr., 199
Felton, C. C., 35
Fendelman, Earl B., 196
Fergenson, Laraine R., 117
Fiction, HDT in, 226
Fiedler, Leslie A., 159

Fields, James T., 15
Figurative language, 164-66, 196, 197, 200
Finland, 221
*First and Last Journeys of Thoreau,* 71
Fitzgerald, Gabrielle M., 195
Flanagan, John, 88
Fleck, Richard F., 90, 118, 200
Foerster, Norman, 97, 100, 101, 112, 208
"Fog," 70
Folklore, 117-18
Foord, Sophia, 9, 27
Ford, Arthur Lewis, Jr., 88
Ford, Nick Aaron, 156
Form, 101, 179-91, 198
Fourier, François Mari Charles, 38, 110, 133-34
Fox, Charles, 43
France, HDT's reputation in, 220
Franco, Francisco, 221
Franklin, Benjamin, 157
Franklin Mint, The, 212
Frederick, Mary P., 153
French literature, 97, 115-16
Freniere, Emil, 26
Freud, Sigmund, 22
Friends of the Earth, 210
"Friendship," 11, 32, 42, 46
Frost, Ruth, 28
Fruits and Seeds (HDT manuscript), 28, 75
Fruitlands, 6, 134
Frye, Northrop, 158
Fugitive Slave Law, 108
Fuller, Margaret, 5, 7, 11, 34, 35, 202
Fuller, Richard, 35, 78
Fussell, Edwin, 82, 118, 158, 218

Galgan, Gerald, 158
Galligan, Edward L., 85, 175, 197
Gandhi, Mahatma, 42, 136, 221, 224
Garber, Frederick, 153
Garrison, William Lloyd, 39, 41, 48, 58, 110, 120
Gates, Michael, 114
Geller, L. D., 28
"Gentle Boy," 5, 26, 70
German literature, 97, 115
Germany, HDT's reputation in, 220, 224
"Getting a Living." *See* "Life Without Principle"
Gierasch, Walter, 116
Gilman, Albert, 166, 196
Gilpin, Rev. William, 101, 117
Gimlin, Joan S., 159
Ginsberg, Allen, 210
Gleason, Herbert, 87
Glick, Wendell, 28, 39, 49, 56, 58, 76, 77, 79, 80, 81, 83, 85, 92, 109, 110, 112, 120, 135-36, 156, 161, 195, 222
Goethe, Johann Wolfgang von, 43, 97, 115, 220
Gohdes, Clarence, 26
Gookin, Daniel, 44

Government, HDT on, 40-41, 48-49, 57, 76, 137-39, 157, 197. *See also* Politics; Reform
Gozzi, Raymond, 22, 29
*Graham's Magazine*, 40
Grammar, English, 167
"Gratitude," 76
Gray, Asa, 128, 154
Greece, 221
Greek literature, 67, 94-97, 115
Greeley, Horace, 6-7, 12, 17, 27, 40, 202, 203, 222
Green, Eugene, 117
Greene, David Mason, 198
Greene, Maud Honeyman, 28
Greenough, Horatio, 201
Griffin, William J., 201
Griswold, Rufus Wilmot, 212
Gruber, Christian, 106, 109, 118
*Gulliver's Travels* (Swift), 52
Gura, Philip F., 87, 102, 117, 153, 159
Guthrie, Harold N., 197

Haddin, Theodore, 200, 223
Hall, Bishop Joseph, 100, 116
Hall of Fame (New York University), 210
Halleck, Reuben P., 215
Harber, Kenneth, 87
Harding, Brian R., 116, 198
Harding, Walter, 22-23, 24-30 *passim*, 72, 77, 79-89, *passim*, 112, 152, 154, 156, 159, 165, 196, 222, 223, 225, 226
*Harivansa*, 45, 93
Harlan, Richard, 128
Harpers Ferry. *See* Brown, John
Harris, Kenneth, 78
Hart, James, 217
Hart, John, 212
Harvard University, 2, 3, 33, 35, 45, 90, 92, 93, 94, 111, 112, 118, 119. *See also* Education
Hawthorne, Julian, 213
Hawthorne, Nathaniel, 6, 9, 27, 102, 112, 120, 201
Haymaker, Richard E., 196
Hayward, John, 44
Hazard, Lucy, 216
"Haze," 70
Hazlitt, William, 36
Heckewelder, John G. E., 104
Hemans, Felicia, 101
Hendrick, George, 25, 29, 113, 223, 224
Henry, Alexander, 44
"Herald of Freedom," 39, 79-80
*Herald of Freedom*, 12
Herbert, George, 100
"Hermes Trismedistus," 37, 79
Hermit, HDT as, 142-43
Herodotus, 95
Herr, William A., 81, 139, 156, 157
Hicks, John, 77, 81, 155, 156, 222
Hicks, Philip M., 164, 196

Higginson, Thomas Wentworth, 73, 213, 215
"Higher Laws," 151, 159
Hildenbrand, Christopher A., 225
Hill, E. B., 207
Himelick, Raymond, 117
"Hindoos," 76
Hindu literature. *See* Oriental literature.
Hinton, R.J., 58
Hippies, 210
History: local, 102, 117; transcended, 162-63. *See also* Natural history
Hoagland, Clayton, 26
Hoar, Edward, 7, 64
Hoar, Elizabeth, 27
Hoar, Judge, 73
Hoch, David G., 114
Hodges, Robert, 197
Hoeltje, Hubert H., 26, 27, 115, 118, 223
Hoffman, Michael, 158
Hollis, C. Carroll, 28
Homer, 95, 101
"Homer. Ossian. Chaucer," 37, 79
Homoeroticism. *See* Sexuality
Horace, 95
Hosmer, Alfred, 90, 223
Hosmer, Fred, 90, 207
Hosmer, Herbert, 90
Hosmer, Horace, 25, 207, 223
Houghton Library (Harvard University), 80
Houghton Mifflin, 28, 73, 206, 207, 208, 209
Hourihan, Paul, 5, 26, 81
Houston, Howard, 200
Hovde, Carl F., 81, 112
Howard, Leon, 218
Howarth, William L., 73, 77, 86, 89, 118, 125, 152
Howes, Abby Willis, 215
"Huckleberries," 75, 89
Hudson, W. H., 196, 220
Hudspeth, Robert, 27
Huffert, Anton, 26, 115, 159, 222
Humor, 62, 65, 67-68, 83, 173-78, 197
Hunter, John Dunn, 118
Huntington Library (San Marino, California), 49, 50, 71, 90
Hut (HDT's), 27, 55, 85
Hyman, Stanley E., 85
Hyperbole, HDT's use of, 121-22. *See also* Style

Idealism. *See* Transcendentalism
"Il Penseroso," 33, 100
Imagery, *See* Symbolic imagery
Immortality, 155
"In Adam's fall," 132
India, HDT's reputation in, 221, 224
Indian, American, 45, 64-65, 87, 90, 96, 103-04, 118, 146-48, 158-59, 169
Indian notebooks, 76, 90, 103, 118
Individualism. *See* Government; Politics; Reform; Solitude; Transcendentalism

"Inspiration," 70
Ireland, HDT's reputation in, 220
Irish, 159
Irving, Washington, 102
Italian literature, 98, 116
Italy, 221
Ives, Charles, 201

Jackson, C. T., 65
Jacques, John, 152
Jamblichus, 95
Japan, HDT's reputation in, 221
Japp, A. H., 29, 219
Jesuit relations, 102, 103, 118
Jeswine, Miriam A., 94
Johnson, Edward, 54, 102
Johnson, Paul David, 82
Jones, Anna, 34
Jones, Buford, 116
Jones, Joseph, 28
Jones, Samuel Arthur, 27, 80, 207, 222, 223
Josselyn, John, 65, 102, 117
*Journal*, 54, 81, 87, 89, 92, 99, 101, 118, 153, 157, 161, 190, 196, 198, 200; as source for published works, 10, 32-49 *passim*, 58-66 *passim*, 206; publication history of, 72-75, 207, 209; Transcendentalism in, 109, 125-26, 152
Jung, Carl Gustav, 200

Kaiser, Leo, 35, 78, 79, 200
Kaplan, Nathaniel, 114
Karabatsos, James, 81
Katahdin. *See* Ktaadn, Mount
Katsaros, Thomas, 114
Katz, Jonathan, 30
Kavanaugh, James V., 201
Keats, John, 101
Keiser, Albert, 118
Keller, Michael, 155
Kern, Alexander, 110, 119, 120, 122, 152
Kerouac, Jack, 210
Kertesz, Louise C., 115, 200
Ketcham, Ralph, 156
Kettler, Robert, 84
Kim, Kichung, 114, 154, 196
King, Martin Luther, Jr., 42, 136, 210
Knapp, Ella, 207
Knight, Grant C., 217
Knortz, Karl, 220
Koopman, Louise, 26
Kopp, Charles C., 155
Koster, Donald N., 119
Kouroo, artist of, 144, 161-63
Kraitsir, Charles, 153, 197
Krutch, Joseph Wood, 29, 52, 108, 127, 152
Ktaadn, Mount, 87, 126-27, 152
"Ktaadn and the Maine Woods," 63, 64, 87
Kwiat, Joseph J., 33, 78, 106, 118

Labor, 140-41
Lacey, James F., 224

"L'Allegro," 33, 100
Lamb, Charles, 36
Lambert, L. Gary, 116
"Landlord, The," 36, 37, 79
Lane, Lauriat, Jr., 78, 80, 84, 85, 155, 159
Language (HDT's): use of figurative, 164-66, 196, 197, 200; knowledge of foreign, 97; levels of usage, 167, 168-69, 170, 196; nature as symbolic, 182-83, 198
Lanier, Sidney, 112
LaRosa, Ralph, 197
"Last Days of John Brown, The," 58, 85, 178
Law, HDT on. *See* Government; Politics
Lawrence, Jerome, 211
"Laws of Menu, The," 36, 79
*Laws of Menu, The,* 93, 94, 114
Lawton, William Cranston, 214
Leary, Lewis, 87, 226
*Leaves of Grass* (Whitman), 13
Lebeaux, Richard, 23, 30, 119, 158, 212
Lebrun, Jean Munro, 25
Lectures, 8, 9, 14, 27, 36, 40, 41, 43, 46, 48, 56, 58, 60, 61, 62, 63, 64, 66, 75, 76, 79, 80, 100. *See also* Concord Lyceum
Lee, Robert E. (playwright), 211
Leisy, Ernest E., 116, 117, 216
Lemmon, Leonard, 213
Letters, 32, 38, 39, 40, 69, 72, 88, 205. See also *Correspondence of Henry David Thoreau; The Familiar Letters;* and *Letters to Various Persons*
*Letters to Various Persons,* 69, 88, 205, 206
Lewis, R. W. B., 155
Lewisohn, Ludwig, 217
*Liberator,* 39, 48, 57, 58
"Life Misspent," 76
"Life Without Principle," 60, 61, 62, 86
Liggera, Joseph J., 196
Limnology, 85, 129, 154
Lincoln, Abraham, 137
Lind, Jenny, 193
Linstromberg, Robin, 79, 157
Literary criticism (HDT's), 177-79, 198
Literary style. *See* Style
Locke, John, 33, 106, 109, 153
Long, Larry R., 117
Long, William J., 215
Longfellow, Henry Wadsworth, 71
Loomis, Grant, 115
Lorch, Frederick W., 80, 179, 181, 198
Loskiel, George Henry, 103
Lost Journal (1840-41), 89
Loudon, John Claudius, 59
"Love," 46, 82
Lowance, Mason, 120
Lowell, James Russell, 14, 15, 19, 24, 30, 44, 64, 65, 71, 107, 171, 173, 203, 206, 213, 216, 222, 223
Lowell, Robert, 68
Lownes, Albert, 82, 90
Lucas, Alec, 154

Lucretius, 95
Lunt, Dudley, 81, 86, 87
Lyceum. *See* Concord Lyceum
*Lycidas* (Milton), 100
Lyon, Melvin E., 198

McAleer, John, 87
McAtee, W. L., 154
McCarthy, Joseph, 210
McElrath, Joseph, Jr., 77, 83
McGill, Frederick T., 27
McGrath, Anne, 226
McGuire, Errol M., 120
Machines, HDT on, 158. *See also* Progress
McInerney, Peter, 200
McIntosh, James, 115, 117, 126, 152, 190, 201
McKay, Glen W., 156
McKee, Christopher, 25, 26, 82
McLean, Albert, 27
MacMechan, Archibald, 216
MacShane, Frank, 114
Macy, John, 208, 215, 216
Madden, Edward, 81
Magnus, John L., 112
Maiden, Emory, Jr., 68, 87
Mailer, Norman, 196
*Main Currents in American Thought* (Parrington), 208
*Maine Woods, The,* 9, 32, 63-65, 66, 67, 73, 86-87, 126, 152, 159, 205
Malthus, Thomas Robert, 157
Mann family correspondence, 72
Mann, Horace, Jr., 14, 88
Manuscript Edition, 31, 73
Manuscripts (HDT's), 89-90, 226
*Marble Faun* (Hawthorne), 6
Marble, Annie Russell, 18-19, 29, 61
Marovitz, S. E., 114
Marsh, James, 101
"Martyrdom of John Brown," 58, 84. *See also* Brown, John
Marx, Leo, 85, 152, 158
Marxist readings of HDT, 82, 208
Massachusetts Agricultural Society, 129-30
Mathers (Puritans), 120
Matthews, Brander, 213
Matthews, J. Chesley, 98, 116
Matthiessen, F. O., 78, 85, 116, 150, 180, 198, 209, 210
Maxfield-Miller, Elizabeth, 27
Mazzini, Carla, 201
Meltzer, Milton, 30, 155
Melville, Herman, 102, 183, 201, 221
"Memorial Poem," 16, 17
Mencius, 41
Metaphors. *See* Figurative language
Metcalf, Henry A., 79
Meteorology, 129, 154
Metzer, Charles, 198, 201
Meyer, Michael, 27, 86, 156, 157, 208, 223
Mexican War, 40, 211

Michaux, F. André, 65
Middlesex Agricultural Society, 14, 58
Military, HDT on, 48
Miller, Arthur, 210
Miller, Perry, 30, 74, 89, 119
Miller, Sarah McEwen, 88
Milton, John, 33, 99, 100, 116
Minnesota, 15, 28, 61, 71, 72, 88
Mitchell, Donald G., 214
Modern Language Association, 76, 211, 218
Moldenhauer, Joseph, 84, 176, 197, 199
Moller, Mary Elkins, 159
Monadnock, Mount (New Hampshire), 9, 28
Money, HDT on, 140-41. *See also* Economic thought
*Moon, The,* 63, 86
"Moonlight," 63, 86
Moral law, 135-36. *See also* Government; Transcendentalism
More, Paul Elmer, 115, 208
Morgan Library (New York City), 47, 74, 90
Moser, Edwin L., 33, 78
Moss, Marcia, 27
Mott, Wesley T., 120
Mozart, Wolfgang Amadeus, 193
Mueller, Roger, 79, 114
Mungo, Ray, 82
Munroe, James, & Co., 11, 42, 43, 49, 203
Murray, Donald M., 159
Music, HDT on, 192-93, 201
"My Prayer," 70
Myerson, Joel, 25, 26, 117, 156
Mysticism and HDT, 113, 132, 155
Myth, HDT's use of, 95, 96, 98, 112, 115, 118, 146, 186-89, 200-01

Nabokov, Vladimir, 191
Nagley, Winfield E., 158
Narasimhaiah, C. D., 114
Nash, Roderick, 158
*National Anti-Slavery Standard,* 203-04
National Endowment for the Humanities, 76, 211
Natural history, HDT's interest in, 11, 34, 44, 52, 58-59, 75, 107, 127-30, 153-54, 204. *See also* Nature
"Natural History of Massachusetts," 34, 35, 78, 200
*Natural History of Selbourne, The* (White), 52
Nature, HDT's view of, 116, 117, 123-30, 145-46, 153-54, 182-83, 198. *See also* Natural history; Transcendentalism
*Nature* (Emerson), 108, 109
*Nature Essays,* 86
Nazism, 220
Nelson, Truman, 85, 156
Neptune, Louis, 64
Neufeldt, Leonard, 30, 119, 158
Newcomb, Charles King, 42
Newcomer, Alphonso G., 214
"New England Native Fruits," 76

New Humanists, 208
New York Public Library, 74. *See also* Berg Collection
*New York Times,* 210
*New York Tribune,* 6-7, 12, 27, 58, 203
Newspapers, HDT on, 49, 58
Nichol, John, 213
Nichols, E. J., 222
Nichols, William W., 153
Nietzsche, Friedrich Wilhelm, 220
"Night and Moonlight," 61, 63, 86
Norse Mythology, 98
Norway, 221
Nostalgia, appeal of, in the 1930s, 209
Novels, HDT on, 91, 161
Noverr, Douglas A., 112, 155
Notebooks, Thoreau's, 76
Nye, Russell B., 119

Oedipus complex, 22
Oehlschlaeger, Fritz, 223
Oliver, Egbert S., 120
"On the Duty of Civil Disobedience." *See* "Civil Disobedience"
Optics, 154
Organic functionalism, 193-94
Organicism. *See* Style
Orians, G. Harrison, 217
Oriental literature, HDT on, 12, 44, 45, 79, 92-94, 96, 112, 113
Orpheus, 95, 200-01
Orth, Michael, 199
Osgood, Joseph, 5
Ossian, 100, 117
O'Sullivan, J. L., 38
Ovid, 95
*Oxford English Dictionary,* 129, 154

Pacifism, and HDT, 136-37
Paganini, Niccolò, 193
Page, H. A. *See* Japp, A. H.
Painter, F. V. N., 214
Painting, HDT on, 127, 191-92
Palladius, 95
Pancoast, Henry S., 214
Pantheism, 203. *See also* Religion
*Paradise Lost* (Milton), 100, 116
"Paradise (To Be) Regained," 38, 79, 133, 135
Paradox, HDT's use of, 173, 175-76, 197
Parker, Theodore, 56
Parrington, Vernon L., 208, 216
Parsons, Thornton H., 196
Pastoral, HDT's use of, 82, 85, 115, 158
Pattee, Fred Lewis, 214, 215
Paul, Saint, 151
Paul, Sherman, 77, 96, 114, 115, 116, 118, 125, 146, 152, 181, 186, 195, 201, 210, 222
Payne, William Morton, 215
Peabody, Elizabeth, 9, 41
Pederson, Lee A., 196
Pellico, Silvio, 98, 116

Pencil-making, 2, 10, 204
Peple, Edward, 26
Perry, Bliss, 216
Persian literature. *See* Oriental literature
Persius, 10, 95
Personality. *See* Psychological approaches to HDT
Pfennig, Hazel, 222
Phenology, 75, 129, 154
Phillips, Wendell, 12-13, 39, 160. *See also* "Wendell Phillips Before Concord Lyceum"
Philology, 153
Photography, 127
Picturesque, in literature, 101, 117
Pilgrims, 120
*Pilgrim's Progress* (Bunyan), 52, 120
Pillsbury, Parker, 110
Pindar, 95. *See also* "Translations from Pindar"
"Places to Walk To," 76
Plato, 128
"Plea for Captain John Brown, A," 56-58, 85-86, 136, 147. *See also* Brown, John
Pliny, 95
Plutarch, 95
Poems (HDT's), 26, 32, 43, 69-71, 72, 75, 88, 132, 161; compared with prose, 163; organic form of, 179-80. See also *Collected Poems of Henry Thoreau*
Poetry, HDT referred to in, 226
Poger, Sidney, 82, 120
Poirier, Richard, 218
Polis, Joe, 65, 87, 147
Politics (HDT's), 109-110, 115, 132-39, 155-56. *See also* Government; Reform
"Politics" (Emerson), 41
Poll Tax, and HDT, 27, 40-41
Pomeroy, S. G., 25
Porphyry, 95
Porte, Joel, 26, 82, 106, 153, 158, 159
Pottawatomie massacre, 156
"Preaching of Buddha, The," 36, 79, 93
Primitivism, 144-45, 158
Princeton Edition, 63, 64, 74, 75-77, 79, 80, 88, 89, 211
Prinzinger, A., 220
Progress, HDT on, 38, 144-45, 158
"Prometheus Bound," 35, 78, 95
Prose. *See* Style
Protestantism, 110-11, 120, 157
Proverbs, HDT's use of, 84, 197
Psychological approaches to HDT, 22, 23, 29-30, 156, 211-12
Puns. *See* Wordplay
Puritanism, 97, 110-11, 120
*Putnam's Magazine,* 46, 66, 67, 202

"Quaker Graveyard in Nantucket" (Lowell), 68
Quarles, Francis, 100, 116
Quick, Donald G., 154

Quinn, Arthur Hobson, 218
Quoil, Hugh, 37
Quotations, HDT's use of, 43, 65, 76, 79, 92, 112, 117

Railton, Stephen, 153
Raleigh, Sir Walter, 36, 43, 100, 116, 161. *See also* "Sir Walter Raleigh"
Reading (HDT's): in American literature, 102-03, 117; in Emerson, 107-08, 119; in English literature, 98-101, 116-17; in European literature, 97-98, 115-16; in Greek literature, 94-97, 115; at Harvard University, 106-07, 118-19; in language theory, 119; in natural history, 128-30; in Oriental literature, 93-94, 112, 113-14; record of, 91, 111-12; in travel literature, 104-05, 118; use of, 92
Reaver, Russell J., 197
Redpath, James, 56, 85
Reform, HDT and, 38, 39, 53, 54, 56-57, 85-86, 109-10, 133-37, 155-56
"Reform and Reformers," 76, 89
*Reform Papers,* 79, 80, 83, 85, 86, 89
"Reformer, The," 76
Reger, William, 84
"Relation of the Individual to the State, The," 41
Religion, and HDT, 2, 26, 44, 47-48, 58, 65, 68, 110-11, 130-32, 155, 197
Republican party, 134
"Resistance to Civil Government." *See* "Civil Disobedience"
Reynolds, R. C., 83, 84
Rhetoric, HDT's use of, 81, 83, 84, 119, 155, 165, 175-76, 197. *See also* Style
Rhoads, Kenneth, 193, 201
Ribbens, Dennis N., 112
Ricardo, David, 157
Richardson, Charles F., 213
Richardson, Robert D., Jr., 201
Ricketson, Anna, 28, 223
Ricketson, Daniel, 12, 28, 101, 110
Ricketson, Walton, 28, 223
Ripley, George, 222
Robbins, Roland, 85
Roberts Brothers, 16
*Robinson Crusoe* (Defoe), 52, 116
Rogers, Nathaniel P., 39, 160
Rohman, Gordon, 83
Roman Catholicism, 47-48, 118, 155
Romanticism, European, 97-98, 115
Rose, Edward J., 119
Rose, V. T., 152
Rosenthal, Bernard, 86
Ross, Donald, Jr., 84, 196, 197
Rourke, Constance, 217
Rousseau, Jean Jacques, 97, 115
Roy, Rajah Rammohun, 113
Ruland, Richard, 84, 113, 223
Ruskin, John, 101
Russell, Jason A., 118

Russia, 221
Rutherford, Mildred, 213
Ryan, George E., 159
Ryan, Kevin, 159

Salomon, Louis B., 152, 159
Salt, Henry S., 18, 29, 173, 219, 224
Sampson, H. Grant, 88
Sanborn, Franklin Benjamin, 13, 15, 17-18, 20-21, 28, 33, 56, 69, 71-72, 78, 79, 83, 85, 86, 88, 94, 98, 103, 206-07, 223
*Sankhya Karika,* 94
Satire. *See* Humor
Sattelmeyer, Robert, Jr., 82, 87, 113
Say, Jean-Baptiste, 157
"Sayings of Confucius," 36, 79, 93
Sayre, Robert, 87, 90, 103, 104, 118, 147, 148, 158
Scandinavian literature, 98, 116
Scatology, 197
Schiller, Andrew, 28
Schneider, Richard J., 153, 154
Schoolcraft, Henry Rowe, 103
Schuster, Eunice M., 157
Science, HDT and, 11, 14, 28, 59, 106, 125, 127-30, 153, 154
Scott, Sir Walter, 101, 219
Scottish Common Sense philosophy, 33, 106, 118, 119
Scriptures, Sacred, HDT on, 93, 100, 117
Scudder, Townsend, 218
Sculpture, 191-92
Sears, Lorenzo, 214
"Season, The," 3, 32, 78
Seelye, John, 115, 158
Seldes, Gilbert, 216
"Self-Reliance" (Emerson), 108
Sensuousness (HDT's), 109, 124, 150-51, 153, 164, 193
Sentences (HDT's), 171-73, 196
"Service, The," 34, 78
"Seven Against Thebes, The," 36, 79
Sewell, Edmund, 5, 26, 70
Sewall, Ellen, 4, 26, 70, 74
Sexuality, and HDT, 26, 30, 46, 82, 151, 159
Seybold, Ethel, 35, 78, 95, 115
Shakespeare, William, 71, 99-100, 116
Shanley, J. Lyndon, 49-50, 51, 83, 152
Sharma, Mohan Lal, 113
Shattuck, Lemuel, 117
Shear, Walter L., 198
Shelley, Percy, 101
Shepard, Odell, 89
Sherwin, J. S., 83, 84
Sherwood, Mary, 87
"Sic Vita," 70
Sierra Club, 210
Silver, Rollo, 89
Simon, Myron, 196
Simms, Thomas, 49
"Sir Walter Raleigh," 36, 79
Skelton, John, 71

Skwire, David, 197
Slavery. *See* Abolitionism
"Slavery in Massachusetts," 48-49, 57, 83, 108, 198
Slethaug, Gordon, 115
Slotkin, Richard, 158
Smith, Adam, 157
Smith, Bernard, 217
Smith, Edwin S., 156
Smith, George W., Jr., 116
Smith, Herbert F., 157
Smith, John, 100, 116
Smith, John Sylvester, 155
Smith, Marion W., 87
Smithsonian Institution, 129
"Smoke," 70
Smyth, Albert, 213
Snyder, Gary, 210
Social criticism (HDT's). *See* Economic thought; Government; Politics; Reform
"Society," 9
Solitude, HDT and, 54, 66, 106, 141-44, 157, 158
Sophocles, 41, 95
South America, 221
Southworth, James, 101, 117
Spain, 221
"Sphinx, The," 76
Spirituality. *See* Transcendentalism
Spring, Marcus, 13
*Spring,* 220
Springer, John, 65
Spurgeon, Caroline, 116
Sreekrishna, Sarma, 113
Stansberry, Gloria J., 199
Staples, Sam, 8, 40
Stapleton, Lawrence, 89
State, the. *See* Government
Staten Island, 6, 7, 13, 27, 36, 43, 72, 100
Stein, Geretrude, 196
Stein, William Bysshe, 94, 113, 114
Stern, Madeleine B., 29
Stern, Philip Van Doren, 83
Stevens, Wallace, 190
Stevenson, Robert Louis, 24, 30, 66, 219, 224
Stewart, Randall, 222
Stockton, Edwin Jr., 199
Stoehr, Taylor, 157
Stoicism, and HDT, 69, 150, 205
Stoller, Leo, 59, 75, 86, 126, 152, 154, 156, 157
Stovall, Floyd, 217
Stowell, Robert, 25, 77, 81, 118
Strabo, 95
Strachner, S. D., 113
Straker, Robert, 88
Strivings, Suzanne, 87
Structure, literary: *See* Form
Style, HDT's literary: Emerson's compared with, 51, 108, 166-67, 196, 198, 199, 201; etymological basis of, 170-71, 175, 197;

figurative language in, 164-66, 196, 197, 200; form in, 179-91, 196, 198, 201; humor in, 173-78, 197; life related to, 160-61; and manual labor, 168; mythic basis of, 95, 96, 98, 112, 115, 118, 146, 186-89, 200-01; nature as symbolic language in, 182-83, 198; paradox in, 173, 175-76, 197; sentences in, 171-73, 196; symbolic images in, 182-85, 198-200; HDT comments on, 177-79; vocabulary in, 168-71, 196
"Succession of Forest Trees, The," 14, 58-60, 75, 86, 154
Sullivan, Louis, 194
*Summer,* 10, 73, 206
Sumner, Charles, 11
Surveying, 10, 27, 28, 59, 106, 111, 204
Swanson, Evadene Burris, 72, 88
Sweden, 221
Swedenborg, Emanuel, 98, 116
Sweetland, Harriet, 28, 88
Swinton, William, 28
Symbolic imagery, 182-85, 198-200

Tacitus, 58
Tanner, Tony, 190, 201, 218
Taoism, 114
Tasso, 98
Taylor, Horace, 153
Taylor, J. Golden, 174, 197, 200, 222
Taylor, Walter Fuller, 217
Taxes. *See* Poll tax
Teaching (HDT's), 3-4, 26, 54, 148-49, 159
Temmer, M. J., 116
Templeman, William, 101, 117
Tennyson, Alfred, 101
Thatcher, George, 64
Theme in literature, HDT on, 160-61
Theophrastus, 95
Therien, Alek, 27
"Thomas Carlyle and His Works," 40, 80, 101, 173-74
Thomas, Robert K., 153
Thomas, William, 88
Thompson, Wade C., 152, 179, 198, 200
Thoreau, Cynthia (mother), 1, 25, 107
Thoreau, David Henry, baptized as, 32
Thoreau, Helen (sister), 1, 2
Thoreau, Jean (grandfather), 1
Thoreau, John (brother), 1, 2, 4, 5, 7, 13, 22, 23, 25, 42, 107
Thoreau, John (father), 1, 2, 7, 10, 107
Thoreau, Maria (aunt), 8, 40, 41
Thoreau, Sophia (sister), 1, 2, 15, 25, 63, 66, 69, 73, 150, 205
*Thoreau Journal Quarterly,* 226
Thoreau Lyceum, The, 226
"Thoreau Newsletter," 209
Thoreau Society, The, 209
*Thoreau Society Bulletin,* 226
Thorpe, James, 84
Ticknor & Fields, 12, 15, 49, 61, 203, 205, 206

Tillinghast, T. A., 199
Timpe, Eugene, 223
Todd, Edgeley, 119
Tolstoy, Leo, 221
Tomlinson, H. M., 43
Torrey, Bradford, 73, 128, 207
Tranquilla, Ronald E., 120
Transcendentalism, American, 33, 92, 97, 101, 121; studies of, 119-20, 198, 201; and HDT's principles, 38, 44, 46, 57, 58, 62, 70-71, 82, 110, 114, 122-27, 132, 143-44, 152, 153, 161-63, 174, 182, 193
"Transcendentalist, The," (Emerson), 143-44
Translations (HDT's), 35-36
Translations, 78, 79, 82
Translations of HDT's works, 220-21, 223-24
"Translations from Pindar," 35, 78
Transmigration of the Seven Brahmans, The, 45, 82, 93, 113
Travel literature, HDT's interest in, 104-05, 118
Trent, William P., 215
Tuberculosis (HDT's), 10, 13, 14
Tuerk, Richard, 184, 199, 200
Typee (Melville), 102

Uhlig, Herbert, 154
Underwood, Francis, 213
Union Magazine, 63
Unitarianism, 2, 4, 131
United States Information Service, 210
University of Illinois Library, 223
Unrue, Darlene, 116
Urbanski, Marie, 226
Urbanization. See Cities
Utopian communities, HDT on, 38, 133-34

Van Anglen, Kevin, 79
Van Doren, Carl, 217
Van Doren, Mark, 24, 29, 210
Varro, 95
Vergil, 95
Vermont, 9
Vietnam War, 210-11
Violence, HDT on, 135-37, 156. See also Brown, John; Reform
Vocabulary (HDT's), 168-71, 196
Vocation, HDT's writing, 150-63, 195
Vogel, Stanley M., 115

Wade, Joseph, 154, 225
Wagner, C. Roland, 156
Wakeman, Stephen H., 90
Walden, 11, 12, 15, 42, 60, 126, 180-82, 186, 203-04, 205, 212-23 passim; discussed, 49-55, 161-63, 180-90; studies of, 77, 83-85, 114, 195-201, et passim
Walden Clubs, 219
Walden Edition. See Manuscript Edition
Walden Pond, HDT at, 8, 23, 49, 50, 54-55, 96

"Walk to Wachusett, A" 35, 78, 79, 200
Walker, Eugene, 85
Walker, Linda K., 200
"Walking," 60-61, 86
"Walks and Talks in Concord," 16. See also "Country Walking"
Walters, Frank, 90
Walton, Izaak, 100, 116
Walpole, Horace, 69
Ward family correspondence, 21, 72
Ward, Prudence, 4
Ward, William, 113
Watkins, Mildred Cabell, 213
Watson, Marston, 63
Weber, Max, 157
Week on the Concord and Merrimack Rivers, A, 10-11, 27, 31-32, 36, 37, 49, 60, 100, 126, 180, 183, 203, 205; discussed, 42-45, 189-90; studies of, 77, 81-82, 112, 114, 159, 200, 201, et passim
Weiss, John, 3
Welch, Donovan L., 88
Welker, Robert H., 37, 78, 154
Wells, Henry, 71, 88
Wendell, Barrett, 214
"Wendell Phillips Before Concord Lyceum," 39, 80
West, Michael, 84, 197, 200
West, HDT on, 158, 199
Westminster Review, 219, 224
Whaling, Anne, 90, 99, 116
"What Shall It Profit?" See "Life Without Principle"
Whately, Richard, 119
Wheeler, Charles Stearns, 54
Wheeler, Ruth R., 25
Wheelwright, Thea, 87
Whitaker, Rosemary, 82
White, E. B., 209
White, Gilbert, 154, 164
White, Viola, 89, 90
White, William, 225
White Mountains (New Hampshire), 9, 26, 82
Whiter, Walter, 197
Whitford, Kathryn, 28, 59, 86, 154
Whitford, Philip, 154
Whitman, Walt, 13, 28, 95, 102, 109, 121, 142, 150, 151, 161, 170, 190, 198, 201
Whittier, John Greenleaf, 71
"Wild Apples," 61-62, 86
"Wild Fruit," 75
Wilderness, HDT on, 60, 86, 146, 152, 158
Wiley, B. B., 12, 98
Wiley & Putnam, 42
Wilkins, Charles, 113
Williams, Paul, 88
Williams, Stanley T., 216, 217
Willis, Lonnie L., 117, 118
Willson, Lawrence, 83, 102, 117, 118, 120, 154, 155, 158
Wilson, Alexander, 128

Wilson, John B., 154
*Winter*, 10, 73, 206, 220
"Winter Walk, A," 37, 38, 78, 79, 198
Witham, W. Tasker, 218
Witherell, Elizabeth K., 77, 88
Wolf, William J., 154, 155
Women, HDT and, 4, 5, 9, 11, 21-22, 26, 27, 159
Wood, James P., 82
Woodlief, Annette M., 85, 119
Woodress, James, 226
Woodson, Thomas, 26, 80, 83, 157, 196
Wordplay, 84, 175-76, 197
Wordsworth, William, 101, 117, 177
Work, HDT on, 140-41
World War II, and HDT's reputation, 209
Worthington, John, 87

Wright, Frank Lloyd, 194, 201
*Writings of Henry David Thoreau*, 76
*Writings of Thoreau, The. See* Manuscript Edition

"Yankee in Canada, A," 46, 82-83
*Yankee in Canada, with Anti-Slavery and Reform Papers, A*, 46, 104, 205
Yeats, William Butler, 220
*Yeoman's Gazette*, 34
Yippies, 210
Yoga, 93, 94, 113, 114

Zahniser, Howard, 86
Zen, 221. *See also* Oriental literature
Zimmer, Jeanne, 27
Zimmermann, J. R. von, 115